POLITICS AND GOOD GOVERNANCE

(A Study of the Chief Ministers of Bihar :
From S.K. Sinha to Nitish Kumar)

POLITICS AND GOOD GOVERNANCE

(A Study of the Chief Ministers of Bihar : From S.K. Sinha to Nitish Kumar)

L.N. SHARMA
Former University Professor and Head
Department of Political Science
Patna University, Patna (Bihar)

REGAL

REGAL PUBLICATIONS
New Delhi - 110 027

POLITICS AND GOOD GOVERNANCE
(A Study of the Chief Ministers of Bihar :
From S.K. Sinha to Nitish Kumar)

ISBN 978-81-8484-269-2

Typeset by
RAHUL COMPOSERS
New Highway Apartments, Lakshmi Niwas
760, Pocket-D, Lok Nayak Puram, New Delhi - 110 041

Printed in India at
MAYUR ENTERPRISES
WZ Plot No. 3, Gujjar Market, Tihar Village, New Delhi - 110 018

Published by
REGAL PUBLICATIONS
F-159, Rajouri Garden, New Delhi - 110 027
Phone : 45546396, 25435369
E-mail : regalbookspub@yahoo.com, regaldeepbooks@yahoo.com

Contents

Preface

This book aims to study the office and position of the Chief Minister (CM) in the specific context of Bihar in the institutional context of his role in promoting good governance. Good governance refers to democratic and constitutional governance as well as to the governments' role in the uplift of economic, human and infrastructural variables such as Gross Domestic Product (GDP), per capita income, health care, educational and communication facilities, amenities available to children and expectant mothers, Information Technology (IT), nutritional level particularly of babies, sense of security, political participation of all adults and women empowerment, etc. All these variables are dependent upon the mechanics and quality of governance particularly of the state governments under different CMs at different points of times.

During Nehruvian era and in particular, under the advice of Mahalonobis, the Union government laid emphasis upon Central planning and national development. But Indian leadership missed the crucial lesson of nation-building of the pre-independence days when it came to govern the Country. Lala Lajpat Rai, Jawaharlal Nehru, S.C. Bose, V.B. Patel and G.B. Pant, etc. rose to higher positions in national politics and governance, having acquired their first hand experience in municipal governance and politics. But this practice was discontinued after independence. The 73rd and 74th amendments to the Constitution have added attention to the significance, financial viability and functional delineation of

Panchayati Raj Institutions (PRIs) and Urban Civic Bodies (UCBs) respectively. Prime Ministers (PMs) and CMs talk of increasing the powers of PRIs and UCBs. But the state list of the Constitution (seventh schedule) includes local self-government of village administration, municipal bodies and other local authorities. These bodies operate within the functional domain of states; and states manage, help in and even control most (barring a few) of their functions. Thus the quality of delivery at the bottom depends upon the quality of governance provided by CMs. It is with this perspective that we propose to operationalize the concept of political leadership in terms of effective political executive in the state government, that is, the CM and the Council of Ministers with particular reference to Bihar from 1937 to 2012. We shall explain in the Introduction (Chapter I) why we have chosen Bihar as a case study, though we have taken note of important cases from other states of the country as well. Bihar has emerged from a well-administered to a backward to a resurgent state and we span the spell of long innings under which this office was held first by S.K. Sinha and now-a-days by Nitish Kumar. Though Mohamad Yunus was the Premier of Bihar between April 1, 1937 and July 19, 1937, he held the office in the capacity of the leader of the Muslim independent party and his was only an interim government. Hence, we count J.K. Sinha as the first Premier of Bihar.

The idea of writing this book suggested itself because of the complete absence of any treatise which covered the entire gamut of Bihar politics from 1937 to this day. A shorter period within the interconnected and long history of growingly representational politics of different segments of society could not have done full justice to the sensitive subject. In the absence of the whole picture, the short picture would have lost its *raison d' etre* and relevance in the continuity of historical development and more particularly, the mobilization of social forces could not have been explained in relation to the role of changing CMs.

A word why we chose to write on what we have written on. Contrary to popular belief, privatization did not only encourage private investments, foreign trade and sale of consumer goods. It placed tremendous strain on state governments to supply ration to those sections of people who were below poverty line (BPL) or to use funds of Mahatma Gandhi National Rural Employment Guarantee Scheme (MGNREGS) fairly and judiciously. If the Right To Education (RTE) Act was to be implemented, state had to monitor *Sarva Siksha Abhiyan* (education to all) in a big way particularly to entice the hungry and clothless *Dalit* children not to drop out from the primary schools. Several schemes related to health care, sanitation, elimination of child labour, distribution of loans, prevention of domestic violence, to name a few, put serious strains on the finances of state governments. The heads of the Central Government and their heirs were keeping their shoulders off by merely saying repeatedly that they sent huge funds but only 10 to 15% reached the targeted groups. Nandan Nilekani, thought it fit to cite these estimated figures in his book *Imagining India* but he along with the biggest leaders and CMs maintain stony silence and do not say where and why such huge funds are siphoned off in the pipelines. The nefarious role of contractors, politicians and bureaucrats is a well-known fact and also well-known is the fact that CMs dared not deprive them of the booties because they were their ex-as well as prospective election agents. The local bureaucracy and police since 1977 in Bihar have been helping leaders in booth-capturing and bogus voting. Local chieftains contribute to election funds. The CMs, therefore, help all of them to siphon off money of development, welfare or road constructions—a part of which returns back to them in the name of election funds, no matter what the People's Representation Act stipulates. Some of the contractors are also local criminals (*rangdars*) who, too, are useful at the time of or between elections. The ex-Election Commissioner of India, S.Y. Quaraishi carried his promise to curb the role of *rangdars* or criminals in conducting the *Vidhan Sabha* elections in Bihar, 2010. But the question begs itself: why did CMs do not spend money well when the complainant, Rajiv Gandhi himself had been appointing CMs of all the Congress-ruled states and Rahul Gandhi who has put the estimated figure of Ill-spent money at a higher point has the power to ask the CMs of Congress-ruled states to see to it that the funds reach the needy and targeted groups and are managed in such a way that they reach the targeted groups? These questions beg answers. People look to CMs, would be CMs, PM and would be PMs for answers to a question which has ruined the lives and destinies of a large number of people residing in the sub-continent, particularly in the backward areas like Assam, Orissa, Chhattisgarh and of course, Bihar and Jharkhand. Our question is addressed as much to non-Congress CMs as to the Congress CMs who may put the questions to the Gandhis or the likes of Nandan Nilekanis who cite them. It is notable that the present CM of Bihar, Nitish Kumar has started an exercise of reviewing and social auditing schemes being run under MGNREGS within four months in all the districts of Bihar since 21-1-2012 to check corruption.

The need to publish this book became paramount in view of the arrival of the second generation of the level of economic reforms which has reinforced economic activities at the regional or state levels and which has mobilized socially immobilized castes (since 1967) and intensified the concept of developmental state. Perceptive scholars like Ashok Lahiri, Assemma Sinha and others have written at length on this point and we need not dwell upon it for long.

Since the CM is the head of the Council of Ministers and the administration in an Indian state under the Constitution of India and is lately all the more in effective control of the ship of the state; and the Governor the nominal constitutional head of the state in normal, non-emergency conditions, it is apt to analyse the office of the CM with all its nuances. In the case of President's rule in a state under Article 356 during the breakdown of constitutional machinery, the governor, appointed by the Centre, is the head of the government for the specified limited duration or when the Centre uses him to suit partisan ends, the governor may play extra-constitutional role. The governors normally play minimal role in development administration. This precisely explains why we have chosen to study the office and position of the CM in state and local administration which is gaining great momentum and wide significance if good governance is to be ensured.

The third chapter is devoted to a discussion of formation of governments and ends with the arrival of the new socio-political dispensation in 1990. In the following chapters, we discuss the CM's in interactive role and conclude the book with a delineation of CM's role in the federal process and in good governance particularly with post-2010 developments.

The book is divided in eleven chapters. In the first chapter where we introduce the topic, named Introduction; we present the context and scope of the book , the setting of the office of the CM, variations in the CM's position and the institutional interactive role of the CM. We present four hypotheses to be tested. We also make a critical overview of the existing literature and end the chapter by presenting a roadmap of what follows in the succeeding chapters. We present the plan of the book at the end of the chapter. In the second chapter, we present an overview of the concepts of the 'Congress' system, coalition politics and good governance.

I am extremely indebted to Prof. M.P. Singh, Professor of Political Science, University of Delhi (Retd.) for his encouragement in the preparation of the book as well as for his erudite comments on previous drafts of some chapters of this book. The model of my book on the Indian Prime Minister published by The Macmillan in 1986 appeared appropriate since for application the model suited its counterpart in the state, the CM. I was profusely encouraged as well as benefited by the suggestions thrown at an interactive seminar (organized on 5-6 March, 2010 by Dr. Chandrakala Padia, Head of the Department of Political Science, Banaras Hindu University, Varanasi and Dr. R.R. Jha, Professor of Political Science in the same Department) by Prof. Mohit Bhattacharya, Dr. Ramashray Roy and Prof. Asok Kumar Mukhopadhyaya. Shri M.K. Gaur, Director, Diwan Chand Institute, Delhi, Prof. S.N. Mishra, Editor, *Lok Prashashan*, Shri B.K. Pandey, Retd. Dy. Director of Bihar Education Service, Dr. Ajay Shankar, Associate Professor, Department of Political Science, Ramjas College, University of Delhi, Dr. Umesh Kumar, Associate Professor, Department of Public Administration, V.K.S. University, Ara, Bihar, Dr. Ashok Kumar Singh, Principal, H.R. College, Mairwa (Siwan), J.P. University, Chapra, Bihar and Dr. U.C. Shukla, Asst. Professor (Senior Grade), Head, Department of Political Science, R.R. College, Mokameh, Magadh University, Bodh-Gaya, Bihar provided useful insights into various aspects of the text. The I.I.P.A. library, Sapru House Library, Jawaharlal Nehru Museum Library and Institute of Constitutional and Parliamentary Studies Library, New Delhi apart from the libraries of the University of Delhi and J.N.U. provided books and journals without which computer and internet facilities generously provided by Dr. Shashi Bhushan Kumar, Asst. Professor (Senior Grade), Department of Political Science, L.N. College, Bhagwanpur, Vaishali, B.R.A. Bihar University would not have sufficed.

I am beholden to my wife, Ms. Krishna Sharma and daughters Sangeeta, Sabeeta and Sushmita, daughter-in-law, Vasudha and son, Dr. Rajesh Sharma who helped me in the preparation of this book. My grandsons, Saksham and Shrikar had to suffer the pangs of separation and deprivation of my company for a long period. Oriental culture comes in the way of thanking them too much, they had to suffer a lot on account of my being busy in unusual hours in preparing and correcting drafts or visiting experts for interactive sessions. No words are enough to compensate for their sacrifices. Lastly, I thank my computer composer, Anil Prakash of Gemini Computers, Patna and publisher, Regal Publications, New Delhi, both of whom did a brilliant job and made it possible to bring the copy of this book before your eyes in the present form.

L.N. SHARMA

1

Introduction

A certain primacy and leadership role of the effective real chief executive is inherent in parliamentary governance. The British cabinet system which India inherited and adopted makes the Prime Minister (PM) the effective head of the Union government; and Parliamentary federal system which we have adopted makes CMs effective heads of governments in Indian states. We have down the line *Pramukhs* or *Mukhiyas* as heads of constitutionally recognized, regularly elected, growingly financially viable and functional PRIs; and Mayors and Deputy Mayors as heads of UCBs. While the former two (union and state government formations) are party-based from Day I, at the third level, elections so far are not party-based, though they are not barred.

Besides the supremacy of the effective executive head, the cabinet's political homogeneity, collective responsibility, and accountability to the lower house of legislature are the basic features of the cabinet system.[1] But all this is theoretical. Things do not operate at the operative level as stated in the text books.

VARIATIONS IN THE CM'S POSITION

When a single party will be in majority in the lower house (to which it is constitutionally responsible), the CM will be more than *primus inter pares*, though not an autocrat. He will be the focal point of state politics and policy making and would wield immense influence and patronage. The working of the party and the imperial Prime Ministerial systems (when Mrs. Gandhi ruled between 1972-77 and 1980-84; and Rajiv Gandhi between 1984-89) precluded the possibility of PM being a colleague in a league of state leaders. There had been strong CMs in several states during Nehruvian days. Nehru's position in Indian government and in the Congress party since 1951 was so unrivalled that he had no reason to feel threatened by the strength the CMs enjoyed in their respective fiefdoms. But Nehru either felt weak after the Chinese aggression or since he wanted to settle his succession, he axed six CMs under the Kamaraj Plan in August, 1963 after procuring the resignation letters of all the CMs of the Congress Party to be disposed off by him. Though the ostensible purpose of the plan was stated to be to draft senior leaders into party work, only the architect (Kamaraj) got a party job (the Presidentship of the party); other five CMs remained without any assigned party work. PM Shastri axed P. S. Kairon and Biju Patnaik, the CMs of Punjab and Orissa respectively against whom charges of corruption had been found to be true in preliminary inquiries. But Mrs. Gandhi and Rajiv Gandhi did not normally allow CMs in Congress-ruled states to stay in their offices for more than two years at a stretch to ward off any threat to their own security in office and to assert their command. The operation of the Congress behemoth in post-*Garibi-hatao* politics (1971-77), in the 'Government that works politics' (1980-84); and in the Rajiv Gandhi Era (1984-89) made CMs beholden to the PM. They were PM's nominees at the first instance and were supposed to function at the PM's behest. They were accountable to the PM; and to the lower house of the legislature or to the people at large only in the formal and legal sense. That was one of the reasons for the Congress Party's electoral debacles generally after a single term of party's incumbency. Imperious Prime Ministerialism eventually led to the rise and growth of regionalism, regional leaders, regional satraps and regional parties. To cite a random example, Rajiv Gandhi, the then General secretary of the Congress party humiliated the then CM of Andhra Pradesh (A. P.), T. Anjaiah at Hyderabad airport in the presence of senior officials and party functionaries; and got him dismissed as CM on his return to Delhi by PM, Mrs. Gandhi in 1982. This is interpreted as one of the reasons for the Congress (I)'s loss of power in that state to the Telugu Desam Party (TDP) soon thereafter.[2]

In the Communist parties, it is an international phenomenon that the party is superior to government in both law and practice. The Party Chairman and its Working Committee take decisions and dictate terms to the government in power. As senior a leader as Jyoti Basu of the CPI (M) who had served a long stint as the CM of West Bengal could not assume charge as the PM of India at a point of time in spite of his willingness to do so because the Working Committee of his party did not permit him to accept the offer. Most of the regional parties, are oriented towards personalities. Personalities like Mayawati, Karunanidhi, Jayalalitha, Laloo Prasad, Mulayam Singh Yadav, Nitish Kumar, Narendra Modi, Patnaik, etc. are supreme leaders of their parties following the Congress (I)'s pattern. Laloo Prasad trusted only his politically naïve and barely literate wife, Rabri Devi, to succeed him as the CM of Bihar in 1997 when he had to go to jail to face prosecution by the CBI on the orders of the Patna High Court. Siboo Soren's writ ran largely in his party; so does Mamata's or ran N.T. Rama Rao's in their respective states at one point of time or another.

In coalition governments, not only the position of the CM (or PM) is comparatively weak; political homogeneity and collective responsibility of the cabinet are also "casualties".[3] The PM or CM's position is linked to his capability to manage, accommodate and take along with him his pre-or post-election partners, pander to them, settle the internecine conflicts (including clashes of personalities and egos), make the government survive and administration deliver outputs to the civil society and for all these acts, the PM or the CM has to draw upon an enormous amount of energy, time and talent. All the eight Indian states which came to be ruled by coalition governments in 1967 were marred by internal dissensions from their very inception and hence, by inherent instability. Six coalition governments were formed between 1967 and 1969 in Bihar, President's Rule was imposed thrice thereafter; and there were thirteen changes of government between 1967 and 1972. The longest that any government lasted for was around 300 days and the shortest was 4 days. Instability continued till the Congress came back with single party majority in the lower house of legislature in 1972 in the state of Bihar.

The relationship of governor *vis-à-vis* coalition CMs is of a genre different than it has had *vis-à-vis* single party majority CMs. Between 1967 and 1971, some of them got the chance to assert themselves; they adopted different yardsticks at different times in inviting leaders to form governments as CMs. Some governors acted at the behest of the Centre. Sarkaria Commission Report enumerated a large number of cases in which CMs were dismissed without substantive or justifiable reasons when different parties ruled at the Centre and in the states concerned. The Supreme Court (in Bommai Judgement delivered in 1994) censured the Union government for blatant misuse of Article 356 on most occasions including those just referred to. The Supreme Court directed that CMs should be dismissed by the governors only after ascertaining their strength on the floor of the lower house.

The opposition parties could not combine for a substantial period to govern in 1967-71 but they learnt the lesson to unite and coalesce. They improved upon the 1967 model subsequently and organized opposition conclaves. By and by, regional satraps and parties emerged in several states and captured power. Since 1989, the Union government has been in the coalition or minority mode. The PM cannot dictate terms to CMs. In 1966 and 1967 when Congress PM was weak, CMs of the Congress party played role as PM-makers. Since 1989, because the PM is the head of a minority or a coalition government most of the times, some of the CMs are assertive, vociferous and take independent stands. They vent their feelings strongly against the meagre or uneven allocation of grants or distribution of funds to their states or if their proposals are not processed in due time by the Centre. When the Centre passed the National Investigative Agency Act, 2008, the press reported that some of the non-Congress CMs like Narendra Modi and Nitish Kumar in a specially convened meeting in Delhi by the Home Ministry told strongly that public order was a state subject; and such a measure should not have been enacted by the Union government without consulting them a-priori. The non-Congress CMs particularly Nitish Kumar opposed the centre's proposal of constituting National Counter Terrorist Centre (NCTC) on the ground that it would dilute and circumvent federalism.

The position of the CM has kept varying like a pendulum since 1967. However, India's long experience with coalition has come to convince the analysts that coalition politics is not an aberration; it is a contingent and normal mode of governance in India deriving its sustenance from India's diverse political culture which shapes its contours. However, with the slowdown of economy, the centre is accusing the coalition politics for policy paralysis or delay in execution of policies and schemes.

CONTEXT OF THE BOOK

Bihar started as one ot the best administered states in 1946 and as one where land reforms measures came to be introduced at the first instance. Most of the developmental projects and schemes funded by the Centre, international agencies or philanthropist organizations were implemented at the level of the state. The oft-repeated argument that non-action and bad or delayed implementation is the Achilles' Hill of governance in Bihar is more true of the period between 1961-2005. The responsibility for the shocking position in post-1961 scenario would no doubt, lie on the shoulders of the CMs of the period concerned. If the CMs were administratively competent, capable, efficient and above all, honest; the pipelines would not have absorbed the huge amount they did and government's large funds would not have been siphoned off. Some former CMs of Bihar[4] of this period faced serious charges of corruption and reportedly stashed enormous amount of black money in several countries of the world. Even when Bihar came to boast of "good governance" in 2005-08, one Excise Minister of the cabinet openly came with the charge of corruption in his own department; and his charge was corroborated by competent authorities. People talk of corruption in many collectorates even today. CAG's report refers to irregularities in account-keeping from 2002 to 2008, and also in the purchase of stamps. In order to avoid misappropriation of funds at state levels, the funds meant for *Jawahar Rojgar Yojana* (JRY) etc. have been routed directly to the PRIs but the report of rampant corruption in the implementation of MGNREGS (all-over India) reached the ears of the Chief Justice of the Supreme Court of India, K. G. Balakrishnan. He thought it fit to make a pointed reference to it in a printed speech[5]. The supervisory role of the CM in controlling fiscal management and in preventing fiscal vagaries in such schemes is paramount. Jean Dreze warned Nitish Kumar about the "dismal laggard in the implementation of MGNREGA in Bihar." Bihar was behind even Jharkhand with less than ten days of work per household per year in terms of annual employment generation. The figure remained much the same in the first four years of Nitish's rule proving that the huge demand for work in Bihar went unmet[6]. In Purnea and Madhubani districts, this scheme generated as little as one or two days of work per household per year. Lack of strict monitoring at all levels and the massive staff shortage made the implementation of the scheme "lame"[7]. Other reasons were that *Gram Panchayats* were not allowed to play an active role in selecting or implementing MGNREGA works, there was non-involvement of women at the *Gram Panchayat* or block levels and above all, there was lack of swift action against those found guilty of indulging in fraudulent acts or misappropriation of funds. The latest effort of Nitish Kumar to make officers to visit each panchayat, analyse the on going work—the pace of work, spending on MGNREGA projects, ensure payment to workers in contact with *Rozgar Sevaks* may improve the working of MGNREGA projects in Bihar. Tamil Nadu has emerged as an MGNREGA success story because it is a well-governed state with a genuine commitment to implement social welfare schemes like ICDS, mid-day meals, public health and so on. Bihar will have to improve the implementation at all levels to ensure good governance.

The CM, Nitish Kumar (since 2005) had assured that he

would increase administrative powers of *Gram Panchayats* and lift the cap of Rs. 1 lakh on the works that could be done directly by the *Panchayats*. Through the BDOs and block engineers at the administrative level; and by getting Bihar's 8442 *Gram Sabhas* reinvigorated through community organization's consultation; enthused, active, participation and people's involvement at both planning and involvement levels; Nitish Kumar or for that matter, any CM could help. The cause of rural development can be accelerated through obtaining popular checking of fund expenditure, site supervision, material checking, checking of payment to labour and elimination of child labour, enforcing the right to information, the right to education, consumers' protection, etc. Broadband connectivity, e-governance, harvesting rain water, catching fish through satellite announcement and women's empowerment, availability of electricity at all times, etc. have been integrated as parts of the total scheme of rural development in Gujarat. These experiments need to be replicated in Jharkhand, backward areas such as Assam, Bihar, Orissa and Chhatisgarh, etc.

THE INSTITUTIONAL INTERACTIVE ROLE OF THE CM AND SCOPE OF THE BOOK

The Indian states, with some exceptions, share a common constitutional law, a common constitutional framework and a common administrative law. Therefore, the state administration, under the federal structure as provided in the Indian Constitutional Law occupies a similar position of importance so far as rule-making, rule-application, rule-adjudication and execution of developmental programmes are concerned. The office of the CM is the focal point of policy-making and policy execution. The CM is the lynch-pin of state's administration. A CM is largely responsible for affecting structures, processes and outcome of the state's political, economic and social values; and plays various roles intimately connected with all the important areas of state's governance. Though some of the responsibilities have now been transferred to the PRIs and UCBs through the 73rd and the 74th amendments of the Constitution of India, it is upon the CM that the responsibility for efficient operation of the administration of the land under his survey falls. The officials of blocks, *anchals* and the districts work directly under the state; and they act as the helpers and controllers of these local bodies. So it is the responsibility of the CM to see that his state level officials such as the secretaries, DMS, (District Magistrates) and D.D.Cs (District Development Commissioners), etc. help PRIs and UCBs prosper; and function efficiently, effectively and democratically.

Besides being the head of the state administration, the CM is also the leader of his party and the people and the chief spokesman of the state. In the performance of these manifold duties, he has to draw upon and combine all his sources of authority. The success and failure of state administration and even some functions of the union administration with which he is concerned depend on the efficient functioning of his office. Failure in any of his major tasks may weaken his authority which may result in his inability to perform his duties in totality.

Since the CM represents the apex of the ruling hierarchical power structure and wields great authority and shapes the style of governance in the state, he is largely responsible for the state's quality of governance. He receives accolades if there is good governance and conversely, denunciations for mal-governance, the onus for over-all performance of the government ultimately lying on him. He tries to make the Centre a scapegoat but generally fails in throwing the buck. He blames disasters like drought, flood or monsoon for bad results but cannot convince the public if he fails to manage those natural disasters.

As the effective head of the executive, the CM interacts with the formal and dignified head (the governor) but the relationship is tenuous when the party composition of governments ruling the Centre and the states is different. The governor in such cases does not remain so formal as he is when a single party dominates the lower house of legislature. This book will focus on the institutional matrix comprising the CM and his interactions with the governor, the cabinet, the legislature and the party etc. on the one hand; and on the interactive socio-political situation and techniques of power manipulation used by the CM and his role in development and interactive role with the Centre on the other. The book will attempt to analyse the various nuances of the role of the CM, the bases of authority with which he interacts, the style of his functioning and his art of the management of the government. Power of the CM is related to the personality of a CM or to his capacity to arrogate power by using various techniques of power. Situations, other personalities of the time and some other factors play a significant role in the exercise of his power. We shall also probe how far the social heterogeneity and plurality of regional, occupational, religious, caste and other interests were reconciled and accommodated by incumbents of the CM's office. We have sought to examine the dynamics of Chief Ministerial power from the aforesaid angles. This book will deal both with (i) institutional and (ii) social interactional roles of the CM. The central focus, however, will be on politics and aspiration for good governance as reflected by the leadership style and performance in office by the Chief Ministers of Bihar from S.K. Sinha to Nitish Kumar.

THE CASE FOR STUDYING BIHAR

The context of breakdown in a backward state (to use James Manor's title of an article on Bihar[8]) is a special reason to make a study of the institution of the CM in the specific context of Bihar. Bihar since 1960s had been a byword in development administration circles for socio-economic-political backwardness. The state had been suffering from anaemia due to the disinterest of NRIs in making investments in trade and industries in Bihar (despite exhortations by some CMs to do so). Bihar earned the reputation of being "the graveyard of development projects that succeed elsewhere but fail"[9] here attracting the sobriquet of the "fourth world" for it. There are some other features that make Bihar a cogent case for study. This poor but populous state, at present, divided into 9 divisions and 38 districts is, according to 2001 Census, demographically predominantly rural. Out of its total area of 94163 sq. km; 01804.64 km only fall in the urban fringe, the rest 92354.40 sq. km fall in the rural hinterland. Populationwise, out of a total of 8,29,98,509 people, 7,43,14,709 are inhabitants of rural areas; According to the figures of 2011, 88.7% people live in rural areas. Whereas a meagre 86,21,800 people reside in the urban centres. According to the figures of 2011, Bihar had only 139 urban centres i.e. only 6% area is urban where 11.3% people reside. Literacy rate according to 2011 Census Report is merely 63.82% out of which male literacy rate is 73.39% and female literacy rate is 53.33%. The Union government has raised the number of BPL people to 90 lacs after much wrangling but the Government of Bihar, contesting the figure, presents its case for more ration on the ground that 1.5 crore people are below poverty line in Bihar and cites Saxena report in its favour. Tendulkar Committee has suggested that Bihar has over 1.25 crore BPL families. The total figure of BPL families in rural areas comes to 57.22%. The figure would go above 1.25 crore after the inclusion of urban families. According to a report of the Central Statistical Organization, the growth rate of Bihar between 2004-05 and 2008-09 had risen to 12 percent which made Bihar state to have the highest growth rate in India at present. In 2011, it achieved the growth rate of 14.15 percent and in a still more economically attractive figure. 2012, it achieved the rowth rate of 13.1% the highest in India. Yet, we cannot ignore the fact of the plight of the poor who are by any account, numerous in Bihar and their miseries, insurmountable.

The Budget-Eve Economic Survey for 2009-10 reported on 25.2.2010 that agriculture had received 0.2% negative growth. The incomes of 52 per cent of all Indians (who depend on agriculture) have fallen to that extent. Bihar's rural poor had suffered a greater decline in income. The failing monsoon of 2010 affected the plantation of paddy and drought conditions created decline in income of farmers. The gaping holes in development are wider in Bihar due to non-utilisation or wrong utilisation of grants and shortage of service providers at different levels. The CMs face the perennial challenge to ensure better value for every rupee spent on development programmes. It may be recapitulated that Bihar's per capita income was Rs. 10,570 according to the Central Statistical Organization Report submitted on 1.5.2009. In 2002-03, Bihar's per capita income was Rs. 6,394 and in 2006-07, it was Rs. 9,432. The Economic Survey report, 2008-2009 found that the number of families below nutrition intake in 2004-05 was 2.7%

and BPL was 41.4% of the total population in Bihar. In the state of Bihar, the number of low weight children below the age of three was 58.4%. Only one-fourth people in Bihar have access to public convenience and toilets. The responsibility devolves upon the CM of Bihar to develop Bihar and make it achieve the status it had in the 1950s. Good governance in the absence of amenities to poor women and children in the spheres of literacy, health, nutrition and sanitation remains a futile claim.

RETROSPECT

V. Krishna Ananth, a journalist of Chennai argues that both Nehru and S.K. Sinha looked to the interests of the bourgeoisie and local landlords who were the traditional vote banks of the Congress party. But the overwhelming opinion is that S.K. Sinha was a 'progressive' leader who introduced substantive land reforms legislations at the early period of Bihar's history.[10] As he and his group consisting of K.B. Sahay in the beginning championed the cause of *zamindari* abolition; peasants, agricultural labourers, small and medium *zamindars* and urban middle class got attracted towards them. Though dominated by rich peasantry, this faction broadened its mass base. However, S.K. Sinha favoured the growth of agricultural capitalism and he wanted to do away with the constraints and hindrances in the way of the growth of productive forces in agriculture.[11] Sinha was, not so much enthusiastic about post-*zamindari* agrarian reforms, a section of leftists argues.[12] Yet, leftists grant credit to Sinha for getting the Bihar Tenancy Act passed in the early years.

Atul Kohli advances the thesis in *Democracy and Development in India*, 2009 that governments between 1967 to 1987 symbolize "increasingly governmental ineffectiveness".[13] He maintains that comparatively speaking, "there was a lull";[14] and money lending and sharecropping were within tolerable limits in Bihar during the early phase of independence (47-66).[15] Agrarian struggles by *Kisan Sabhas* under the leadership of Swami Sahajanand, Karyanand Sharma and other leaders of some leftist groups had been launched since pre-independence period. S.K. Sinha, the premier of Bihar who had himself been a member of *Kisan Sabha* (20 July 1937–31 October 1939) introduced measures of land reforms as the CM during 1937-39 and after 1946. After independence, Bihar was the first state to abolish *Zamindari*. Before his death in 1961, he introduced Land Ceiling Bill in the house. Consolidation of holdings, though done in U.P., has, however, not been taken up in Bihar to-date.[16] Land records, too, have not been updated (a measure almost all the states in India have taken up and Nitish Kumar has got a Bill passed in the winter session of legislature, 2011 to take it up at this late stage now); *benami* ownership is still in vogue and *Karmacharis* demand money and take long time even in issuing land receipts to the poor land owners atleast till the Right to Services Act came to be implemented by Nitish Kumar. Karmacharis yet take the plea that land register has been lost. Amendment to *Bataidari* Bill after submission of D. Mukhopadhyaya Committee Report or implementation of it opened a Pandora Box even in the Financial Year 2009-10; and Nitish Kumar and his colleagues were hard put to explaining particularly to please the newly emergent landowning classes of *Kurmis, Yadavs, Kushawahas*, and the traditional land owners among *Bhumihars* and *Rajputs* that no *bataidari* bill had been planned and it was not going to be implemented, though the electorate who had voted against him in the 18 seats of by-election to the Vidhan Sabha held in 2009 probably on this score refused to be convinced and failed to shed their fear, the love for land being ancestrally ingrained in them.

Bihar took pride in calling itself to be a well-administered state in the 1950s.[17] It was ruled peacefully during the tenures of S.K. Sinha and B.N. Jha (1961-63), but tempers started running high during the regime of K.B. Sahay (1963-1967). People started murmuring against mal-development, rising prices, unemployment and corruption since 1963-64.

Corruption has been the bane of Bihar politics (to begin with Congress politics) right from pre-independence days. Even a stalwart like S.K. Sinha was charged with wrong doings like settlement of Bettiah (Sathi) lands, passing orders for the sale of molasses (which were scarce then) to benefit the then Excise Commissioner and a relative of Mahesh Prasad Sinha (who was close to the then C.M.), Ram Prasad Narain Sahi. The charges of wrong settlements of iron and cement to suit vested interests were made. Mahatma Gandhi and Sardar Patel had condemned such incidents. Ministers of the post-independence era including the then, CM K.B. Sahay faced the Aiyar Commission of inquiry which found some of the charges to be true. Things came to such a pass by 1980s that a large number of MLAs turned criminals and served periods in jails along with the Chairmen and members of Bihar Public Service Commission, Bihar University Commission, etc. In the 1990s, the incumbent CM himself was chargesheeted by the CBI, sent to jail for weeks together, facing several cases, his relatives broke law every now and then, innocent children were kidnapped for ransom at the behest of MLAs and ministers and some say, at the instance of even the then CM. So corruption existed even at the level of CM from the beginning to the end and percolated down to ministers, bureaucracy, lower civil service, police, PWD and so on. Growing immerisation and the tendency of consumerism added to the menace.

Immediate post-independence leaders, in any case, stand in better light than their successors. S.K. Sinha led *Dalit's* entry into Baidyanath Dham Temple, Deoghar reflecting his (though belonging to upper caste) commitment to the upliftment and empowerment of *Dalits*. S.K. Sinha was known for his scholarship and he had donated his personal collection of 17,000 books to the public library in Monghyr in 1959 which is now named after him Sri Krishna *Seva Sadan*. His inaugural address to the All-India Political Science Conference delivered at Patna on the 27th December, 1960 was nationally acclaimed as a piece of erudition. The letters of exchange between Sinha and Nehru entitled *Freedom and Beyond* contain exchange of views on several national and social issues. Almost all the development projects be it on the irrigation front or on industrial front were done by the excellent pair of Sri Babu and Anugraha Babu. They include several river valley projects like those on Koshi, Aghaur, Sakri and others. They brought Bihar on the agricultural as well as the industrial map. Several heavy industries like Barauni Oil Refinery, HEC Plant of Hatia, Bokaro Steel Plant, Barauni Fertiliser Plant, Barauni Thermal Power Plant, Maithon Hydel Power Station, Sulphur Mines at Amjhaur, Sindri Fertiliser Plant, Kargali Coal Washery, Barauni Dairy Project, etc. were all started since the Second Five Year Plan during S.K. Sinha's tenure as CM.

S.K. Sinha had immense contribution to the cultural and social development of the state. It was he who established the Rajendra *Chatra Niwas* at Calcutta for the Bihari students and the Anugraha Narain Sinha Institute of Social Studies at Patna. Lok Rangshala of the Bihar *Sangit Nritya Natya Parishad,* Sanskrit College at Patna, Ravindra Bhawan at Patna, Bhagwan Buddha's statute at Rajgir *Venu Van, Vihar* as well as an orphanage at Muzaffarpur were opened by him.

Binodanand Jha (18 February 1961 to 2 October 1963) belonged to a priestly class, he was pro-peasant. But his tenure was, by and large, uneventful. He had to resign under the Kamaraj Plan before he could accomplish much. As a personality, his successor, K.B. Sahay (2 October, 1969 to 5 March, 1967) was credited to be associated in the crusade for land reforms. He belonged to Hazaribagh and his crusade had much to do with his animosity towards the *Raja* of Ramgarh. He became the C.M. of Bihar in 1963 with the support of the son of A.N. Sinha and an eminent leader in his own right, S.N. Sinha (who later became the CM of Bihar) who then was Deputy Chief Minister and served as Education Minister.

The Aiyar Commission which was appointed to look into 189 charges against five Congress ministers and one Congress CM forund that while some charges were trivial, "quite a large number" were "substantial in character".[18] The Commission found charges of favouritism and casteism against K.B. Sahay, Mahesh Prasad Sinha, Satyendra Narain Sinha, Ragvendra Narain Singh and Ambika Saran Singh correct. The Government of Bihar filed cases against the accused which dragged on for years and caused immense damage to their political standing. The Mudholkar Commission of Inquiry indicted a CM for appointing a minister and allocating him the portfolio of mines when the said minister was himself a big mine-owner in Bihar. The minister served his own interest and the interest of his family rather than that of the state.[19]

Till the separation of Jharkhand in 2000, Bihar had plenty of coal and other minerals but became it bereft of after the separation, those minerals. Biharis, in need of more wages and better educational and employment opportunities, migrate temporarily or permanently to other states where they are treated as "unwanted" and even assaulted despite constitutional protection to all the citizens of India to work and settle anywhere in the territory of India. However, with the increase in construction activities, agricultural operations, MGNARGA related activities and other rural works, migration of Bihari labour to Punjab and Haryana at cheaper rates has come down.

Bihar is yet marked by "feudal" barbarities, caste-based electoral animosities, alliances, caste atrocities and violence,[20] communal strife (abated after the bloody communal riots of Bhagalpur in 1989) and rising cases of Naxal activities and Maoist attacks. Filled with disgust at the occurrences of such violent acts every now and then, H.V. Kamath, the then editor of the *Illustrated Weekly* (of then called Bombay) had once argued in his journal that Bihar had to be saved from Biharis.[21] The glaring fact staring our face is that now Biharis need to be saved from Maharashtrians, Assamese, Karnatakawallahs, Delhites and many other *statewallahs*. Bihar is in dire need of development and infrastructure to provide maximum employment and education to Biharis within Bihar's boundaries if Biharis have to maintain self-respect. The role of CM becomes crucial as the steersman of the ship of the state which has to be rowed skilfully and tactfully to attain self-respect for its people through the attainment of the cherished goal of development and socio-economic justice which is possible only through good governance.

The CM of Bihar since 2005, Nitish Kumar has been spearheading a movement with the support of almost all the parties that Bihar be granted the status of a "special category state" like the other eleven so declared states of the country like Arunachal Pradesh, Assam, Manipur, Meghalaya, Sikkim, Tripura, Uttarakhand, etc. That the things have come to such a pass needs an over-view. If the growth rate of Bihar is the highest in the country and Bihar is making strides in trade and transport, the demand for special status may not be acceptable to the National Developmental Council which has already refused to concede it despite strong political presure being mounted for the same by the Government of Bihar since 2005.

POLITICAL HISTORY OF BIHAR (1947-67)

Between 1947 and 1967, there was political stability and advancement of Bihar due to the following reasons:

(i) administrative efficiency and integrity;
(ii) Industrialisation (two out of the three state-owned plants: Bokaro Steel Plant and Heavy Steel Plant, Ranchi have been transferred to Jharkhand after the partition of Bihar in 2000);
(iii) Institutionalization-Institutions like Netarhat School and Birsa Agricultural University were established by the state government, they ran well and produced good results; and
(iv) Passage of land reform laws introduced a shift in the status of tenants and sharecroppers. The tenants since then turned into agricultural labour whose percentage swelled from 25% in 1951 to 48% in 1971.

We may, however, note that one potent reason of political stability and one-party-dominance between 1947-67 was that a narrow elitist political order consisting mainly of upper caste leadership and co-opted OBC, SC, ST and Muslim sub-leadership ruled between 1947-67. There was lack of social and political mobilization of the Other Backward Castes (OBCs). Ram Manohar Lohia's thesis about backward class political mobilization in 1967 exhorted the slumbering OBCs to unite and make attempt to capture power. Lohia envisaged that only a coalition government can replace the hegemonic (Brahmanic-upper caste) rule of the Congress party. Bihar did not shed its semi-feudal character even after the *zamindari* abolition. Land ceiling laws, *bataidari* laws or other laws pertaining to land reforms were not properly implemented. They became the instruments for the *Karamcharis* of the *Anchal* to get their palms greased by the affected parties; and to boot, the big sharks holding thousands of acres of lands as *benami* owners took the help of courts and advocates to get remedies. Politicians helped the rich; the left parties made noises and organized rallies but failed to produce meaningful results. The CMs preferred to look the other way or patronized the big land holders; so the big and *benami* land holders made hay.

The cliché that politicians depend upon the poor to get their votes; and upon the rich to procure their money to spend or stash characterized the political scenario in Bihar particularly after the days when the euphoria and spirit of sacrifice generated by the freedom movement among the Congressmen led by the CM (S.K. Sinha) and his affable and able Deputy CM (A.N. Sinha) started waning by and by. Development and good governance started being neglected after the two stalwarts left the scene. Bihar became a victim of neglect of agriculture, irrigation, energy security, rural development, communication infrastructure and industrial development. No subsidies were granted to the families belonging to the lower strata of the population to cope with under-development. Old mechanisms were inadequate to implement new tasks and they were not replaced. The administrative machinery was not revamped; law and order was not maintained properly; corruption was not eradicated; education, health, sanitation and other measures of well-being were not ensured to people at large. Therefore, Biharis failed to lead a meaningful, harmonious and prosperous life. The duty of translating these dreams into realities devolves upon the CM and his cabinet and the CMs failed in performing the aforesaid tasks.

Even in 2008-12, Extremely Backward Castes (EBCs), *Pasmanda* Muslims and *Mahadalits* were arduously organized by Nitish Kumar so that more benefits of reverse discrimination might reach them.[22] Just as the Hindu society was divided between forwards and backwards, Muslim society which once boasted of equality among its members was sought to be divided by vested interests between forward Muslims (including *Ashrafs*) and backwards or *Dalits* (*Pasmandas*). *Pasmanda* Muslims had not become either a Deputy Collector or an M.L.A. till a pretty long time. *Pasmandas* resented that if a Hindu S.T. converted into Christianity, he retained S.T. status but a Muslim tribal lost his S.T. status if he converted into another religion.[23] Nitish Kumar exploited these sentiments of *Pasmandas* to suit his electoral interests. He assiduously cultivated the support of EBCs who constituted 33% of the population and of Mahadalits. This showed that he has had been adept in social engineering.

It is for a CM to decide to unite or divide, to develop or keep under-developed the state he governs. For political reasons, he may be tempted to divide the civil society and thereby, keep the state under perpetual under-development and encourage corrupt-criminal-contractors and conspirators. But in that case, his rule will neither be politically viable nor stable and his reputation as an expedient politician will place him low in the category; and he will never acquire the status of a statesman which good governance, done in perpetuity in actual practice, may provide him for good. Aspirations for good governance and social engineering may cut across each other after a given point.

POLITICAL HISTORY OF BIHAR (1967-2012)

Few states in India offer such multi-sided experiences of instability of governments and of experiments in disparate kinds of political coalitions as did the state of Bihar between 1967-1990. Political inability of the late sixties had added to the traditionally caste-based politics of the state which since the early years of the sixties, had been marked by the phenomenon of leaderlessness or backward caste mobilization. The elections following the adulthood of India's parliamentary experience reduced Congress's majority in India; and Bihar was a typical case. Congress emerged as a minority party, several opposition parties led by intermediate castes or OBCs gained in significance. One Extremely Backward Caste leader and two *Dalits* got chance to become CMs. None of the parties, however, was in a position to form a government by itself.

Closer examination reveals two factors that were at work in Bihar between 1967 and 2012: the disarray within the congress party, and the growing power conflict between the forward and the backward castes followed by the experiment of forging an alliance of convenience between upper castes and some intermediate castes, EBCs, some Dalits and some Muslims as had been tried by Mayawati in UP in 2007. The rising significance of the non-upper castes was clearly manifested in the fact that seven of the nine CMs during 1967-72 did not belong to the twice-born castes. Within the newly emergent castes which captured power, there has been intra- and inter-elite conflict which made it difficult to achieve any degree of governmental cohesiveness. The early 1970s are viewed as a period when the intermediate/backward castes were rising slowly to challenge the power of the forward castes, culminating in the 1977 victory of the backward castes under the leadership of Karpoori Thakur who belonged to an extremely backward caste.

The anti-Congress extra-parliamentary protest movement reached a crescendo in 1974 under the leadership of Jayaprakash Narayan (affectionately called JP), himself belonging to upper caste. Given the political nature of the anti-Indira rebellion and emergency, a fair amount of Bihar's activism during that period may be understood more as a political conflict than as a socio-economic struggle. The end of national emergency brought the Janata Party to power in Bihar. Karpoori Thakur, a socialist and an associate of Charan Singh, and popularly identified as a leader of the backward castes in Bihar, emerged as the State's CM. After his death, the mantle fell on Laloo Prasad who empowered the backward classes and gave them dignity and social status but was trounced after a 15 years' rule by him and his wife by Janata Dal (United)—Bharatiya Janata Party combine led by Nitish Kumar. Nitish Kumar for the first three and half years as CM projected his image as *Vikash Purush* (raised state's revenues, excise collections, took a large number of good decisions through cabinet, made big budgets, improved public order and the condition of roads, though not so much eased energy availability) but with election eighteen months away (held in October-November, 2010), he started cobbling up caste combinations of EBCs, *Mahadalits* and *Pasmanda* Muslims, etc. but this eroded the confidence of his old voters who orchestrated their resentment in the Assembly by-elections of September, 2009 in which his combine had to cede 9 out of 18 seats to Laloo-Paswan duo while JD (U)-BJP remained restricted to only five seats.

Instead of starting the process of introducing the *bataidari* bill, had he initiated the process of computerizing land records in the early period of his rule (for which funds had been provided by the Centre), making land receipts and mutations up-to-date, he would have made a success story. He contented himself by getting a bill passed in December, 2009 to get land disputes passed through speedy trials. He should have tried his hand at consolidation of holdings or introducing measures to increase the productivity of land earlier. He became a late-starter by passing a law about it in late 2011. The decision of the Patna High Court indicating "irregularities" made in keeping accounts between 2002 and 2008 by the Government of Bihar malaffected the "fair" image that Nitish Kumar had started his innings of governance with. His image got a nosedive when the CAG in another report pointed out Government's defaults in revenue collection through stamps. Though the High Court later absolved the Government of the charges, it did not clean the stains.

Nitish Kumar takes a soft approach in the rift between the landed and the landless class and even favours taking a "soft approach" towards Naxalites. It was an indication lack of proper security and failure of law and order that an anti-Naxalite, the leader of *Ranvir Sena,* Brahameshwar Singh popularly called *Mukhiya Ji* was killed on 1. 6. 2012 creating wide indignation among his supporters. Earlier, soon after the Janata party came to rule in 1977, much social upheaval had been caused by reservations. Rioting in 1978 following Karpoori Thakur's declaration of reservations for OBCs in government jobs reached the same high level as in 1974 during the JP movement the year before the emergency was proclaimed. As a result, Karpoori Thakur's government was forced to resign under pressure. Janata government under Ram Sundar Das which ruled till 1980 did not pursue the policy of reservations for backward classes. Shifts in national politics led to an electoral defeat of the Janata Party and to the re-emergence of Congress in 1980. Prominent non-Marxist scholars like Francine Frankel see the "backward class movement" led by Karpoori Thakur as an organisation of the poor which is a double assault on the caste system and the class structure.[24]

We have made an attempt to explain the process of breakdown of political and social order in Bihar. We make no implicit assumption that the old order of the fifties and even of the mid-sixties was desirable and the turmoil of the seventies or of the decades thereafter is not. The seemingly stable political rule in the 1950s and 1960s was rule by a narrow elitist political order. Challenges to the power of the few elites drawn from four Hindu Castes grew in both the civil society and the state resulting in considerable turmoil. Broadening the power base necessarily entailed violence and turmoil. Change took place simultaneously at the social, economic and political level (and not sequentially as in England) and so naturally there have had been visible signs of unrest and turmoil.

Significance of the Study

This book in hand is significant from both practical and academic viewpoint. Since this is the least researched area of the subject, it fills a gap in the existing literature on the Indian political system. Secondly, it caters to the need to make an analysis of exploring the causes of Bihar's increasing political turmoil and also caters to the need of looking at the theory and practice of good governance from a critical, comparative and objective viewpoint.

The erosion of authority of CMs during the imperial Prime Ministerial Governments of Mrs. Gandhi and Rajiv Gandhi (1972-77 and 1980-89) adds another dimension to the office of the CM. The authority of CMs suffered grievously at the hands of Mrs. Gandhi when she was at the helm of affairs in the country in 1972-77 and 1980-84. She began foisting her own choices on the state legislators and a result, CMs began to be made in and exported from New Delhi. The country saw the spectacle of Ghansham Bhai Oza (1972) being despatched to Gujarat, P.C. Sethi (1972) to Madhya Pradesh, Nandini Sathpathy (1972) to Orissa, Siddhartha Shankar Ray (1972) to West Bengal and H.N. Bahuguna (1973) to U.P. etc. Understandably, she would select persons as had no political base of their own, for this alone would effectively ensure their looking up to her for survival and support. If any CM showed any signs of independence in his or her functioning, he or she was immediately replaced on one pretext or the other as was the case with Nandini Sathpathy, Jagannath Mishra and Bahuguna. The average tenure of the CM of Bihar has been very short: less than two years. If we exclude the period of Laloo Prasad and Rabri Devi combined (March 1990 to November 2005); the average tenure of the Chief Ministership will come down to about 1.2 months.

This short-tenure headship of governments hampered the development of federal structure in India. In the late 1980's and onwards, with the growth of regional parties, the operation of federalism drastically changed. The CMs who in the earlier phase of Centre-state relations used to be subservient to the Central government started exercising effective strength in relation to the Centre and dictate the Centre in bargaining in several matters. In Chapter IX, we have examined how in the same set-up and within the same constitution, things have changed a lot. There have been interesting changes in the past couple of decades and they have vastly affected the federal structure of the country. We have explored if they have led to genuine federalism or created Centre-state imbalance and deadlocks.

Caste combination or belongingness to 'dominant caste' makes a lot of difference for CM's stability. Governmental stability is closely related to the caste composition of the legislature which CMs lead Caste composition of different successive houses affect the continuance and working of the office of the CM. The strength of the party in the legislature had bearing on the stability of the CMs; for example, that of Laloo Prasad with minority in 1990 and with majority in 1995. Performance in general, i.e. the quality of governance has relationship with the tenure of CMs.

Personality cult has relationship with the tenure of CMs. Laloo Prasad during his tenure as the CM had acquired the position of a hero with a personality cult and mannerisms of his own. The stability of Laloo Prasad during his first term (1990-95) was credited to his manipulative style and ability to cause defections in the opposition parties. Laloo's success by a huge margin in the 1995 Assembly elections proved that besides having grip over Muslim-Yadav (MY) votes, he commanded the votes of a large number of EBCs and *Dalits* as well. By 1995, he had emerged as a *massiah* of the downtrodden sections of society. During his second term, his stability was credited to his party's honeymoon with the Congress, one of the opposition parties. The relationship between the CM and the opposition parties during coalition period (1967-71) which had been tenuous required delicate tension-management on the part of the CM. Laloo Prasad showed that he possessed the skill of political management and thereby ruled in his first term when his party, the *Janata Dal* was in minority in the Bihar

Vidhan Sabha, and the Congress Party thereafter was just the follower of the *Janata Dal* which was in command on its own.

This study treats the state as a robust social actor. It attempts to develop a state-oriented explanation of the crisis of governability of the CM in a developing democratic country. The concern of this study goes back to the analytical issue of "political stability". The explanation for political stability in the specific case varies from those generated by other approaches both developmental and Marxist. The primary focus of analysis here is neither "social mobilization", leading up to growing demands by social groups in a "modernising" society nor class conflict. Rather, the main concern is with the patterns of politicization that result when the CMs attempt to and actually influence the life chances of many social groups. The breakdown of political order in contemporary India puts into question the future capacity of the Indian state to govern. Organisational decline within the Congress party and many other disputes contributed to the erosion of established pattern of authority but an alternative pattern of authority did not emerge. The institutional vacuum in the periphery helped explain a number of political trends including coalition instability and substantial fluctuations in the "political mood" and in electoral outcomes, limping local government (even after constitutional protection) and the emergence of personal rule, often with ruffians as *de facto* local leaders.

This book applies the modified and revised conceptual framework of Rajni Kothari[25] and Stanley A. Kochanek.[26] The modification or revision became essential in order to suit the changed socio-political dynamics of the post-1967 period of Bihar. Kochanek's sub-title of the book "The Dynamics of One Party Democracy" did not fit the multi-party democratic coalitional dynamics of the post-1967 era. The concept of 'dynamics' inheres from Karl J. Deutsch who in his book *The Nerves of Government*[27] likens the chief executive of the state to a steersman of the ship. Both successfully "control" and communicate the followers they work with. Neutstadt[28] echoes the same point more democratically avoiding the "control" syndrome and saying that the power of a chief executive consists in the power to persuade or cajole his fellow advisers and workers to achieve the agreed upon collective goals. But

Kochanek's use of the word has a more distinctive connotation for our study since we refer through the concept of dynamics to forces, factors and changes which impinge upon the states (or the CMs) which are in action or motion. A robust or strong political actor does not so much control the forces as he successfully manipulates, mobilizes and recognizes them; and his own strength or weakness is correlated with his successful or weak interaction and sensitive recognition of those forces. Thus while we have gone close to Huntington's correlation between institutionalisation and mobilization, we have tended to hypothesize that leadership's theory of mobilization is correlated positively to an understanding and manipulation of the emerging aspiring, demanding and to an extent, even commanding (Rudolph and Rudolph's concepts) forces.

HYPOTHESES

(A) The Status of the CM is Shaped as much by Political Dynamics as by the Formal Constitution

Political dynamics includes interplay of factors such as factions, political mobilization of forces, and operation of the federal system. They appear to shape the working of the office of the CM. It is the political dynamics which shapes and mould the status or the personality of the CM. Carl J. Fredrich's concept of constitution as a process that limits and restrains the government effectively and regularly is in tune with this hypothesis which highlights the limiting and guiding role of the forces. A sea change has taken place in the position of the CM in the Centre-state relations. The CM who at one time was reduced to the position of a puppet of the Central government started wielding real powers, and even dictated the Centre if and when essential after 1989.

(B) While the Office Remains the same, Changes in the Style and Pattern of Management Account for different Contrasting Features of Governance

Governance does not only include efficiency in managing the governmental or administrative agencies but it is itself the outcome of the capacity of the government to identify itself with the emerging, demanding and commanding forces in the society, to translate those demands into viable issue- areas fit for decision-making, framing of laws or rules and implementing them so as to deliver goods and benefits to the targeted groups. Seeking balance between aspirations and their fulfilment without unduly straining the treasury and without adversely affecting the condition of the disadvantaged and growingly vociferous groups accounts for the success of the leaders. That is what good governance aspires for.

(C) Governance is a Function of both Mobilization of Forces and Management of Structures

The Congress party under Nehru used the rhetoric of socialism. State leaders under him like S.K. Sinha were pragmatic enough to take the advantage of having the halo of being freedom fighters of long standing as well as being supporters of Nehru's move to champion the cause of socialism at party's Avadi session and bring in Mahalanobis to put in heavy dose of industrialisation through Public Sector Units (PSUs) in the Second Five Year Plan. But neither Nehru nor the state leaders offended either the national bourgeoisie or the rural land owners. Therefore, the Congress party bagged the support of the upper castes as well as the OBCs, SCs, STs and the Muslims till 1962. The Congress party was rightly characterized as an omnibus, a mass party, open like an umbrella or the nation as a whole. The system before 1967 has been called by Rajni Kothari and W.H. Morris-Jones as 'one-party-dominant-system' or 'the Congress system'.[29] Lohia, in addition to alternative mobilization of OBCs, held the Congress regime responsible for mass unemployment, corruption and rising prices which were induced by continued bad monsoon for consecutive two years leading to famine-like conditions before the Fourth General Elections to the *Lok Sabha* and Assemblies. The argument of bad governance appealed to the Indian masses in general who threw the Congress out of power in 1967 in nine states including Tamil Nadu. But the coalition governments which succeeded the Congress were so weak and instable that they could not manage to rule and failed to survive leaving space for the Congress (I) to stage a come back by 1972.

(D) The Character of The Legislature and CMs Changed with The Rise of Regionalism

The autonomy of the state leadership was in doubt till sub-nationalism or regionalism became the battle cry and regional satraps emerged independent of the Central control or will. Social composition of the legislature and the social origin of CMs underwent a marked change as regionalism surged ahead with the breakdown of the Cngress monolith in 1967.

REVIEW OF LITERATURE

W.H. Morris-Jones, Rajni Kothari, Stanley A. Kochanek, Atul Kohli, Sudipto Kaviraj, Norman D. Palmer, S.R. Maheshwari, S.C. Gangal, V. Krishna Ananth and H.M. Jain have provided useful insights on the functioning of the Indian political system. The field of the CM's office has been enriched by their contributions. But there are various books which deal specifically with state politics in India. Atul Kohli in *Democracy and Discontent: India's growing crisis of Governability*[30] explains the roots of the crisis. A highly interventionist but ineffectual national government and weak political parties are characterised by him as two factors in India's governability crisis which contribute towards making India's democracy the "wrong" type.

Francine R. Frankel and M.S.A. Rao's *Dominance and State Power in Modern India*,[31] Vol. I set out an interactional framework of society-state relations where castes, ethnicity and dominance were treated as structures and processes interacting with each other and with increasingly growing powerful state institutions. The comparative studies provide an explanation of how state policies undermine the religious legitimacy of the hierarchical social order and at the same time, facilitate the manipulation of linguistic, communal, caste and ethnic loyalties to diffuse class polarization. The analysis shows that subordinate low caste-cum-class groups are mounting increasingly militant challenges to the hold of the upper castes and classes over state institutions which have provided the most important avenue of social mobility in modern India which also provides an explanation for Bihar.[32]

Iqbal Narain's *State Politics in India* (both written independently and an edited volume) are pioneering works in the field of state politics which provide an insight into understanding of constitutional and political functionaries and processes within the state. He has typified the politics of the state of Bihar since 1967 in a very demonstrative manner. The turmoil of Bihar is seen as a product of two related but independent struggles; a political struggle for control of the state pitting the forward castes against the backward castes, and a socio-economic struggle of the landless lower castes and outcastes against the land owning forward and already rich or neo-rich backward castes.

S.R. Maheshwari in *State Government in India*[33] makes a comparative study of the machinery of governments in the states and UTs and their functioning. Its particular focus is on policy making and public administration at the state level in India. Starting with the analysis of the constitutional position accorded to the states in India, it surveys the various efforts directed to the modernisation of the old system. It analyses the formulation and manifestations of regionalism. It pinpoints the thrones in intergovernmental relations and uncovers corruption at various levels in a candid analysis of the functioning of the state and local governments.

L.N. Sharma in *The Indian Prime Minister*[34] illustrates that while the makers of the Indian Constitution had the British model in mind, during subsequent years of practice, the office developed a distinct style, partly because of the socio-economic condition of the country, and partly because of one party dominance and the personalistic traits in India's political culture. He points out that one can achieve a basic understanding of Indian politics and the working of the Indian political system through the changing power equations and levels of dynamic interactions between the Prime Minister and myriad other institutions and forces. He develops an angle to see the Prime Ministership as a vantage point from which one can dissect the working of the politics of a country. His angle leads one to the position that the Chief Ministership, similarly, is a vantage point to study and meaningfully examine state politics.

A few illuminating articles published in illustrious newspapers are also valuable contributions to the literature on this topic. V.V.P. Sharma in "Chief Ministers as he saw Them" in *The Hindustan Times*, June 10, 1997 emphasised that a very high amount of illegal and excess withdrawals skyrocketed during the *Janata Dal* regime and this compromised the position of the CM *vis-à-vis* Central ministries and intelligence agencies and judiciary. Instances of granting extensions of the CBI's probe at the initial stage and the ill-attempted cover-up job tarnished the image of the state governments leading credence to the view that high-level executive itself is the fountain of corruption and nepotism.

Niranjan Mohanty in "Bihar Blues: A Riches to Rags Story" in *The Times of India*, Dec. 12, 1997 throws useful insights on the growing ineffectiveness and political violence in Bihar. He agrees with Atul Kohli's thesis that the intensity of conflict in Bihar was due to long traditions of elite factionalism, unusually weak political parties, recurring agitations and mass mobilizations, persistent effort to make access to the state's resources, and pattern of caste domination that made "caste appeals both attractive and dangerous".

Books have also been written by former Governors like Sri Prakasa entitled *State Governors in India* and D.C. Pavate who entitles his book as *My Days as Governor*. An edited book by R.R. Diwakar recounts personal experiences of governors in personal and authentic terms and throws useful light on governor-CM relationship. Yet, one laments the dearth of serious academic literature on state politics, particularly the office of the CM which keeps researchers and interested readers at great disadvantage.

While there is a growing need for a careful study of the institution of the CM of Bihar, there is hardly any good book on this subject. A few monographs have come out but they do not throw light on the basic and dynamic powers of the C.M. Mahamaya Prasad Sinha is the only CM of Bihar to have written a book. He entitles his book as *Jab Main Mukhya Mantri Tha* (When I was Chief Minister). The book is a memoir and as the name of the book itself suggests, it covers the period of his short tenure as CM but it is not a systematic treatise and lacks academic objectivity. In contrast, the book by a Janata Party CM of Himachal Pradesh, Shanta Kumar, entitled *Rajniti Ka Satranj* is fulsome. This book deals with the period when he was the C.M. of Himachal Pradesh and highlights his performance and grievances.

To another category lie books written on the CMs. A book entitled *With West Bengal Chief Ministers* written by a bureaucrat, Saroj Chakravarty, talks authoritatively about the CMs and their relationship with other important personalities of the state as well as of the country he had come into contact with or had seen them working from close quarters. Another book entitled *Profile of a Chief Minister* is written by Munni Lal who deals with the days of Bansi Lal when he was the CM of Haryana. Sagar Ahluwalia's book *Anna: The Tempest and the Sea,* and T.V. Kunhi Krishnan's *Chavan and The Troubled Decades* belong to the category where writers author books to glorify their ego *et rex meus.*

Autobiographies written by A.N. Sinha entitled *Mere Sansmaran* and by Rajendra Prasad entitled *Autobiography* help to an extent in understanding the office and powers of the CM of Bihar. *State Politics of India* and *The politics of Power* written by Paul R. Brass; and *Defections and State Politics in India* written by S.C. Kahyap dealing with defection politics, fractional politics as well as the performance and processes of the Congress as well as coalitional governments in states are stimulating. An unpublished thesis submitted to Patna University by Mazhar Hussain entitled *Office and Powers of Chief Minister: A study of some Aspects of Indian Administration* (1979) presents comparative study of CMs of the Indian states and their constitutional and various aspects and interactive role in state administration and politics. Arjun Sharma's unpublished thesis entitled *"The Chief Minister of Bihar: Office and Powers"* submitted to Patna University in 1986 under the guidance of the present writer is a valuable addition to the knowledge on the subject.

The highest credit goes to Iqbal Narain for leading the Jaipur School of Political Science to making pioneer studies of politics of states particularly of Rajasthan. G. Ram Reddy and K. Sheshadri followed up with brilliant studies of politics of Andhra Pradesh. Dhami studied the attitude of Akali leaders in

Punjab. Ramashray Roy and M.P. Singh have done path breaking studies on the dynamics of Congress Party of Bihar. They have made intra-party and factional dynamics centred round caste/party leadership the focal point of analysis of state politics of Bihar. Some useful insights are available in other works on Bihar. Works dealing with bureaucracy and politics by Haridwar Rai, Birkeshwar Prasad Singh and Bishwanath Prasad deal with close dimensions of state and politics L.B. Pandey's book on state executive makes a good discussion of governor-CM relationship. Some helpful dissertations are: Bachoo Sinha's on Committees of Bihar Legislature, Kavita Jha's on Public Undertakings, Maya Devi's on Privileges Committee and B.K. Sinha's on Public Undertakings Committee. These unpublished works provide insights into the working of the sub-system in interaction with the political system in Bihar. Arvind N. Das, Francine R. Frankel, S.N. Sinha, Rudolph and Rudolph and Paul Brass have done pioneering work on political economy and caste/class dynamics in their published works which appeared from time to time. Some other works provide narrative accounts of different periods and are of use to researchers.

Despite various books and relevant documents, none has attempted to discuss what shaped and determined the leadership role and style of the CMs. We need fresh efforts to explain the factors that are involved in bringing about the change in the role, style, background and interactive relationships of the CMs. Hence, this attempt.

RESEARCH METHODOLOGY AND SOURCES

The approach used in this study is historical, comparative and analytical. In carrying out research for the book, the main reliance has been placed on primary sources like Constitution, Constituent Assemble Debates, memoirs, autobiographies, legislative debates and records and reports of the government's committees and departments found in different libraries. I have relied upon secondary sources like books and journals as also upon newspaper articles such as those published in *The Times of India* (Delhi), *The Hindustan Times* (Delhi), *The Indian Express* (Delhi), *The Hindu* (Kolkata) and *The Telegraph* (Calcutta). We have consulted news Archives like the *Asian Recorder* and journals like *The Indian Journal of Political Science, The Indian Journal of Public Administration, Political Science Review* as well as *The Journal of Constitutional and Parliamentary Studies*. We have also collected useful information from Bihar newspapers published in English like *The Hindustan Times* (Patna), *The Times of India* (Patna), *the Indian Nation* (Patna) and *The Searchlight* (Patna) so long as the latter two were published and those published in Hindi like *Hindustan* (Patna) and *Prabhat Khabhar* (Patna). I conducted interviews with some important persons connected with the political processes , some present and former cabinet ministers of the state, some opposition party leaders as well as some old and senior personages who have had the opportunity to watch the political processes of the government from close quarters.

PLAN OF THE BOOK

The next chapter (Chapter II) introduces the concepts of 'Congress' system, 'coalition' system and good governance. In Chapter III, we discuss about the formation of governments. In Chapter IV, we present a broad view of the politics of appointment, background and style of CMs. Chapter V and succeeding chapters are devoted to a discussion of the role and position of the governor *vis-à-vis* the CM; the appointment, power and position of the CMs; and their interactive relations with the governor, the cabinet and the legislature. The next two chapters are devoted to examining the relationship of the CM of Bihar with the people, the party and the media. Chapter IX deals with the CM and the federal process. Then we conclude with delineating the role of CMs and discussing how far their aspiration for good governance was realized. We bring the discussion to recent developments i.e. up to August, 2012. We divide the narrative into different phases of governance and mobilisation in Bihar. The six identified phases are: 1947-67 symbolising Congress dominance, 1967-72 symbolizing a non-Congress Coalition system with new features, style and impact; 1971-76 symbolising imperial Prime Ministerialism; 1977-80 symbolizing a non non-Congress system with pre-party and non-coalitional features, style and impact; 1980-89 symbolizing restored Congress dominant system ending in the emergence of non-Congress dominant system in Bihar, etc. and 1990-2012 symbolizing empowerment of OBCs. This periodisation is relevant and may be used in the study of the CMs' office in other states as well.

NOTES AND REFERENCES

1. V.A. Pai Panandiker and Ajay K. Mehra, Delhi, *The Indian Cabinet*, Konark, 1996, pp. 5-6.
2. V. Krishna Ananth, *India Since Independence: Making Sense of Indian Politics*, Delhi, Pearson, 2009, p. 259.
3. V.N. Gadgil, an M.P. and spokesman of the Congress party ridiculed the working of coalition government in 1996 writing that "the Cabinet speaks in many voices. The sense of direction of unity of purpose, very essential for a proper functioning of a Cabinet, get lost in a coalition government". This, however, may not be true about all coalition governments. We may only note that members of a cabinet in a coalition government should ideally function on a commonly agreed programme or agenda for governance agreed upon by them. For Gadgil's view, see his "*Coalition Politics in India and Abroad*", *Politics India* (Delhi), October 1996, p. 13.
4. While some of the CMs of Bihar had earned the notoriety for being corrupt, Jharkhand's Madhu Koda crossed limits; and disclosures in Enforcement Directorate raids in November, 2009 drew nationwide attention.
5. K.G. Balakrishnan's summary of the speech appeared in *The Times of India* (Delhi) and other newspapers.
6. *The Hindu* (Kolkata), 23.04.2010.
7. *Ibid.*, 25.04.2010.
8. Atul Kohli, "*Breakdown in a 'Backward' state: Bihar*" in *Democracy and Development in India: From Pro-Socialism to Pro-Business*, Delhi, Oxford University Press, 2009, p. 260.
9. Thomas A. Timberg, "*Bihari Backwardness: Does Feudalism Frustrate?*", *Asian Survey*, May 1982, p. 470.
10. V. Krishna Ananth, *op. cit.*
11. Girish Mishra and Braj Kumar Pandey, *Sociology and Economics of Casteism in India*, Delhi, Pragati Publications, 1996, pp. 281-82.
12. *Ibid.*
13. Kohli, *op. cit.*, p. 274.
14. *Ibid.*
15. *Ibid.*

16. Atul Kohli appreciates the role of S.K. Sinha as one who introduced four land reform legislations and was the first in India to implement *Zamindari* abolition. But V. Krishna Ananth writes that leaders like G.B. Pant, R.S. Shukla, Rajendra Prasad, S.K. Sinha and others were in favour of preserving the *status quo* in the social and economic sense. They empathised with the rural elite and in turn, for a large chunk of the upper castes, Congress party was the obvious choice. See his *op. cit.*, pp. 39-40. He repeats this point of view at several other places in this book.
17. Paul H. Appleby, the Ford Foundation consultant visited ten states including Bihar. Appleby profusely praised the administration in India and on some points, said that this was the best in the world. This admiration also, by logic, extends to the administration of Bihar as he saw it in 1953.
18. Report of the T.L. Venkatarama Aiyar Commission of Inquiry constituted under Notification No. 255, dated 1st October by the Government of Bihar, report submitted on February 5, 1970, conclusion on p. 487.
19. Mudholkar Commission of Inquiry, Report on the charges against Fourteen Ex-United Front Ministers, constituted under Government of Bihar Notification No. S.O. 140, dated the 12th March 1986, S.O. 758, dated the 24th of October, 1968 printed by the Superintendent, Secretariat Press, Bihar, Patna, 1970, conclusion on pp. 245-275.
20. Between 1980 and 1984, there had been more politically motivated murders in Bihar than in Punjab. Private caste armies like *Lorik Sena, Ranvir Sena, Bhoomi Sena, The Brahmrishi Sena, The Kunwar Sena* and *The Lal Sena* were founded.
21. Cited in Timberg, *op. cit.*
22. Ali Anwar, *Sar Ke Bal Khari Muslim Siyasat*, Amarte-e-Ahale Ansar Alhind; Patna, 1998.
23. Pasmanda Muslim Agenda: *21Vin Sadi Ki Ore*, Main Office of Pasmanda Muslim Mahaj, Patna, 1999.
24. Francine, R. Franke, *India's Political Economy 1947-77; The Gradual Revolution*, Oxford University Press, Delhi, 1978.
25. Rajni Kothari, *Politics in India*, Orient Longman, Delhi, 1970.
26. Stanley A. Kochanek, *The Congress Party in India: The Dynamics of One Party Dominance*, Princeton University Press, 1968.
27. Karl, J. Deutsch, *The Nerves of Government*, The Free Press of Glencoe, London, 1963.
28. Richard, E. Neutstadt, *Presidential Power*, Delhi: Allied Publishers, 1960.
29. This is the theme of the next chapter dealing with theoretical framework.

30. Atul Kohli, *Democracy and Discontent: India's Growing Crisis of Governability*, New York: Cambridge University Press, 1991.
31. Francine, R. Frankel and M.S.A. Rao, *Dominance and State Power in Modern India*, Vol. I, Oxford University Press, 1987.
32. Iqbal Narain, *State Politics in India*, Meerut: Meenakshi Prakashan, 1967.
33. S.R. Maheshwari, *State Government in India*, Delhi: Macmillan, 1979.
34. L.N. Sharma, *The Indian Prime Minister: Office and Powers*, Delhi: Macmillan, 1976.

2

The Concepts of Congress and Coalition Politics and Good Governance

Indian political system between 1947 and 1967 was conceptualised as one-party-dominant system. Rajni Kothari, W.H. Morris-Jones and Ramashray Roy delineated the features of one-party-dominant system in their articles and books written between 1964-70, though the system had given way to a coalition system in states like Bihar, West Bengal, Uttar Pradesh, Punjab, Haryana, Madhya Pradesh, Orissa and Kerala after 1964. This conception of the system fitted the Nehruvian era; and erosion started after the death of Nehru. After the Congress party split in 1969, this concept did not characterize the governance at the Centre. Mrs. Gandhi's rule was characterized by populism followed by authoritarianism, personality-orientedness and ended by pursuing dynastic succession. Since Bihar followed both the models, these theoretical models apply to Bihar *muta mutandis*.

THE 'CONGRESS' SYSTEM (1947-67)

Constitutionally speaking, India started her experiment of parliamentary democracy as a multi-party system. But some analytical political scientists perceived that the Indian party system was a 'Congress' system.[1] The Congress party for the first time gave to the country a coherent and unified leadership which could speak for the whole of the country. PM Nehru spoke for the nation as a whole, had a powerful identity of his own; and possessed authority and legitimacy of rule. Similarly, the CM of Bihar, S.K. Sinha and his counterparts, B.C. Roy, G.B. Pant, Kamaraj, the Shuklas in West Bengal, U.P., Madras, and M.P. respectively, for their states as a whole and had grip over men and matters in the states they ruled over and had an established identity, authority and legitimacy.

The Congress party had not emerged as a parliamentary party to win elections. Designed originally as an oppositional movement, it played that role right from 1885 to September, 1946 at the Centre and in the process, assimilated contradictory and divergent interests and tried to forge unity among them on the point of gaining freedom from colonialism. Consensus-building was the watchword of this mass party. Even when freedom was achieved and opportunities of universal adult franchise were opened, the older tendencies continued under Nehru and the Congressmen displayed the aura of being persons who had made sacrifices and ultimately, won freedom for the country. Opposition parties were at a disadvantage, and they did not have in their midst charismatic personalities of the type the Congress possessed; and those who left the Congress lost the aura they had when they were inside the Congress party. The Congress continued to play the role of a broad-based movement, involving within itself both dominant and dissident groups. In Bihar, for example, A.N. Sinha represented the perennial opposition leader within the Congress right from 1937 itself; he had the calibre and the strength to always "self-appoint" as the Finance Minister in all the cabinets that the CM S.K. Sinha formed. They contested each other for the office of the CM of Bihar in 1957 only to embrace each other after S.K. Sinha was declared elected and A.N. Sinha continued as usual as the Finance Minister of the state.

It came natural for the Congress to play an eclectic role. Though it took away *bhowli* lands and *zamindari*, passed *bataidari* and land ceiling laws, yet it was near and dear to the land-owning castes and classes because it did not implement them strictly. Central leadership particularly since 1967 started dictating and dominating CMs in the Congress ruled states who could hold office only with the goodwill of the PM, Mrs. Gandhi. CMs till 1972 or in the imperial Prime Ministerial era (1972-77 and 1980-89) in the Congress ruled states were puppets in the hands of the PM. The CMs during this era started their tenure with the feeling that they owed their office not due to their strength in the Congress Legislature Party (CLP) or stature among the people but due to the pleasure of the PM. This generated a psychological complex of dependence and the tendency to do things not at their own bidding but at that of the "determinate human superior".

Both Mrs. Gandhi and her son, Rajiv Gandhi were central to the birth, life, sustenance and ultimately, death of the CM. Although this practice, ensured party discipline and prevented unchecked intra-party dissensions but it weakened the decentralization process in the party and proved a death-knell first to intra-party democracy and finally, to democracy at the national level epitomized by the declaration and the way of implementation of national emergency in 1977-79.

In 1952 and 1957 elections, those who got tickets convassed by making door-to-door visits to electorates' houses and through mass campaigns. By 1977, the familiar method was booth capturing, bogus voting, use of money and bullets to intimidate voter or offering them allurements. Jagannath Mishra of Congress (I) paved the path for securing the support of the police and the bureaucracy for politicians to win elections. The Janata Party with its hoodlums took the advantage of winning the elections through booth capturing and bogus voting; and having won, it pursued the practice of one of its factions—JKD, nominating four CMs and another faction, BJP nominating another four. The then elected CM of Bihar, Karpoori Thakur, was the nominee of BJP faction. The consensus-building was thus gone by as a model of the past.

The government started mobilizing people in new ways. The party acted as an articulator of interests and opinions and as a transmission belt between the government and the people. PM Nehru had not allowed the Congress party to play this role because he feared the recurrence of internal opposition from the likes of Patel and Tandon which he had faced between 1947 to 1950 and also because of his penchant for consensus-building. As the CM of Bihar, S.K. Sinha did not have happy relationship with the President of Bihar Pradesh Congress Committee (BPCC), Mahamaya Prasad Sinha who, after having been defeated by S.K. Sinha's man, Prajapati Mishra in the election to the office of the BPCC President, turned S.K. Sinha's bitter critic, levelled several allegations against him and ultimately, deserted the Congress. In the absence of government-party relations not being congenial enough to transmit people's grievances formally to the government, professional middlemen or intermediaries (*dalals*) entered into the arena to bridge the gap and make money. S.A. Kochanek has referred to this phenomenon in many of his writings.[2] The unified control at the highest level (be it of the PM or the CM) reinforced the tendency to continue and people formed the habit of getting official works done by not directly contacting the concerned officials or the elected representatives but intermediaries who were numerous and who flourished professionally by procuring money from "clients" almost on a daily basis.

The opposition parties, on the other hand, saw their role in a peculiar manner. Ashok Mehta, the socialist leader, openly said that the role of the opposition parties in India should be to cooperate with the ruling party in a critical spirit; it was a "corrective" rather than a competitive role that they should perform.[3] It was only in the mid-sixties, following the fragmentation in the Congress ranks, and taunted by the sparkling ridicule of the dynamic Lohia, that the various non-Congress parties began to adopt the strategy of "opposition" and play their distinctive role in "Indian" or "*Bihari*" style.

Finally, coalition system emerged in eight of the then sixteen states including Bihar in 1967. We shall discuss the characteristics of the 'Congress' system (1947-67) before we take up a discussion of the coalition system begining from 1967.

CHARACTERISTICS OF THE 'CONGRESS' SYSTEM (1947-67)

1. The 'Congress' system was made up of a small elite, homogeneous in social background, mainly upper caste, English-educated, and almost a "one class" ensemble[4]. Opposition groups also emerged from this class. Society was not apolitical as political mobilization penetrated to the bottom. OBCs, lower middle and lower classes joined the broad stream as time moved on. The traditional dominance of lawyers declined in Parliament by 1967 and their place was taken over by farmers and agriculturists. The structure, style and idioms of politics underwent a change as a precursor to further radical changes which were to follow under Mandal politics since 1989 onwards.
2. Political groups fragmented and oppositional activity found its stimulus from fragmentation, dissent and even outright and quick defections and desertions of allegiance to groups, factions, alliances and parties. It was difficult to draw clear lines between government and opposition; both belonged to what Mosca called the "ruling class". It was also difficult to draw clear lines between "government" and "party". The distinctions had blurred because of selfish motivations of politicians to capture power by any means.
3. Re-structuring led to making the system "open". Since the Congress party did not face sufficient challenge until 1967, factions within the Congress acted as opposition parties would have otherwise done. These factions reflected the policy positions and ideological stands as opposition parties do. This accounted for a considerable openness of political communication.[5]

4. Where governmental authority is stable (as was the case in Bihar from 1947 to 1967), factional competition within the party was both possible and permitted. But in India, it has been noted that even where majorities have been insecure but institutionalization weak, it has often led to increased dissidence, lack of consensus and erosion of cohesion.
5. Following the background of nationalist movement, protest movements have gained a certain legitimacy in India. The ambivalent concept of democracy also lends justification to political protest which is normally waged in the name of masses. S.K. Sinha had to deal with students' protest movement in 1955 when a student of B.N. College, Patna and another at Nawadah were killed in firing by the police. When Nehru visited Patna later, he was hooted by the student leaders of Patna University in the midst of his speech in Gandhi Maidan of Patna. Since 1967 and more particularly since 1974, protest movements have gained a certain legitimacy and have been lodged frequently not only in Bihar but all over India.
6. Most of the agitations or protest movements, barring a few exceptions, did not challenge the basic institutions of the system or the values that sustained them until 1967. Rather, they strengthened the values by declaring that the ruling elites had failed to implement them. This is the reason that out of eight CMs who took over charge in 1967 post-Congress era, six were former Congressmen. A distinctive anti-Congress style had not emerged even in 1967. Hence, a continuity in personnel, ideological and pragmatic commitments and even style of politics was perceptible. Institutionalization took place largely within the permissive boundaries of the system.
7. The government became the anchor to the system and its leadership role was legitimized. Even the role of agents and heirs of leaders was legitimized.
8. Intellectual and urban elements presented the critique of government, its working, its ideology and

the values that sustained it. The largely illiterate population participates in the critique in an unsophisticated manner, verbally and mutely but not vocally and organizationally except when they are part of rallies. They are listeners to leaders in mass meetings organized by parties or groups from time to time to show their strength.

9. Personalized networks operate, though their amorphous character has changed and style has shifted. A notable point is that national and state organs of the same party pull in opposite directions. As political mobilization increased, the role of local and regional parties and the number of independents in electoral fray increased.
10. Emphasis on personalities in mediating political relationships grew up. As the Congress system weakened, the concept of coalition emerged.

THE CONCEPT OF 'COALITION'

A coalition is a parliamentary or a political grouping whose stability by its very nature, is threatened in comparison to a party, faction or interest because it occurs in a situation when no single party enjoys an overall majority and disparate elements are cobbled up to create a working majority to run the government.[6] Coalition is, a "co-operative arrangement".[7] One of its benefits is to promote compromises in politics. Everybody should yield something, although mutual surrender is rarely sufficient to guarantee stability or strength for more than a fleeting interval of time. Coalitions tend to curb radicalism and, to liberalise conservatism. Radical parties usually feel that they are expected to yield most and they are usually least inclined to affiliate".[8]

The concept of coalition system has certain implications. First, coalition is made on the basis of a commonly agreed set of principles or agenda which appears useful to the partners of the coalition. Second, coalition means a company, an assembly of groups and not a motley of crowd; it has partners who agree by consent to work together under the given circumstances. Third, coalition system implies the process of give and take. As a result of the tugs and pulls, a point of equilibrium arrives at which the actors agree to lay down their arms in order to unite for the realisation of their goals.[9] Lastly, coalition politics is not a static but a dynamic affair as collaborational adjustments pass through the process of growth and decay.

A coalition system has several operational dimensions. First, it has general as well as particular aspects. Its general aspect means coverage of any situation or the clustering together of various groups of men having any profession or field of activity; its particular aspect is concerned with the formation of a political alliance of various groups or organisations for the specific purpose of sharing power. Second, it has rational or normative and practical or descriptive aspects. Thirdly, a coalition system may operate in a tacit or implied and an express or formal form. While a tacit coalition system implies the role of a single party in power banking on the invisible support or understanding of other party or parties, the latter exhibits a formal alliance of one party with other party or parties with clear and open understanding of give and take. Fourth, tacit coalition system has two sub-variables-proto-coalition and sub-coalition. While the former means the existence of dissimilar partners under the same umbrella acting with accommodative tendencies, the latter makes a situation in which one party in power maintains invisible co-operation with other parties or groups either on the basis of some understanding or on the merits of the issue in question. Lastly, a coalition system may have constructive and/or destructive aspects. The cooperative endeavour of two or more parties may be made for the formation of government with or without any scheme in hand to provide an alternative government.

In fine, a coalition signifies a system where the participants pool their resources and co-ordinate their deployment for the sake of achieving the desired purpose. It is based on the temporary conjunction of interests. Gamson points out that the coalition adjustments "can take place only within the context of mixed motives in which both conflicts and common interests are simultaneously present and must govern the sources of action chosen."[10] He, therefore, defines coalition as "the joint use of resources to determine the outcome of a decision in a mixed motive situation involving more than two units."[11]

CHARACTERISTICS OF 'COALITION' POLITICS (1967-89)

The fourth general election (1967) marked the end of the continued Congress hegemony in Bihar as the Congress party captured only 128 of 318 seats of *The Vidhan Sabha*. Except Bihar, the Congress party lost power in eight other Indian states due to mobilization of social forces and also due to its unpopularity on account of the common perception of the electorate of its non-performance, corrupt governance, responsibility for rising prices and unemployment, etc. The non-Congress parties gained efficacy following Lohia's ideas of unification of non-Congress parties and OBCs. Rich peasants and urban commercials or mercantile bourgeoise had emerged among *Ahirs, Kushwahas* and *Kurmis* who had been making efforts to combine since 1924, first of all in the name of *Tribeni Sangh*. As a result of *zamindari* abolition and developmental planning, they prospered rapidly because they generally participated directly in cultivation without any social inhibitions. Vegetable growers, milk sellers, fishermen and owners of cold storages among them were also making money. They were purchasing land-both in rural and urban areas and educating their wards in schools and colleges. They were running cinema houses and entering in trade, transport and construction business. These castes, especially the neo-rich among them, were attracted towards Lohia's exhortations. Thanks to Lohia's ideas and efforts and Karpoori Thakur's grassroots mobilization, OBCs got united and emerged as a big factor in Bihar politics in 1967. Land speculation also provided fillip to them to make a meaningful and effective dent in politics. The fact that the group of parties could defeat the Congress after three General Elections filled in them a sense of confidence that they could re-gain power if they did not fragment themselves. This also led to issue confrontation, ideological orientation and a greater sense of political involvement among opposition parties borne out of optimism that they were a part of power sharing process and hence, should take responsible policy stands.

Nearly all the non-Congress parties after 1967 have had to resort to coalition-making (among themselves and with

Congress defectors of all kinds, without regard to the fact that such combinations were sometimes not "coalitionable") and therefore, an amorphous and heterogeneous assortment of groups captured power most of the times. Just as the defection of dissident factions within the Congress Party was the prime cause of Congress loss of power in the 1967 elections, the inability of the anti-Congress United Fronts (UFs) to "hang together" led to a toppling of those governments in one state after another. This happened in five states, namely Bihar, U.P., West Bengal, Punjab and Haryana from December, 1967 to February, 1968. On the break up of UFs, a short-lived attempt was made in Bihar and West Bengal to form minority governments of factions that left the UFs with the backing of the Congress Party. In West Bengal, the Congress Party itself officially joined the coalition. In both cases, as the coalition lacked the strength of a strong CLP, the attempt failed.

The Congress party had an advantage over the non-Congress parties. The Congress party, was by its very nature, a "giant coalition", accommodative and agglomerative, adapted to consensus and eclecticism. The opposition parties, while they played their "minority" roles in such a system, could form governments only when they came together to challenge the hegemony of the Congress party. Lohia's scheme of coalition worked out neither to the architect's satisfaction nor came up to people's expectations. The very experiment was not durable from its very start.

The fluidity of political alignments and the rampant opportunism characterized "politics of defection" between 1967 and 1969. This led to discrediting of Lohia's coalition politics and demanded a more discerning approach to coalition-making. The Congress party, on the other hand, took steps to achieve the lost cohesion.[12] As a result, significant changes came about when states faced the "little election" in 1969. In Bihar, in a matter of four months after the 1969 election, two coalition governments, one led by the Congress party and another by dissident Congress groups, came into being but collapsed, and President's rule was imposed the same year. In contrast with M.P. and U.P. (which came under the Congress domain), Bihar remained a faction-ridden state from the beginning due to its sprawling size, disparate population, semi-feudal background and socio-economic backwardness. These facts partly explain political instability in Bihar. The Indian electorate, however, showed a large degree of political awareness and punished both the Congress and the anti-Congress parties, like the *Jana Sangh* and *Samyukta Socialist Party* (SSP) in U.P. and Bihar in 1969 as they failed to provide stable and purposive governments which the electorate wanted them to provide. "Split Voting" at the Parliamentary level favoured the Congress party at the Centre.

The 1969 election forced the realization that the integrating element in India's increasing political diversity is the growing focus of identity with social forces and alienation from the government. The government provides the arena around which both consensual and dissident orientations take place. Opposition may take place from within the government party or from without against the Congress party as well as against other government parties. In Bihar, the Congress lost a few seats in 1968 but due to fragmentation of non-Congress forces, was able to form a coalition government. The role of voter's reprisal, voter's assessment of governmental performance and the ability of alternative alignments to provide cohesive and coalitional teams and the institutionalization of party support and identities became more critical after the 1969 elections.

The Congress party under the leadership of Mrs. Gandhi with the help of her close associates like Chavan tried to build working relationship with non-Congress CMs in the states. The consensus that Mrs. Gandhi worked out between 1967-69 was, according to Rajni Kothari, "more broad-based and in many ways more fluid" than the one brought by Nehru or Lal Bahadur Shastri.[13] The "rightist" parties like the *Jana Sangh* were shedding their earlier extremist positions on language (Hindi) and religion (Hindu and the holy cow) while the *Swatantra Party* declined in strength in Bihar. A left-of-centre consensus was the only natural course which came to be articulated. This articulation, however, was not the consequence of interest aggregation or aggregation of party structures. The "intermediate systems", the regional and local structures brought them about. This explains why since 1967, state and regional parties and even independents have expanded their strength and played an increasing role on Mrs. Gandhi's (the then Congress President's) pressure. The promulgation of President's rule in Kerala in 1959 against President Rajendra Prasad's counsel to the contrary had put a serious block to the consensus-building approach and Nehru's democratic credentials. Mrs. Gandhi, after the 1969 Congress split, was ruling the Union as a minority government with the outside support of the DMK and the CPI and did not pursue the role of a consensus-builder since 1969. She consciously crafted a left-of-centre image for herself through taking token steps like nationalization of fourteen banks, derecognition of princes, etc. She won the 1971 Parliamentary polls by huge majority on the populist slogan of *Garibi Hatao*. Her party re-christened as the Congress (I) won the 1972 Legislative Assembly elections in several states including Bihar by huge majority on the same plank and commensurate image-construction.

The Congress party which since 1969 had not been the party of consensus but of confrontation and opposition, remained somewhat demoralised till 1972, but it had by then gained ten years' experience of competitive dominance. Non-aggregation between the interests of the Centre and states was thus loudly pronounced, and conclaves of opposition leaders were held to put forward revision of Centre-state relations. Yet, the number of constituencies where one party enjoyed a virtual monopoly over its competitors was on the decline. In 1967 elections, a survey showed that a majority of 75 to 90 per cent of those who responded disapproved the Congress record.[14] The two Communist Parties were electorally the most successful in states between 1967-89, though the CPI (M) was trounced in 2011 after 34 years of continuous rule in West Bengal. The Communist Party of India (CPI) was supported in the industrial areas of Bihar in the 1967 elections. The CPI (Marxist-Leninist) entered the electoral fray but did not make much dent. It has remained an agitational cadre party. Associational interest groups except FICCI and some trade unions did not make much dent. PIL cases in courts raised issues of public importance, though they served limited purpose. Traditional family and kinship structures controlled both industrial and political enterprises in succession. Castes and communities played predominant roles. These negative tendencies led some prominent sceptics to doubt the ability of universal adult franchise in India to solve the pressing problems of national integration, security and above all, socio-economic change and development. Jaya Prakash Narain talked of partyless democracy, M.N. Roy pinned hope on People's Committees, Gandhi ji on village as the centre of power from where power would go from down to the upmost layers; and of late, through constitutional amendments, we are pinning hopes on PRIs and UCBs to reach the benefits of development to the doorsteps of the people living below poverty line. But since 1989, at the Centre, we have either minority or coalition governments and in states also, the pendulum moves from one type of agglomerative system to another and a new federalisation system is on in which states have come to play a more effective role and the Union is an ensemble of states.

India has entered into an era of coalitions, but like the Britishers, we regard it even after about 45 years of experimenting with it as "a regrettable necessity".[15] "England", said Disraeli in 1852, "does not love coalitions".[16] Coalitions are detestable and dishonest, Ramsay Mac Donald told the House of Commons in 1928[17]. But they felt that the Westminster model works successfully only if there are no more than two strong parties. Unlike England, India's diversity and heterogeneity provide the example of a society which suits the formation of a coalition government unless the exigencies of a situation (like war, external aggression, internal disturbance, economic insecurity or social unrest) demand otherwise. Nehru and S.K. Sinha were charismatic leaders (Mrs. Gandhi, Laloo and Nitish have had been"populist" leaders) who, with potent organisational structures, socially and politically mobilized the society and were able to establish one-party-dominance or in some years, the latter ran coalition governments. Coalition politics also reflects the earlier consensus-making politics of the 'Congress system' and aggregates the underlying regional and parochial subterranean interests and therefore, the transition from the 'Congress system' to the 'coalition system' is not innovative. That is the reason why after a few years of disappointing experience with the coalition system, it has come to be widely accepted as a system of governance at both the Central and state levels in India. Since various sections of our population are prone to asserting some kind of "identity" of their own, they are more likely to vote for coalitions more particularly at state level elections. The only precaution from the point of view of nation-building is that the tendencies that foster sub-nationalism have to be restrained and kept within limits through parallel efforts to make the presence of states felt in various aspects of socio-economic-political life. This is, however, problematic since market has replaced the state.

When for the first time, one-party governance at the Centre and another party governing the big states like Bihar, U.P., etc. in 1967 came about, the first reaction was one of concern about the adverse effect of coalition governments on political stability and the smooth and coherent working of administration[18]. The apprehensions were proved correct in the case of Bihar where there were nine coalition governments between 1967 and 1972; and the first of these included parties as disparate as the CPI and the *Jana Sangh*, and they ruled withe the outside support of the CPI (M) and the *Swantantra Party*.

CHANGING PARTY CONTOURS AND STYLES

The Congress party continued to occupy the central position even after 1967 but of course, with a marked difference. Many ad hoc groups that once prospered due to the absorptive capacity of the amorphous Congress organisation, proliferated after 1967 and emerged on the map of state politics including in the politics of Bihar. In place of political fragmentation of a 'structured party system' as hitherto manifested by the stable Congress party, an 'atomised party structure' (to use the words of Sartori) came up to demonstrate the political axiom that, by and large, many regional organisations, owing allegiance to local issues and loyalties, rather than national perspectives, dominated the electoral politics.

The non-Congress parties became ruling partners in eight north Indian states including Bihar as a result of the wonders of the fourth general elections that marked a "beginning of break with the past". A set of factors contributed to this mini-revolution. First, the opposition parties changed their tactics drastically. Instead of challenging the legitimacy of the electoral process which made the Congress win, they participated in it seriously enough to shake the Congress fort.[19] Non-Congress parties and groups decided to have electoral adjustments and alliances "not on the basis of all-India issues but on the basis of the all-India grievances".[20] Third, people in general were in favour of a change of leaders who could provide better governance, a more suitable administrative order and establish a more democratic rapport with them. Fourth, people (including the rural masses) appreciated the programmes formulated by the non-Congress parties because they had pragmatic and accommodative orientation. Fifth, the have-nots saw an opportunity opening for them to become the haves in the changing electoral scenario.

The non-Congress coalition mode, however, suffered from inherent instability as the heterogeneous stuff of which it was made had its toll sooner than later. "The participants did not seem to have become used to the ways of collective responsibility".[21] Defections became so common that even respected non-Congress leaders were seen reverting back to the Congress model, relegating ideological considerations to the background. The Bihar *Vidhan Sabha* polls of 1972 signified termination of the non-Congress coalition model as all the non-Congress parties were badly routed by the tempestuous blow of the 'Indira Wave'. The one-dominant-party system of the 1950s and mid-60s was restored with the difference that the former system had the democratic tinge while the 1971-72 to 77 phase exhibited an authoritarian streak. The strength shown by the Indian electorate against authoritarianism in 1977 elections points to the trend that democracy had its roots in India despite illiteracy, poverty, superstitions and lack of exposure to media and international fora. In the parliamentary elections held in early 1977, Mrs. Gandhi's Congress party secured only one seat in all the nine north Indian states put together. Thus non-Congressism was fiercely back to live for not more than three years at the Centre and in most of the states where the U.F. governments were dismissed following the Congress's spectacular victory in 1980 as the *Janata Party* had done in relation to the Congress governments in 1977. The ground given in both the situations, though not very tenable, was that the parliamentary results showed that people had lost faith in state governments and hence, the latter were liable to be dismissed under Article 356 of the Indian Constitution. The role of the opposition parties between 1980 and 1989 was again restricted to making attempts to influencing the policies of the ruling party at the national level rather than challenging its monopoly of power. The Congress party at the national level led by Mrs. Gandhi between 1980-84 and by her son, Rajiv Gandhi between 1984-89 was the arbiter of internecine disputes at the state levels within the party.

CONCEPT OF 'GOOD GOVERNANCE'

World-Bank-sponsored concept of good governance and the goal set by the World Summit for Social Development, 1995 for the governments to realize social and people centred sustainable development pose challenges as well as yardsticks for judging the performance of governments.[22]

States are now known for what they do, what they perform and how much they deliver in the briefest possible period to the people. States to-day vie and struggle to provide Constitutionalism (self-limited, self-restrained and self-controlled effective and regular governance), equal opportunity of development to all, justice-social, economic and political, independent judiciary, *Lokpal* and *Lokayuktas* besides administrative accountability.The Twelfth Report of Second Administrative Reforms Commission (A.R.C.), submitted in February, 2009, makes citizen centric administration the heart of governance.[23] This report identifies the under-mentioned traits as the hallmarks of citizen centric governance:[24]

1. Rule of Law zero tolerance strategy.
2. Vibrant, responsive and accountable institution-making.
3. Decentralization.
4. Transparency.

5. Civil Service Reforms.
6. Ethics in Governance.
7. Process Reforms.
8. Periodic and independent evaluation of services (service ethos), and the quality of governance.
9. Equity.
10. Efficiency.
11. Predictability.

Four pre-requisites for citizen centric governance are identified viz.

(a) Sound legal framework.
(b) Robust institutional mechanism for proper implementation of laws and their effective functioning.
(c) Competent personnel staffing these institutions and sound personnel management policies.
(d) Right policies for decentralization, delegation and accountability.

The Commission suggests the following strategies and processes as well as the tools and mechanisms which can be usefully employed to make the administration citizen centric. These are:[26]

(a) Re-engineering processes to make governance 'citizen centric'.
(b) Adoption of Appropriate Modern Technology.
(c) Right to Information.
(d) Citizens' Charters.
(e) Independent evaluation of servies (Performance Appraisal).
(f) Grievance redressal mechanisms.
(g) Active Citizens participation-Public-private partnerships.

In addition, delegation and simplification of procedures can improve efficiency and bring goverment services to the doorsteps of citizens. A series of service operations can maximize citizens' welfare. Use of management principles such as data, focus on clients/citizens, quality process flow, minimizing the costs of unnecessary complesity can transform government service organizations into more efficient and citizen friendly agencies. A multi-channel single window delivery structure for channelising all types of government services at the local level in the most efficient manner possible using IT technology so that the citizen can access those services easily and conveniently at his doorstep and even on the run through the use of mobile telephony is what one hopes for.

The Twelfth report of the Second A.R.C. raises people's expectations as well as puts forth tasks for the governments to perform if they want stability and sound reputation. Like one day cricket, a citizen now aspires to get his birth-or death-certificate, land receipt, mutation receipt, etc. in six hours after he puts in his form on the counter to receive the same. The government has either to make arrangements for rapid and equitable access to these government services or see his reputation so sullied that he may be thrown out in the mid-term or when he faces the electorate the next time.

A reading of the 13th report of the Second A.R.C. submitted in April, 2009 suggests that the govermment, in particular, should pay special attention to the activities of the following Ministries/Departments:[27]

(i) Rural Development.
(ii) Drinking Water Supply
(iii) Housing and Urban Poverty Alleviation
(iv) Urban Development, and
(v) *Panchayati Raj*

The same programmes are monitored by both the Ministry of Rural Development as well as the Ministry of *Panchayati Raj*. So Sujata Singh cogently comments that the creation of a separate ministry for *Panchayati Raj* at the Union level in 2004 was against the princile of rationality[28]

E-governance is a very much emphasized form of governance in the twenty-first century. National Council for Applied Economic Research in its stydy of the E-readiness of different state governments in 2006 found that Karnataka, Tamil Nadu, Andhra Pradesh, Delhi, Haryana, Punjab, Kerala and Chandigarh were the leaders in e-readiness. Maharashtra, Gujarat, Uttar Pradesh and Goa were aspiring to be leaders.[29] In the "Expectant" category were the states of Rajasthan, West Bengal, Himachal Pradesh, Sikkim, Meghalaya and Uttrakhand. "Average Achivers". were Assam, Nagaland, Andamaan and Nicobar Islands and Lakshadweep. Bihar, Tripura, Manipur, Daman & Diu, Jammu & Kashmir, Dadra &Nagar Haveli and Arunachal Pradesh were placed at the very bottom, in the "Lowest Achievers" category.[30] The situation has changed little though the Union Government has started the Scheme for establishing State Wide Area Networks (SWAN) across the country at a total outlay of Rs. 3334 crores over a period of five years.[31]

The study of Impact Assessment in three state level e-government projects-vehicle registration, property registration and land records was taken up in twelve states across India and the report of the first phase was released on the 19th of November 208 on the MIT website.[32] Given the poor record of e-readiness of Bihar, Impact assessment study of Bihar was not included in this study. However, there is no doubt that through e-governance, Bihar can improve its capacity to provide governance equitably and cost effectively, improve the degree of integration of deprived segments of society, provide business and participate in the provincial and national level digital economics. However, Biharis need not rue their lot since the survey of Asian civil services finds India herself at the bottom. Secondly, data produced by e-governance are amenable to manipulation. For instance, computerized list of beneficiaries includes those who have been facilitated by the implementation of anti-poverty programmes. On several occasions, it has been discovered that the computerized list had names of beneficiaries who did not exist in reality.[33]

Two more points need to be noted in relation to the concept of good governance. Growth in GDP has, of late, been sought to be made out to be an indicator of good governance and judging on that score, Nitish Kumar scores very high having been the CM of a state which in 2010-11 and in 2011-12 has had the highest GDP rate in the country (14.15% and 13.1% respectively). But Amartya Sen and Stiglitz are right in pointing out that these increases in GDP may not reflect the rise in human happiness or even rise in indicators of human index like rates of literacy, nutrition, security of life, food security, sanitation, health amenities and housing facilities available to the needy poor. Pavement dwellers or homeless rural poor go to *Janata Darbars* and *Seva Yatras* to demand a few fundamental rights: the right to shelter in scorching heat or to firewood to "preserve and protect" their bodies from severing cold, to food (ration cards) or to life (protection from police brutality, and criminal extortion by concerned government officials). How can Bihar explain the demand for special status if it has already achieved the highest growth rate already? Quite a few analysts believe that the increase in growth rate, in fact, indicates the fact that a few have grown much richer while a large number are still living in miseries devoid of a decent standard of life and dignity. Neo-liberals, therefore, emphasize on the realization of equity, social justice and prevention of slippage in reaching the goals of development of all or more succinctly, unto the last.

Another fact is that growth may be at a price. Bhutan's growth was estimated in 2008 to be at 21.4% by the CIA World Factbook but much of it had been achieved by displacing people and submerging forests to create dams, thus creating a danger to environment and thus, a challenge to good governance. The growth rate of Bihar reflects the increase in salaries of government employees and flourishing of trade in post-Laloo period and does not reflect the raised standard of living of farmers, wage-earners (a large number of whom belong to the BPL category), widows dependent on pension, nourishment of children who die in large numbers before they reach the age of five or in a word, in the over-all conditions of lives of 70% destitute and deprived sections of the society. So this area is to be targeted for much more benefits of equal development if good governance is the aspiration of both the civil society and the government.

A good sign from the point of view of BIMARU states of the cow-belt is that their civil society and perceptibly, their elected governments have shed their addiction to poor governance. Bihar, Assam, Orissa and Chhatisgarh certainly appear to have shed their addiction to poor governance. These states have provided stable CMs who have been able to raise growth rates in their states almost all of whom were facing extremist episodes from time to time. The only dominating factors in elections between 1952 to 2005 particularly these states used to be caste, religion and particularistic/affection-based relationships. Good governance has laudably entered into the lexicon of electoral politics in the last decade even in these states and the likes of Laloo Prasad, Raman Singh and Digvijai Singh learnt to their dismay and by paying the cost that days when caste combinations alone brought victories in elections were over; People now wanted good governance. As a consequence, the ritual of what Huntington called: procedural democracy" (sham elections, etc.) and the perpetuation of age-old power structure have been replaced, to some extent, by signs of "substantive democracy" as a pre-condition of good governance.[34]

The concept of good governance, both includes and excludes the traditional concept of governance. For both Kautilya and Hobbes state existed to provide security to people and protection of their lives and wealth. Hobbes' state existed to provide security to people and protection of their lives and wealth. Hobbes who made the state a Leviathan, at the end of his famous treatise surmised that people have the right to rebel against the state if it failed to provide security of life to them. Providing security is still the prime duty of modern state and the reputation of Nitish Kumar as one who at least in the begining of his tennure is CM provided good governance depends largely on freeing the state from the clutches of *rangdars*, kidnappers and law-breakers and most perceptibly, on creating the impression that Ministers and MLA/MLCs no longer protected or encouraged the criminals and tried to influence the DMs/SPs to provide protection to those henchmen of politicians who happened to be criminals. Similarly, the beginning of trade and commerce in Europe in the fourteenth century necessitated the migration of traders who needed roads for transporting goods. So construction of roads and flyovers as well as protection from thieves and robbers was the primary duty of the state. Nitish Kumar's reputation for good governance for a large part depended on the fact that he got roads, flyovers, etc. constructed in big spaces across the state. Both these functions are part of the traditional as well as the modern concept of good governance.

A twilight area of the indicator of good governance, because of its significance in the context of developing areas like Bihar, is the adroit use of available resources, both human and financial and reconcile those resources with main priorities. Criticisms are afloat, in general, against improper utilisation of public funds and resources. Kautilya had warned, "Just as it is impossible not to taste honey or poision that one may find at the tip of one's tongue, so it is impossible for one dealing with government funds not to taste, a little bit, of the King's Wealth."[35] He also warns, "Just as it is impossible to know when a fish moving in water is drinking it, so it is impossible to find out when government servants in charge of undertakings misappropriate money."[36] But electoral politics has made it imperative for the elected "King" to arrange for the misapporiation of funds so as to build up enough election funds to get persons of the ruling party or coalition re-elected. Even in the mid-election period, MLAs/MLC want money to get richer. Statistics based on declarations made by people's representatives to the Election Commission are shocking. Two-thirds of the CMs became *crorepatis,* though many of them were nowhere as rich as some of the legislators from their own states.[37] CMs or would-be CMs are reported to have received money from rich manufacturers on the promise of their nomination to the *Rajya Sabha* if they became CMs. MLA Area Fund (abolished in Bihar now) was another source of procurement of money by MLAs. *Mukhiyas,* members of *Panchayat Samiti* and their nominees have also been indulging in making money through taking share in the allotment of contracts, grant of loans under *Indira Awas Yojana,* the allotment of work in MGNAREGS, etc. In a state like Bihar, an indicator of good governance is to provide corruption-free administration and to post, transfer and promote personnel on performance appraisal (and not on caste equations). S.R.

Maheshwari suggests that compulsory retirement of deadwood personnel on reaching certain age would help in the maintenance of administrative standards.[38] Combined training courses in which senior civil servants and ministers should jointly participate may also be helpful.[39] Under the challenges of second generation of the level of liberalization, social services like education, health care, sanitation, nutrition of children, food security and women's empowerment need larger investment and attention. Administration of these require newer skills with increasing use of modern management techniques. Regulation of autonomous private sector also requires new expertise, knowledge and skills. Regulatory bureaucracy on the broad pattern of Independent Regulatory Commission of the USA may be created to impart good governance. All these new innovations in order to be workable necessitate the existence of a refined, well-tuned, depersonalised (to use Max Weber's terminology, the ideal type 'rational authority'), controlled, responsive and responsible bureaucracy working in concert with the CM and Ministers to serve public ends possessing the zeal to provide good governance. Along with the political exceutive, bureaucracy does not merely row, it also steers the ship of the state and takes appropriate steps to reach the destination within the stipulated timeframe. Economic reforms demand specialised knowledge of economics,trade, appropriate technology, alternative energy resources, modern methods of increasing agricultural and horticultural production and industrial advancement, dairy management, etc. While the requirements are heavy, it is disheartening to learn that a report by a well-known consulting firm has given a near-rock bottom-rating to India's bureaucracy (naming it to be the worst in Asia).[40] If the report is to be believed, Indian bureaucracy is performing worse than its counterparts in Vietnam, Indonesia, Philippines and China. Business is not enamoured of India's exalted *babudom*. The licence-permit *raj*-with its maddening ineptiude and scope for graft-does not seem to be over. The privileged tribe of officials is primarily blamed for unease in doing business. Meant to be the "steel frame', civil servants are viewed as uncivil blockaders: they preside over systemic inertia where red tape is generally removed by palm greasing.[41]

Is Bihar an exception to the bureaucratic malfunctioning depicted above? Perhaps not and that explains investor wariness in Bihar despite exhortations by successive CMs. Some analysts go to the extent of commenting that *babus* had become unaccoutable till they were punished by the present C.M. in some of the cases of blatant misconduct brought before him in his *Seva Yatras* or in general, under the Bihar Special Court Act (2009). The general feeling is that irresponsibility of bureaucracy flows from a *mai-baap* culture of the people and condonation or connivance by the political masters in the lapses by the bureaucrats or some refer even to the politician-bureaucrat-contractor-traders alliance with the share of benefits as the benchmark of running the alliance. Investors are spooked by shoddy infrastructure, regulatory mazes, delays and administrative obstructionism. *Lokpal* or *Lokayuktas* cannot expose job-secure mandarins to their stick and bring them to the table or send them to the field to provide good governance. Administrative, police, judicial and electoral reforms are the key to satisfy our aspirations for good governance. There are many honest, efficient bureaucrats in Bihar who can shine if they are professionalized *via* better training, stricter selection, talent sponsorship and competitive appraisal systems linking rewards to competence. For good governance, the steel frame must be rattled.

It is not enough for bureaucracy or even the CM to be accountable, transparent, responsive and responsible. Howsoever industrious or knowledgeable the CM may be, he ought to recapitualate the old wisdom enshrined in Kautilya's dictum that a state is not just made up of *swami* but of *saptang*.[42] The King must act in concert with the *amatyas, mantries*, spies, *mitras* and last but not the least, *Acharyas* and value their advice. As one prudent US President said, his power consists in his ability to persuade and motivate colleagues and co-ordinate as a leader so that the collectively agreed goals can be executed in time, exactitude and quality. *Rajniti* is to be controlled by *Lokniti* and *Acharyakul,* to use Acharya Vinoba Bhave's term. *Dandniti* is to be applied with caution and justice.

Of late, citizens charters, protection to whistleblowers, Right to Information, Declaration of Assets by the Chief

Executive down to the lowest employees annually and their posting on the website, Protection to human rights and anti-corruption measures have become part of the administrative scheme in response to the growing pressure for good governance. But people's representatives are as yet resistant to popular measures like *Lokpal* Bill (they have been resistant for as long as 43 years and even if they existed, were by and large toothless) and Women's Reservation Bill is still hanging in Parliament. The evolution of resistant Parliament which wrongly talks, of 'Parliamentary sovereignty' whereas the members of Constituent Assembly talked of people as sovereign is a reckless development. The executive is much too over-burdened. Legislative surveillance, judicial review, audit control, financial advisory system in ministries may ensure administrative accountability. But for good governance, they must be reinforced and supplemented by the mass media, responsible political parties, public interest groups, sound electoral process and watchdog organisations existing in the society. The emergence of civil society and N.G.Os is a welcome development.

Notes and References

1. Rajni Kothari, "Form and Substance in Indian Politics", *The Economic Weekly*, Vol. XIII, June 3, 1961, ..., "The Congress 'System' in India", *Asian Survey*, Vol. IV, No. 12, December 1964; ..... "Party Politics and Political Development", *Economic and Political Weekly*, Annual Number, February, 1967; and ...., *Politics in India*, Orient Longman, New Delhi, 1970.
2. Stanley, A. Kochanek, *The Congress Party of India, The Dynamics of One-party Democracy*, Princeton University Press, 1968; and *Business and Politics in India*, University of California Press, 1974.
3. Ashok Mehta, *Politics of Planned Economy*, Hyderabad, 1953.
4. Gopal Krishna, "One Party Dominance- Development and Trends" in *Party System and Election Studies*, Occasional Papers of the Centre for the Study of Developing Societies, New Delhi, 1967.
5. W.H. Morris-Jones has diagrammed this view in his "Dominance and Dissent", *Government and Opposition*, Vol. 1, No. 4, August, 1966.
6. L.P. Singh, "Learning from Experience", *Seminar*, June 1984, pp. 14-15.
7. O.P. Minocha, "Chalition Government- Experience and Prospects",

Fortieth Annual Conference of Members of IIPA, Delhi, Indian Institute of Public Administration, October 27, 1996, pp. 10-11.

8. Fredrick Austin Ogg, "Coalition" in *Encyclopaedia of the Social Sciences*, Vol. 2, p. 600.
9. J.C. Johari, *Indian Government and Politics* (Seventh edition), Jalandhar: Vishal Publications, 1983, p. 879.
10. W.A. Gamson, "Coalition Formation" in *International Encyclopaedia of the Social Sciences*, Vol. 2, p. 531.
11. *Ibid.*
12. W.H. Morris-Jones, "The Indian Congress Party: A Dilemma of Dominance", *Modern Asian Studies*, Vol. 1, No. 2, 1967.
13. Rajni Kothari, Politics in India, *op. cit.*, p. 197.
14. *Ibid.*, p. 203.
15. V.N. Gadgil, "Coalition Politics in India and abroad", *Politics India*, Vol. 1, No. 4, Delhi; Vimot Publisher, October 1996, p. 10.
16. Cited in *Ibid.*
17. *Ibid.*
18. "The Problem", *Seminar* (Delhi), June 1994.
19. Rajni Kothari, "The Congress System on Trial", *Asian Survey*, February, 1967, pp. 11-12.
20. *The Times of India* (Delhi), February 15, 1967.
21. N.C.B. Ray Chaudhury, "The Politics of India's Coalition", *The Political Quarterly* (London), July-September, 1969, pp. 279-91.
22. Two good papers on the concept of good governance are: Mohit Bhattacharya, "From Good Government to Good Governance: Changing Profiles of Public Administration in the Developing Countries". *Public Administration Association of Nepal (PAAN) Journal*, Vol. 10 & 11, Jan./Feb. 2000, Sept./Oct. 2000, pp. 339-352; and Neelima Deshmukh, "From Good Governance to Good Government for 21st Century with Special to India" in *ibid.*, pp. 353-63.
23. Government of India, Second Administrative Reforms Commission, Twelfth Report, February 2009, p. 1.
24. *Ibid.*
25. *Ibid.*
26. *Ibid.*
27. Sujata Singh, "Reforms in Governance", *Indian Institute of Public Administration*, New Delhi, 2009, p. 14.
28. *Ibid., p. 15.*
29. *Ibid.*, p. 24
30. *Ibid.*
31. *Ibid.*, p. 29.
32. *Ibid.*, p. 33
33. Mohit Bhattacharya, *op. cit.* p. 342.

34. L.N. Rangarajan (ed. and tr.), *Kautilya's The Arthashastra*, Penguin Books India, 1992, Part VI Civil Service Regulations, pp. 251.
35. *Ibid.*
36. *India Today*, New Delhi, Feb. 17--23, 2009, p. 34.
37. S.R. Maheshwari, "Developing New Administrative Culture in the Context of Good Governance", *A Key-note Address Presented in PAAN*, November 4, 2000, p. 6.
38. *Ibid.*
39. *The Times of India*, Patna (Editorial), 13-01-2012.
40. *Ibid.*
41. For a detailed analysis, see L.N. Sharma and Susmita Sharma, "Kautilyan Indicators of Good Governance", *Indian Journal of Public Administration*, Vol. XLIV, July-September, 2000, No. 3, pp. 265-70

3

The Politics of Formation of Governments

It is wrong to think that voters in Bihar polarize on the basis of caste, class or party alone.[1] If it were so, Karpoori Thakur's *Lok Dal* would not have obtained only 18% of the popular vote in 1985. We find evidences of the ineffectiveness of the state and increase in agrarian conflict in the civil society in Bihar. Governments of Bihar have remained ridden with caste loyalties and political factionalism.[2] After 1967, in the Congress party, high command's writ rang. The Congress which was the single largest party was invited to form the government in 1967 but its leader, Mahesh Prasad Sinha refused to do so reportedly at the suggestion of the high command of the party. In a nutshell, the relationship between the PCC and the national party leadership, factional politics and inter-party dynamics played distinctive role in the appointment of CMs.

COALITION GOVERNMENTS FORMED (1967-72)

The first coalition ministry under Mahamaya Prasad Sinha was installed on March 5, 1967. It was a *Samyukta Vidhayak Dal*

(SVD) Ministry consisting of the CPI, SSP, PSP, *Jana Sangh* and the *Jan Kranti Dal* (JKD). Mahamaya's address to students as his *'jigar ke tukre'* aroused hooliganism among students who wanted the right to use *chits* in examination halls. The Deputy Chief Minister, Karpoori Thakur's decision of making students pass without English at the Entrance level made education vernacular. It is not that boys and girls belonging to the middle class gave up receiving education in English; a lot of them went out of Bihar to receive the advantages of better educational opportunities. Karpoori Thakur, knowingly or unknowingly, neither served Hindi nor the poor, he paved the way for the creamy layer of both the upper and middle classes to receive education in English; and those belonging to lower classes to read books and magazines of lower standards which were published mostly from Patna, Agra, Meerut or Jaipur. The high quality standards of teaching imparted in some of the best known colleges of India located in Patna, Ranchi or Muzaffarpur came down once for all. Karpoori Thakur unlocked the key to another method to help the backward classes. In his second *avatar*, he sought to reserve seats in government jobs (in 1978) so that they could find compensation for the infirmities for a part of which he was himself responsible. Karpoori Thakur was the first leader in Bihar who made sincere efforts to introduce social justice by introducing provisions of reservations for OBCs in government jobs as per the recommendations of Mungeri Lal Commission.

Mahamaya government took other important decisions of consequence. His government instituted Aiyar Commission of inquiry against Congress ministers to probe into alleged charges of corruption by Congress ministers when in office. The Congress leaders, then sitting in opposition, branded it as 'a political vendetta'. However, it was an important step in the corruption-ridden state.But Mahamaya Prasad Sinha's ministry became a victim of crisis fomented by the SSP leader, B.P. Mandal. Instead of resigning his *Lok Sabha* seat in deference to the wishes of SSP's top party leaders including Lohia, he adhered to his claim of having a seat in the Sinha Cabinet. Feeling frustrated, he formed a group of his own henchmen and named it *Soshit Dal*. Taking advantage of the situation, the

Congress leaders entered into an alliance with the Mandal faction and defeated the Sinha ministry on January 25, 1968.

Since B.P. Mandal was not a member of any house, the governor of Bihar declined to invite him to form government. Hence, a nominee of Mandal, Satish Prasad Singh was appointed as the CM for four days for the sole purpose of advising the governor to nominate Mandal to the Legislative Council. This way, path was paved for the appointment of Mandal as the CM. S.P. Singh got Mandal appointed as the CM of a minority government banking on the support of the Congress party and did nothing else. The Congress party was invited to form the government. But it declined saying that it would support Mandal's government. The whole exercise looked hanky panky but the constitutional functionaries allowed it to happen that way.

On January 28, 1968, *Soshit Dal* ministry with Mandal as the CM was sworn in. The Congress dissidents posed a problem as some of them clamoured for berths in the ministry while 15 MLAs led by B.P. Shastri desired ouster of the Mandal government. The latter alleged that the *Soshit Dal* had "no Constitution, no ideology, no programme of action and no code of conduct". The half-hearted support of the strife-ridden Congress party failed to save this ministry when a no-confidence motion tabled by Karpoori Thakur of the SSP was carried by 165 votes to 148 on March 18, 1968. This was the second fall of a government in Bihar within thirteen months; the ministry of Mandal lasted only for 47 days.

On March 22, 1968, a UF Ministry came into being again this time under the leadership of Shastri with the support of Binodanand Jha (who had been CM in 1961-63). This UF and *Lok Tantrik Congress Dal* Ministry soon became unpopular owing to the unfair demands and pressure of the *Raja of Ramgarh*, a leader of the Janata Party and a member of the erstwhile cabinet. Certain civil cases were pending against the Raja in the Calcutta High Court and he was persuading the then CM, Shastri to give him political protection against judicial onslaughts. The *Raja* also aspired to become the Deputy CM but Shastri resisted his demands and overtures. Feeling disappointed, the Raja looked towards the Congress party which was much too eager to topple the UF ministry by any means. An alliance between the Congress, the *Soshit Dal* and *the Janata Party* was forged which brought about the fall of the Shastri ministry in 96 days, that is on June 25, 1968. It led to the imposition of emergency in the state of Bihar under Article 356.

Elections took place for the *Vidhan Sabha* in February 1969 but that did not improve matters since no party secured absolute majority once again. After intense political activity, the Congress party managed to requisition the support of *the Janata Party, BKD, Jharkhand Party, Soshit Dal, Swatantra Party* and six independents as a result of which a coalition ministry led by Sardar Harihar Singh came into being on February 26, 1969. This Congress-led coalition ministry faced rough weather soon when the leaders of the *Soshit Dal* and *Swatantra Party* desired slackening the process of inquiry against former Congress ministers as well as insisted on the re-allocation of portfolios. The distribution of portfolios was a matter of so much tussle that 21 of 33 members of the ministry remained without portfolio for over a month. *The Hindu* (Madras) reported on June 13, 1969 that "the meetings of the Congress Legislature party are turned into regular battle fields .... The administration has come to standstill and the state is sinking deeper into the morass of financial bankruptcy. The government seems to have hardly any time to attend to pressing problems of state wholly preoccupied as it is with the problem of how to keep itself in office." Some important Congress leaders added fuel to the fire by demanding ouster of the *Raja of Ramgarh*. As internal bickering heightened, Sardar Harihar Singh ministry fell in four months i.e. on June 19, 1969 even before the allocation of portfolios could be finally completed.

Shastri was installed as the CM of UF Government for the second time on June 22, 1969 for two weeks. The cracks between the major partners like the *Jana Sangh, the SSP, the CPI* and *the PSP* continued. The CM alleged that the *Jana Sangh* was behaving almost like a "dictator" and was opposing the inclusion of non-Hindus in the government. Whatever may be the truth, the fall of the second Shastri ministry came about in July. Once again, the state was placed under President's rule that was revoked on February 16, 1970 when a Congress (R)-led coalition ministry under Daroga Prasad Rai came into being with the support of the *BKD, Soshit Dal, the PSP, the CPI* and *Jharkhand Party*. Rai was an *Ahir* with a clean image and progressive views. He appointed a Backward Class Commission to explore whether reservations for backward classes could be made in government services and in admissions in educational institutions. It was headed by Mungeri Lal, a former General Secretary of the BPCC and a minister who belonged to the Dusadh community. This Commission proved to be a forerunner of the Mandal Commission. Later, there developed a rift between Rai and L.N. Mishra, a protégée of PM Mrs. Gandhi: The process of internal dissension within the constituents of the coalition went on unchecked as a result of which D. P. Rai's government had to quit in 10 months, i.e. on December 18, 1970 after it was defeated in a trial of strength in the *Vidhan Sabha*.

Thereupon, a new SVD Ministry under the leadership of Karpoori Thakur of the SSP assumed office on December 22,1970 banking on the support of *the Congress (O), the SSP, Swatantra Party, Jana Sangh, Janata Party, BKD, Soshit Dal* (Mandal faction), Rebel *PSP, Hul-Jharkhand* (Richard faction) and some independents. The "Indira Wave" sweeping 1971 Lok Sabha polls came as a rude shock to this ministry. The leaders of the Congress (R) formed a new alliance called Progressive Vidhayak Dal (PVD) consisting of the CPI, SSP, *Soshit Dal* and *Jharkhand* Party under the leadership of Bhola Paswan Shastri. The trend of counter-defection to the side of the Congress was so quick that it portended imminent danger to the Shastri Ministry which could not survive. Ultimately, the last coalition Ministry of this period (67-72) went the usual way leading to the restoration of the Congress rule in the state of Bihar which lasted till 1977.

THE CONGRESS HEGEMONY (1972-77)

The defeat of Daroga Prasad Rai Ministry from Chief Ministership had proved that Bihar Congress was a party of careerists and opportunists. However, with the Congress (R) obtaining absolute majority, the practice of CMs being nominated by the then PM, Mrs. Gandhi started. Kedar Pandey was nominated as the leader of the CLP of Bihar after the CLP authorised her to do so.[3] Pandey brought order and regularity in school and college education and examinations but did nothing substantial to carry forward land reforms or regenerate the industrial economy of the state. His ministry was torn by factional conflicts. He did not have a free hand in conducting the affairs of the government. He asked seven of his ministers to resign but all of them refused to oblige him. The oath taking of ministers took a bizarre turn which showed that ministers lacked faith in him. The high command then ordered Pandey to quit and he could remain in the chair only between 19.03.1972 to 02.07.1973.

In the elections to the Vidhan Sabha held in March, 1972, the Congress party secured 52% of votes. The suggestion was made by the central observer, Sidhartha Shankar Ray to the CLP to authorise Mrs. Gandhi to nominate the leader. The CLP unanimously passed a resolution to that effect and Mrs. Gandhi nominated Abdul Ghafoor who was not a member of the Legislative Assembly at the time of his nomination (though he was a member of the Legislative Council and its Chairman). He was elected to the Assembly soon in a by-election. Though Ghafoor was honest, he neither possessed administrative skill nor political tact nor did he possess any social or political base. He failed both to handle satisfactorily the unprecedented floods which devastated Patna and to control the rising prices and worsening economic scenario. Ghafoor's position became further untenable in the wake of the J. P. Movement. Since he had no wherewithal to cope with the movement, the administration was paralysed and all developmental activities came to a standstill. His failure to protect the life of L.N. Mishra was used by his opponents as a stick to beat him up. He was ultimately forced to resign on the 6th April, 1975.

Following the exit of Ghafoor, Jagannath Mishra was unanimously elected leader of the CLP (with the blessings of Mrs. Gandhi and her son, Sanjay) and continued as the CM for two years up to June, 1977. J. Mishra was neither a freedom fighter nor a man of standing either in public life or in political organization. Age-wise, he was the youngest CM (if we exclude Satish Prasad Singh). But he indulged in populism and met a large number of party workers every day. He tried to endear himself to the Muslims by declaring Urdu as the second official language of the state. He introduced various schemes for the benefit of college and university teachers, introduced old-age pension and speeded up the implementation of land reform measures for weaker sections, though he disfavoured the recommendations of Mungeri Lal Commission.

THE *JANATA* CMs (1977-79)

The *Janata Party* secured an unprecedented 68 percent of the popular vote, thanks to the enthusiastic support of the police forces, the bureaucracy, students, youth and landholders from both upper and backward castes. Criminals entered the fray in a sizeable number. Voting irregularities were reported in about 80 constituencies. *Dalits* and members of extremely backward castes were prevented from voting by the *Bhumihars, Rajputs* and *Ahirs*. No surprise, the Congress secured less than 23% of votes polled. The *Janata* Party formed government with Karpoori Thakur as the state's CM in 1977. But the government had a coalitional character in view of the fact that the *Janata* Party was a conglomerate alliance of several heterogeneous elements. The 214- member *Janata* Legislature Party (JLP) was distinctly divided into three factions- 84 MLAs were loyal to the Congress (O) leader, S.N. Sinha; the Lok Dal leader, Karpoori Thakur commanded the loyalty of an equal number of MLAs (including the Socialist Party loyalists); and the rest belonged to the *Jana Sangh*. No consensus to elect the CM could be possible. In the election of the CM that followed within the party, the *Jana Sangh* faction supported Karpoori Thakur who was elected CM on June 21, 1977. The *Janata* Party had promised job reservations for backward castes in its election manifesto of 1977. *Rajputs* and *Bhumihars* did not object then since they were not sure of the victory of the Janata Party. But after the landslide victory of the party and installation of Karpoori Thakur as CM, Thakur proceeded to undertake to introduce the representation of backward castes in government services. This created stiff opposition from upper caste men even at the cabinet level. The backward castes took to streets when Thakur wanted to strike a compromise formula. In retaliation, the upper castes too took to streets. As soon as the Karpoori Government notified its decision on 10.11.1978, another round of agitation by upper caste youth started.

The ruling *Janata* Party turned into a divided house. In the elections to *Prakhand Samitis* and their *Pramukhs* in 1978, bloody clashes on caste-lines took place all over the state, leaving around a hundred persons dead. The upper castes did not want to lose their dominance, prestige, economic and political power to backward castes; so they put everything at stake. The reservations in government jobs involved only 18,00 posts. So what was more important from the point of view of upper castes was to stop the emergence of rich among the backward people as a power wielding group in the society. Karpoori Thakur had triggered this evolution. Due to high voltage political turmoil and weak party organization, the government of Karpoori Thakur faced storm. Rich peasants belonging to the backward castes had become oppressive towards *Dalit* labourers and refused to pay even subsistence wages to them. This led to a number of bloody attacks on *Dalits* particularly by *Kurmis*. One of them at Belchchi attracted nation wide attention. These incidents repelled *Dalits* who joined hands with upper castes to pull down the Thakur Ministry. A no-confidence motion was passed against Thakur on 19.04.2002; and on 21.04.2002, Ram Sundar Das (a *Dalit* socialist) was elected the CM of Bihar. Since the Congress (I) did not choose to dislodge Das as the next *Lok Sabha* election (1980) was due, he continued to rule till the election to the Bihar Legislative Assembly for seeking fresh mandate of the people was held. In 1980 elections to the Bihar Assembly, the Congress rule was revived. Soon after, the Das Ministry was dismissed and President's rule was imposed.

CMs AFTER REVIVAL OF CONGRESS RULE (1980-89)

The persuasion or pressure of the Central unit of the Congress party on Kedar Pandey paved the way for the re-election of Jagannath Mishra as the CM on June 7, 1980. The blessing of Sanjay Gandhi was again the most important factor in his re-election. He lost favour of the party high command when Rajiv Gandhi took over as the General Secretary of the party. Mishra found himself defenceless against a host of charges levelled against him. He was compelled by the party high command to vacate the office which he did on 14.08.1983. Mrs. Gandhi and the high command, thereafter, chose a state leader then in central politics, C.S. Singh, as the state's CM because the party was looking for a non-controversial CM who could refurbish and improve the image of the party in Bihar. Singh was conservative and had no sympathy for the weaker sections of the society. He did not attend to the task of completing the unfinished task of land reforms. In his opinion, taking up the issue of sharecroppers and agricultural labourers can have destabilizing implications for state's politics. During his regime, the incidents of agrarian violence increased and spread in many areas. Dissidents mounted their campaign against Singh and accused him of promoting extra-constitutional centre of power, consisting of kins and some government officials. Singh could not show much output; he pulled the cart of the government any how till the next general election of *the Vidhan Sabha* in 1985 after which the choice fell upon Bindeshwari Dubey due to his allegiance to New Delhi (now under Rajiv Gandhi).

Though Dubey was a trade union leader of long standing, he was not pro-poor as a CM. He did not tackle the problem of inequitable land relations due to which the poor nursed grievances against him. He was old agedand had weakness for his relations. Above all, he failed to bring peace and order in the rural areas. Agrarian violence proved a tough nut to crack for him. In North Bihar, particularly in Champaran; kidnappings, dacoities and murders became rampant under his rule. The killings of fifty persons (mostly Rajputs) in villages of Dalel Chak and Baghaura in the district of Aurangabad shocked people. This kind of situation demoralised police and the civic administration. The developmental work also came to a halt and corruption increased under his regime.

Rajiv Gandhi continued the practice of changing CMs at frequent intervals like his mother, Mrs. Gandhi. Dubey was replaced by Bhagwat Jha Azad (a central government minister from Bihar) on 14.02.1988. Azad was not a pragmatic leader.

He nurtured grand ideas but did not know how to implement them. For example, he wanted the state of Bihar to get rid of *mafia* gangs but used wrong tactics to do the same. He placed powerful caste leaders of his own party up in arms against himself. Bureaucrats were unhappy with him for he had stopped the March Loot. Inspite of all these shortcomings, his bold statements, laudable intentions and actions endeared him to the people at large. His tour of the areas affected by Naxalism even at the risk of his safety earned him goodwill. He was one of the few CMs of Bihar to hold that the root cause of Bihar's violence was non-completion of the task of land reforms. But Azad had to give way to S.N. Sinha on 11.03.1989 who, in turn, made way on 05.12.1989 for three months' stint of Jagannath Mishra (06.12.1989 to 09.03.1990). Mishra has been the last CM of the Congress party in power so far.

Satyendra Narain Sinha and Jagannath Mishra struck death blows to the already growing weak Congress party. Sinha's only asset was that he was the son of A.N. Sinha. He was not a freedom fighter and he was widely known as a *Rajput* landlord and a leader of *Rajputs*. By the time he became CM, he had lost the drive and initiative to take the state to bigger heights. During his regime, law and order came to a lower ebb and the state slipped in chaos and anarchy. In this situation came the Bhagalpur communal riots between Hindus and Muslims in October, 1989 as a big avalanche which washed away both the CM and the Muslim base of the Congress (I).

Jagannath Mishra was brought in just to sign the instruments of surrender after the impending defeat. In the *Lok Sabha* elections in December 1989, the Congress (I) secured only 4 out of 54 seats in Bihar, whereas the newly created *Janata Dal* secured 32 seats. *Janata Dal* scored victories in the Lok Sabha constituencies of the last three CMs: Bhagwat Jha Azad, Satyendra Narain Sinha and Jagannath Mishra. The son of an ex-CM, Kedar Pandey and the wife of an ex-CM, Chandra Shekhar Singh were defeated. The *Vidhan Sabha* elections which took place during the first quarter of 1990 saw the Congress seats come down to just 71 as against 196 in 1985. The *Janata Dal* Legislative Party (JDLP) was more representative and in tune with the socio-economic realities of the state.

THE NEW POLITICO-SOCIAL DISPENSATION

A contest for leadership of the Janata Dal Legislature Party (JDLP) took place in 1990 in which Laloo Prasad trounced his rivals, Raghunath Jha and Ram Sundar Das. Laloo's victory opened a new phase in the history of Bihar. He formed the government with the help of the CPI, CPI (M) and other small parties to begin with. The son of a cowherd, rustic looking, unsophisticated entrant to politics without previous administrative skills,though an alumnus of Patna University was initially dismissed by the established politicians and caste overlords as an ephemeral phenomenon but he went from strength to strength and between him and his novice and barely literate wife, Rabri Devi, held the CM's office from 1990 to 2005.

The emergence of Laloo Prasad was brought about by a constellation of several factors. After Lohia and Charan Singh, Devi Lal was the champion of backward castes. From the very beginning of the formation of the *Janata Dal,* Devi Lal projected Laloo as the future leader of the JDLP in Bihar. The CPI and the CPI (M) already had a broad seat agreement with the *Janata Dal*. Laloo's emergence marginalised established leaders of backward castes on the one hand and old socialist stalwarts on the other. Young leaders came to the fore. Nitish Kumar, an engineer belonging to the *Kurmi* community became the second-in-command of Laloo in the *Janata Dal*. Laloo and Nitish combined brought *Ahirs* and *Kurmis* together which became a formidable combination in many areas, incapable of being defeated by upper castes, already divided across a number of political parties. OBCs who were sought to be mobilized since long got fully mobilized in North India and Laloo Prasad as CM was the champion of their mobilisation in Bihar. Referring to the first terms in the caste names of forward castes, Laloo was said to have exhorted backward castes in these terms, *"Bhura Bal Saaf Karo"*. Later on, he started denying having said so to appease upper castes which emerged as a section to contend with in state politics by 2005. Coalition experiments which had not been a success in 1967-89 period turned towards success by 1990 because leaders at the helm of the coalition government considerably matured by then.

The aggressive posture of Laloo endeared him to OBCs and *Dalits* who had been oppressed, insulted and kept mute by *Bhumihars* and *Rajputs* for long. They were happy that some one was paying back their old tormentors in the same coin. Laloo gave the backward castes voice, dignity and taught them to walk with their heads high. His strategies and mannerisms were designed to keep the forward castes and those among them in the higher bureaucracy demoralized. He asked ladies in the IAS to make poor babies (belonging to *Dalit* communities in particular) to make them have bath and to comb their hair. He delivered public speeches in rustic style and jocular vein, made vernacular gestures so as to make the audience burst into peels of laughter in order to come closer to the sub-alterns. In an age of reality bytes and mass television, he made himself popular among masses by his earthly humour and quick repartees.

Laloo was the icon of the youth in particular. The spread of Hindi and that of the network of the IPF and Naxalites consolidated his social base. To cap it all, he identified himself solely and exclusively with the cause of anti-communalism which endeared him to Muslims. As CM, he took firm steps to control the spread of communal riots in Badaki Gulani village in Nawada district, Jamshedpur, Bhagalpur, Ranchi and Hazaribagh. He was always the first to arrive at the places of communal occurrences. He took decisions and announced them on the spot. The *Ramnavami* used to pass off peacefully because of the anticipated prompt measures. As CM, he even observed a day long fast for communal harmony on one of such occasions. He gave a *carte blanche* to officers of civil administration and the police in these terms, "*Jo bhi badmashi kare, danga fasad kare, usko thok do.*" Thus Muslims got safety, if not welfare and development. His commitment to secularism reached its peak when he halted the *Rath Yatra* of the veteran BJP leader, L.K. Advani in Samastipur while the latter was on way to Ayodhya to rebuild the Ram temple in October 1990. Laloo arrested and detained Advani (who was acting to reply to the *Mandal Card*) while other leaders of the country had not dared touch him. To add to his feat, he did not allow communal peace to be disturbed which Advani and some BJP leaders were threatening would happen if the government dared stop Advani's *Rath Yatra*. Bihar remained free from communal disturbances even after the demolition of the Babri Masjid. Sociologically, secularism was buttressed in Bihar by Muslim-Yadav combination crafted by Laloo Prasad. *Ahirs* had been playing active role in every communal riot that occurred in Bihar and U. P. against the Muslims between 1880 and 1989. Laloo made them natural allies and secularized *Ahirs* in positive terms providing Muslims safety from *Ahirs*. Earlier, he had also handled Sitamarhi riots (in October 1992) deftly, promptly announced a judicial inquiry and ordered speedy trial of the accused. He had also rendered material help for the repair of mosques and arranged for relief and rehabilitation of the victims. Whenever apprehensions of communal riots arose, *Ahirs* formed a ring of defence around Muslims to protect them from atrocities. Laloo won because of the powerful alliance among Muslims who account for 16.6 percent of Bihar's population and the *Ahirs* who account for 12.7% and a chunk of the 14% *Dalit* votes. However, he did not take prompt steps to bring those guilty for Bhagalpur Communal riots to book–a task which Nitish Kumar performed as the CM of the state.

The announcement by PM V.P. Singh to implement the recommendations of the Mandal Commission in August 1990 to reserve 27.5 percent of the government jobs for OBCs and the agitation against it by the upper caste people, especially the youth galvanized the OBCs led by *Kurmis* and *Ahirs* to identify with the cause of reservations as recommended by Mandal. The OBCs found that they were getting an opportunity to capture state power. Laloo Prasad and his cohorts successfully built an alliance of OBCs on this issue of mutual interest. Thereafter, Laloo did not remain a mere upstart *Ahir* leader. He got the loyalty of fishermen by providing them facilities for fishing in rivers and government tanks and *chaurs*. He got the loyalty of *Pasis* by making the tapping of toddy tax-free. He pleased *Dalits* by his decision to change the name of the Bihar University to Baba Saheb Bhimrao Ambedkar University. He permitted and encouraged the *Ahirs* to bring their cows and buffaloes to Patna and keep them in the sheds constructed by the government through the Patna Regional Development Authority. In this way, the *Ahirs* were grabbing city's valuable public land.

By a feat of political acumen, Laloo's minority government survived between 1990-95. In the 1991 Lok Sabha election results, the *Janata Dal* (J.D.) captured the maximum number of seats. The results increased his political stature since he had vanquished all his political rivals. During the rest of his tenure, Laloo concentrated on consolidating his support base. He announced the establishment of *Charwaha Vidyalayas*. This, too, was the pretext to gift away the valuable farm lands to OBCs in general and *Ahirs* in particular. When he developed some differences with the C.P.I., he politically managed to hijack an influential C.P.I. leader from Gaya and made him an M.L.C. He split the I.P.F. and hijacked a number of its legislators while he forced Raghuath Jha, the supreme leader of the S.G.P. in Bihar to surrender to him.

In order to win over *Dalits* (who looked to OBCs with suspicion), Laloo anointed four *Dalit* leaders (including Ramai Ram, the President of the Bihar J.D. unit) as *Shankaracharyas*. A resolution was passed, demanding appointment of lower caste people in temples and maths, as priests. A senior *Dalit* I.A.S. officer, Pancham Lal made a scathing attack on Laloo's show of anti-Brahmanism. After this, Laloo concentrated on visiting *Dalit basties* and telling the inhabitants of the virtues of keeping themselves clean and get their wards educated so that they could rise socially and economically. He got houses constructed for *Dalits* under the *Indira Awas Yojana* under his supervision. He revised Karpoori Thakur's and Lohia's anti-English orientation of education. He found that over 91 per cent felt that English should be made a compulsory language and more than 89 per cent felt that the abolition of English would create problems in employment for their wards.

Quite a few elites were engaged in building a personality cult round Laloo. A group of nine persons emerged around him when he was CM who managed the affairs of the state as well as the party and some of them brought bad name for Laloo. From the middle of 1993, Laloo Prasad came under pressure from both inside and outside the party. There were agitations all over the state. Ram Lakhan Singh Yadav defected; Nitish Kumar began distancing himself; Syed Shahabuddin, Yunus

Saleem and Abdul Ghafoor fell out with him on the issue of the recognition of a private medical college at Katihar. The Supreme Court judgment excluding the 'creamy layer' from the purview of the Mandal Commission's recommendations made the richer segments of the OBCs lukewarm towards Laloo. Laloo Prasad was being criticized for having criminalized social and and lumpenized the political life of Bihar. The BJP tried to show to *Kurmis* and *Koeris* that while socially, culturally and educationally, they were more advanced then *Ahirs,* Laloo had marginalised them. In a *Kurmi Chetana Maha Rally* organized on 12.02.1994 in Gandhi Maidan (Patna), Nitish Kumar's speech gave an impression that the *Kurmis* were on the verge of separating themselves politically from Laloo. In 1993, caste rallies of *Kushwahas, Telis, Banias* and *Nishads* were held. All of them were demanding a bigger share in the cake power and more economic opportunities but they were agreed that upper castes should not be allowed to grab power again. A good number of people resented the kind of control Laloo's kiths and kins like Sadhu and Subhas Yadavs, etc. had come to exercise over the party since 1994.

The message sent by the caste rallies was misunderstood by Nitish Kumar who broke away from the J.D. to contest election in 1995 for Bihar Vidhan Sabha from his newly constituted *Samata Party* which made no dent. The BJP, the Congress (I) and the C.P.I. (M.L.-Vinod Mishra group) also went into a mirage. The CPI and the CPI (M) which did not leave the company of Laloo were better off. The journalists and expert analysts who had predicted doom for Laloo in the 1995 Vidhan Sabha elections found their predictions falsified. Laloo had emerged victorious with two-thirds majority and the Samata Party was almost wiped out.

The psephologists ignored the fact that several small castes like Nonias, Lohars, Dhanuks, Kahars, Kanduks, Binds, Mali, Berai, Bari, etc. were still with Laloo and were able to vote, thanks to Sheshan and the deployment of para-military forces and observers. The same was the case with the *Dalits*. Fourteen Koeris were elected on the ticket of the J.D. Muslims, *Ahirs* and *Dalits* continued to vote for Laloo. Laloo's dictum that development means adequate share in its fruits for non-upper castes and the right to live with self-respect and dignity yet appealed to these backward castes, *Dalits* and Muslims. Laloo put forward his native theory of development Stung by being left behind in the IT boom, he averred that computers were anti-poor.

After returning to power with an absolute majority in 1995, Laloo changed his tune and tried to appear sober, considerate and realistic. During 1990-95, he largely indulged in acts of bravado and gimmicks. After 1995, he took up the cause of propelling the economy on to the path of development; solve the problems like unemployment, poverty and lawlessness. He tried his hand in attracting private investors, both Indian and foreign, and visited foreign countries to invite Non-Resident Indians (NRIs) to invest in enterprises in Bihar. A 'Bihar Development Run' was organized on 11.06.1995. A new industrial policy aimed at attracting private sector investment was announced. Laloo Prasad as the CM, emphasized the need to cut short the bureaucratic tangles faced by private investors. He assured that he will himself look into the problems of foreign investors. Documentaries were prepared to boost tourism. But he did not succeed in his plans because the bad law and order situation and the bad conditions of roads in Bihar scared the entrepreneurs. Criminal gangs, armed *senas*, drug mafias, kidnappers and smuggling gangs operated with the patronage of politicians. Within a decade, two district magistrates of Gopalganj district were killed in broad daylight. In central Bihar, Naxalites had been operating freely for two decades. One MLA was murdered in Patna and another was attacked. Laloo did nothing to control the criminals. He did nothing to tackle the problem of land reforms and re-organize agricultural economy without which neither rural violence could be checked nor agricultural production or living standards of the people of Bihar could be increased. Bihar's industrialisation under Laloo remained a distant dream. For industrialization, electricity is a must which had been in very short supply. The record of Rajya Transport Corporation and the Housing Board had been dismal.

Yet, Laloo had become so megalomaniac that he believed that he or his wife would continue to rule Bihar for twenty years at a stretch. This was not to be. His personal rule was cut short when the CBI chargesheeted him. The enormity of the animal husbandry and fodder scams started surfacing and Laloo started getting entangled in scandals which involved misappropriation of billions of dollars of fund given by the World Bank. Laloo was alleged to have played an active part in letting them happen. The CBI took him to "judicial remand" on 30.07.1997 for 134 days in fodder case and on 28.10.1998 for 73 days and lodged him in State Guest House. When objections were raised to his being lodged there, he was shifted to the Beur Jail in Patna in Disproportionate Assets Case. But so far, he has not been judged guilty in any of the cases. However, since the RJD had become his pocket organization (J.D. was re-named as R.J.D. at a later stage), he retained the office of the party president and handed over charge of the office of the CM of Bihar to his wife, Rabri Devi (who had read up to class V in her village school). Laloo ruled the state of Bihar by proxy for the next seven to eight years. He ruled the state from behind the curtain. When Laloo was not available, one of the trusted bureaucrats was assigned the task of procuring the signature of Rabri Devi on dotted lines. Rabri's three brothers were ministers. All the three of them had serious criminal charges against them from murder to kidnapping to extortion. Nepotism flourished. Rabri Devi was mute in the *Vidhan Sabha, Vidhan Parishad* and in public meetings in the early years of her political career. The opposition mocked at her predicament but for Laloo's ministers and cohorts, life was as usual.

In 2000 election to the Bihar Vidhan Sabha, Laloo saw his grip over both his vote-bank and his cohorts going down substantially. From a party with iron-grip over the Bihar electorate, R.J.D. failed to get even a simple majority. He had to rely on the support of independent candidates almost all of whom were hardcore criminals and history-sheeters like Suraj Bhan Singh. Laloo's RJD itself was full of history-sheeters like Shahabuddin, Pappu Yadav, etc. Kidnapping continued to run as industry and criminals ruled the roost. Development was an alien word in the state. Nobody wanted to invest in the state, even those who had been engaged in trade or commerce since long in Bihar started fleeing.

Resentment against Laloo-Rabri rule led the Kurmis, disgruntled elements among OBCs and Muslims who had become tired with his caste and lawless politics and absence of development and land reforms to combine. A major chunk of the 13 per cent upper castes who were waiting to retaliate jumped in 2005 Vidhan Sabha elections with all the power and strength at their disposal. JD (U) led by Nitish Kumar had combined electorally with the BJP to defeat Laloo-led *Janta Dal* supported by the CPI and the CPI (M). In this election, Rabri Devi as CM had to make way for JD (U)-BJP coalition government of Nitish Kumar as the election had given a fractured mandate.

Nitish Kumar as the CM lived with the lexicon of development and good governance for the first three and half years in office in politics. Atal Bihari Vajpayee lost election in 2004 and failed to get another term of PM on the slogan of 'Shining India', though Manmohan Singh got the second term on the slogans of "Incredible India", growth rate and Indo-US Nuclear deal. CMs like Chandrababu Naidu who was identified with starting the I.T revolution in the Hyderabad lost in 1999; and S.M. Krishna was also voted out of power inspite of good development records of both, though Laloo continued to win even when he did not care to implement development programmes. Nitish Kumar as the CM announced soon after taking oath as the CM that he would provide "good governance" to Bihar and repeatedly told in public that if he failed to fulfil this solemn promise and could not deliver impressive output, he would not go to the electorate to ask for a second term as CM in 2010.

Nitish took up the task of restoring law and order in right earnest. About 45,000 accused were convicted through speedy trials between 2005-09 of Nitish's rule. However, according to a report of the National Human Rights Commission for 2007-08, the Commission received a total of 4595 cases of human rights violations from Bihar. Of them, 560 cases were related to custodial deaths, while six were encounter deaths. Bihar, under Nitish, achieved a surprising growth rate of 14.15% and 13.1% in 2011 and and 2012 respectively the highest in the Country as per the report of the Central Stastical Organization. Christened as a *'Bimaru'* state, the growth rate of Bihar averaged 8 per cent during 2004-05. It did better during 2006-07 (during Nitish's regime) and now it has reached the zenith. GDP had in fact, started growing at the rate of 6.9 per cent between 1999-2000 (during Rabri's rule) itself. Secondly, growth is driven mainly by the services and in the tertiary sector. Thirdly, increase in growth rate (as economists like Schiltz and Amartya Sen warn) does not correspond with increase in human development. Under Nitish's regime also; education, health, sanitation, industry, generation or distribution of electricity, nutritional intake and availability of jobs to the unemployed have not considerably improved despite his occasional spurring of seminars for making a "resurgent" Bihar and despite his efforts to attract NRIs to invest in industrial enterprises in Bihar in the changed scenario so far as the condition of roads and law and order are positively reported about. No industrial enterprise worth the name has been established and the British High Commissioner, Richard Saggy attributed this disinterest or non-investor friendly attitude to lack of "a clean and transparent administration".[25] He added that corruption was a very big drawback for foreign investors who want both clarity and transparency in governance.[4]Richard was, however, appreciative of Nitish Kumar's "global aspiration", programmes and public delivery system.[5]

Nitish Kumar and his colleagues have been demanding since Day I of assuming office that since Bihar is abysmally poor, it should be granted "special category status". The data cited by them exposes the extent of continuing poverty despite the rhetoric of resurgence in Bihar. The per capita income has continued to be Rs. 12,643 against the national average of Rs. 37,400. Women's literacy rate continues to be round 35% compared to the national average of 55% in spite of the visible fact of appointments made of *Shiksha Mitras,* the distribution of cycles and uniforms to school-going girls under *Mukhya Mantri Yojana,* and proposed appointments of more *Vikas Mitras* in each *Panchayat* (rural) and ward (urban). According to the data presented by International Food Policy Research Institute, Bihar ranks among the alarming category *vis-à-vis* hunger. The growth rate of agriculture being negative, agricultural income coming down (in predominantly rural Bihar) due to lack of provision of irrigational facilities round the year or HYV seeds, no better result can be expected so far as the field of agricultural production is concerned. Disparity and disparaging inequality are writ large in the growth story some of which data is false and manipulated as proved by Shankar Acharya in his book *India and Global Crisis* (2009). In human development index, Bihar stands on the 22nd and in educational index, on the 35th position, next only to Pondichery. Higher education has got the worst deal. Absence of toilets in primary schools, pathetic amenities and poor education standard is forcing many girl students to drop out from Bihar schools. Even on regular days, the presence of students in primary schools are less than 50% -96.4% of schools lack of proper teacher-student ratio.

Abhijit Sen, Plan panel member, however, pets Nitish Kumar for bringing poverty down from 62.3 percent to 55.7 percent in rural Bihar and for doing better on poverty reduction in 2006-09.[7] The fact, however, stands that 12 districts of Bihar are to date "highly food insecure".[8] Bihar's poor female literacy rate—33.64% is the most significant factor in aggravating food insecurity and child mortality in the rural regions.[9] Absence of access to doctors and safe drinking water also enhances it. Nitish has, however, used craft in managing the state's development even if the funds did not come handy from the Centre. The state's credit absorption capacity has gone high. NABARD plans to grant a credit of 75% more than what it gave to Bihar in the last fiscal year. It includes crop loan, credit in agriculture and allied activities, non-farm sector, agro and food processing as well as micro-financing for the self-help groups. Road connectivity in the state's food-prone zones covering health centres, schools and bridges are also being focussed. Primary Agriculture Credit Societies are being formed. Clubs of small farmers, sharecroppers and landless people are being formed to provide credit linkages to them. When PM Manmohan Singh did not provide a special package for the reconstruction of the flood-devastated Kosi region and rehabilitation of its displaced people in 2008 despite calling it a "national calamity", Nitish's government approached the Work Bank through the Centre which conveyed its readiness[10] to undertake work the first phase of which has started. Nitish Kumar, at long last, managed to get the Centre to double the special assistance package to Rs. 20,000 crore during the 12th Five Year Plan (2012-17).

Nitish's most notable achievement has been in taking up the job of construction of roads and flyovers in a big way.

According to an agreement reached in 2005, CPWD had to get 1705 km and Ercon International Ltd. 330 km of roads by March 2010.[11] Bihar State Road Development Corporation Ltd. (BSRDCL) managed mega highway projects in a short span. BSRDCL executed projects worth Rs. 541 crore in 2008-09 and earned a profit of Rs. 23 crore. Its turn over was about Rs. 544 crore. In the past, corporations were being shut down in Bihar as they were running in the deep red but Nitish made corporations run smoothly and earn profit. Encouraged by the success of corporations, Nitish Kumar plans to set up new corporations. Nitish Kumar had dreamt that a person travelling from different places in the state could reach the state capital within six hours. To achieve this goal, he embarked on the scheme of building a network of smooth roads, highways, flyovers, express routes, paths, tunnels, routes, streets and bridges all over the state. Asian Development Bank (ADB) provided a soft loan of Rs. 2,000 crore in phase-I for the construction of various roads. The state government did the job well, finished in time and submitted utilisation certificates in earnest. ADB was so impressed that it invited the representatives of the BSRDCL to present papers in a Conference in Mumbai on the manner of functional management and quality control employed by the Bihar unit. People of Bihar are, in general, appreciative of the efforts made on the front of construction of roadways under the regime of Nitish Kumar. In all, 3,000 km state highways and 9,000 rural highways were constructed between 2005-10.

It has to be noted, however, that people talk about the fact that the extent of corruption including payment of commissions in the construction of roads and flyovers, etc. or that pay-offs for getting any work done at the level of secretariat, collectorate, *anchal* or *panchayat* has increased in Nitish's regime than it was in Laloo-Rabri regime. One plausible explanation for this is that no roads were being constructed during Laloo-Rabri regime because *rangdars* demanded *rangdari* tax before the contractors planned to reach the site to start the work; so the contractors abandoned the idea of doing the construction work due to fear of more and more such demands coming to them. In the government offices also, RJD's *dalals* commanded the deal. In Nitish's regime, citizens have to contend directly with the sharks in the bureaucracy or clerkocracy. MLA/MPs, ministers or party workers had, of course, been initially asked by Nitish Kumar to refrain from influencing the officials. During Laloo-Rabri regime, Laloo-Rabri themselves faced scams, the PWD Minister faced coaltar scam, other ministers faced charges, Laloo's kins were a law unto themselves and his *navratnas* made arbitrary decisions. Their relatives had earned such a bad name for breaking law and order and kidnapping for ransom that Patna High Court once called his rule "*jungle raj*". But it is an irony that the ghost of corruption continued to persist in the so-called era of "good governance" justifying the tittle of the book that the state is still aspiring for good governance.

Nitish Kumar himself inspected a construction site in Kankarbagh and found sub-standard materials being used. He asked the police to lodge FIR against the concerned contractor and cancelled the ongoing contract with the government. Internecine conflicts in both the constituents of the ruling JD (U) and BJP coalition created a bad show. It also clearly showed that coalition *dharma was* neither observed nor formally respected by Nitish Kumar as the head of a coalition government. The very fact that the CM had to do this work personally indicates that his minister and bureaucrats of the department were hands -in-glove with the corrupt contractor. The performance of the cabinet ministers, apart from that of the CM, is not laudable. Bureaucracy has extended its tentacles too far, thanks to the support of the CM. Political elements feel ignored and bypassed. The cause of political education is lost.

Nitish Kumar blames the Centre for non-release of funds for *Pradhan Mantri Gramin Sadak Yojana* (PMGSY), MGNAREGA or for making available to the state 800 to 850 M.W. of electricity whereas it is duly allotted 1600 M.W. and its actual need is of 3,000 M.W. The Centre has not undertaken any major work of electric generation during Nitish's regime rather takes the plea that the state should generate the same and maintain its transmission and distribution network in a manner so as to avoid frequent breakdowns. Nitish Kumar argues that he had arranged Rs. 653 crore from its resources to continue work on PMGSY which came to standstill due to non-availability of fund from the Centre. The state had to do work of disaster management and assess the damages to the houses in the tornado that affected Purnea, Araria, Katihar and Supaul areas in 2010, the Centre's help was not available. But Nitish Kumar has much to account for. The warnings of the then Chief Justice of India, Balakrishnan about the prevalence of "rampant corruption" in the implementation of MGNREGS and of Dreze should caution an already corruption-ridden state like Bihar. The inefficiency shown in the appointment of two lac primary school teachers (leading to the dismissal of 15,000 of them due to false certificates and so on) were preposterous. Similarly, the purchase of computers worth Rs. 17,00 crores for schools without provision for power or manpower to operate them amounts to wasteful expenditure of precious public funds

Due to socio-economic disparity and deprivation, Naxalism is spreading in more and more areas of Bihar. The banned CPI (Maoist) has been targeting railway property in Danapur Division stations. The railways have suffered a substantial loss in the past years due to extremist attacks at different places under this division. Maoists targeted Narganjo railway station in Jamui district of Bihar seven times under Nitish's regime. Jhajha station which was attacked by Maoists on 13.4.2008 claimed six people's lives. Jhajha-Jamalpur section has become a Maoist-dominated area. The Government of Bihar has done precious little to control this menace of Maoism either through socio-economic development of the areas concerned or tightening law and order machinery there at least. Chidambaram, the then Union Home Minister, complained[12] that Nitish Kumar, the C.M. of Bihar, neither cared to attend his meetings scheduled in Kolkata to discuss the important issue of Naxalism nor was he willing to meet him to discuss the matter. Nitish Kumar had demanded three times the number of officers his officials had petitioned for. The then Union Home Minister wanted to discuss what Nitish Kumar's plans were since he exceeded the demand for Central forces by three-fold from what his officials demanded but Chidambaram complained that he received no reply from the CM. This strategy of throwing the blame on the Union for not making adequate funds or forces available to fight the Naxalist or Maoist menace is not good politics; state government ought to have owned its responsibility to maintain public order within its boundary. The result is that whereas in 2005, five to six districts of Bihar were affected by Naxalism; by 2012, 33 out of

38 districts are Naxal-affected and police men on duty are often killed while the government looks on. It may be noted that while Nitish Kumar gained some admiration for facilitating speedy trials, the main conspirator of the murder of 58 *Dalit* men, women and children on 1.12.1997 at Laxmanpur-Bathe village in Arwal district, *Ranvir Sena* chief, late Brahmeshwar Singh Mukhiya was not chargesheeted in the last thirteen years. He languished in Ara jail for the last 8-9 years and was at last, set free. The Patna High Court in its judgement absolved him of the charges of murders in Bathani Tola. The government of Bihar has appealed to the Supreme Court against this judgement under public pressure.

A notable fact is that Nitish Kumar made a deliberate turn about in his image projection after three and half years of his tenure. From the height of "*Vikash Purush*", he chose to slide to the downstream of reconstructing an electoral alliance of *Mahadalits* (constituted a commission to study their problems and granted them relief), Extremely Backward Castes (EBCs) and *Pasmanda* (*Dalit*) Muslims which could be supportive in the by-elections to *Vidhan Sabha* (2009) and ultimately, in the election to *Vidhan Sabha* (2010). His cabinet decided to provide three decimals of land or Rs. 20,000 to each *Mahadalit* family for constructing a house. He proposes to appoint 9,600 *Vikash Mitras* from *Mahadalit* castes in each *panchayat* (rural) and ward (urban) to enlist each *Mahadalit* in the Census list, electoral roll and BPL list. Buta Singh, the chairman of the Dalit Commission alleged that the use of the word "*Mahadalit*" is unconstitutional. Ram Vilash Paswan alleged that the establishment of the *Mahadalit* Commission was done with the purpose of excluding his community of *Dusadhs* who constitute 40.2 lakhs of the 1.30 crore S.C. population from receiving funds released by the Centre for S.Cs. And S.Ts. It is difficult to exclude one community from receiving the benefits while permitting other twenty-two or so to receive the same so that they become his vote-banks. Nitish Kumar defends his position by saying that he will include *Dusadhs* also among *Maha-dalits*. Since Nitish Kumar has got his image yoked to the caste syndrome (with which Laloo Prasad and Ram Vilash Paswan along with a host of leaders of Bihar have been associated), he lost the high pedestal of being the "*Vikash Purush*" from where he had begun his journey as CM.

Nitish Kumar lives with the images of one who can do good social engineering as well as provide good governance to people who aspire for it. However, it was a mistake on the part of Nitish Kumar to adopt an ambiguous and confused approach towards the implementation of land reforms. He appointed Bandopadhyaya Commission to suggest measures of land reforms. When Mukhopadhyaya submitted his report by mail, the landed classes consisting now of a lesser number of upper castes and a far greater number of neo-rich among the intermediate castes rose in rebellion. They were filled with the apprehension that after the names of the tillers of the land will be registered in *anchals*, they would become holders of a specified share in the produce and in course of a few years, would themselves become owners of the land depriving the original owners the right to sell or bequeath the land to their successors. Nitish constituted a committee under the chairmanship of Land Reforms Commissioner to study the pros and cons of the Report but by that time, the misgivings of the landed classes had reached a high pitch. The dismal performance of the constituents of Nitish government (securing 5 seats out of 18) in the by-elections to the Bihar *Vidhan Sabha* in 2009 is attributed partially to Nitish's hidden agenda to introduce land reforms. This is evidenced by the fact that in one village in Patna district, out of 21,000 *Kurmis* eligible voters, only 4,000 went to the electoral booth to cast vote, others abstained in protest. Nitish Kumar was forced to deny in the Assembly and in a large number of public meetings that he had any plan to implement the *Bataidari* Act which is already in existence and had been prepared by a previous government. But his opponents in various political parties and a group of disgruntled elements who formed *Kisan Mahapanchayat* had been trying to convince the people that if Nitish got another term as CM in 2010, he would implement the *Bataidari* Act (old or amended).

Bihar has neither done consolidation of holdings nor computerized and updated land records. The old *Khatian* is missing in many cases. (Attempt is being made in late 2011 to update land records and law has been passed to that effect.) A recent attempt to distribute *Bhoodan* lands resulted in police firing in Khagaria killing 16 villagers by their own village men on 2.10.2009 inspiring Avinash Kumar to comment that the Government of Bihar is "illegitimate".[13]

As the 2010 election to *the Vidhan Sabha* in Bihar drew closer, Nitish Kumar started playing the old game of caste-based politics. He led a slew of "*Confidence Yatras*" or *raths* designed to appease different castes and communities. Whereas the "*Karpoori Rath*" was launched with the purpose of reinforcing the positive work done by the government in the minds of the extremely backward communities (EBCs), "*Swavlamban* (self-reliance) *Yatra*" dwelt on various steps undertaken by the NDA government for the uplift of women. "*Nirbhay Rath*" targeted at the *Bania* community and reminded them of the commerce-friendly law and order situation created by the ruling party. "*Aman Rath*" targeted at Muslims to remind them of the riot-free atmosphere during Nitish's term as CM; the purpose had been also to offbeat the vicious disinformation campaigns, for example, undertaken by the upper caste anti-Nitish lobby under the banner of "*Kisan Mahapanchayat*" against Nitish's proposed action to give tenancy rights to sharecroppers. While JD (U) dissidents took out a rally on 9.5.2010; CPI ML) organized a four days' movement ending on 10.5.2010 to procure *Bataidar Kisan Adhikar* i.e. to provide the status of farmers to sharecroppers. Since 2008, Nitish is putting all the eggs on the basket of caste groups, he cannot show to the people that he has ensured the presence of doctors in primary health centres, brought improvement in medicare, sanitation or education. Yet, it is a fact that he was adjudged the Best Chief Minister by the CNN-IBN and HT state of the Nation Poll 2007. *Economic Times* also awarded him with the title of "Reformer of The Year 2009". But the eruption of charge of "irregularities" for not furnishing A/c, D/c vouchers for about Rs. 11,000 crore- a fact which triggered the Patna High Court to observe that the case was fit to be referred to the CBI tarnished Nitish's image of a good administrator with grip over the sinews of administration. The CAG also reported about "defalcation of revenue collection collected through stamp duty and registration fees." Such omissions continued in spite of being pointed out in consecutive CAG reports, the report pointed out. The case was reported in April 2009 but the

Government did not furnish any reply till January 2010. Ceasar's wife is not above suspicion; rather people started comparing these reports of "irregularities" under Nitish with "scams" during Laloo's regime. However, comparisons came to rest with the Patna High Court absolving the state government of the charges in this connection.

We may draw the following conclusions about the working of institutions between the period 1967 to 2012:

1. The office of the governor, considered as a gubernatorial job till 1967 became a tool at the hands of the Centre between 1967-71 to beat and crush non-Congress governments at the state level. The CM, far from being the master of his ministry became loyal to the co-ordination committee (in the case of the non-Congress parties) or in the case of Congress party, the PM's most loyal men in the state. Collective responsibility became a misnomer as different ministers pulled in different directions.[14] Neutrality of the civil services was replaced by Mrs. Gandhi's penchant for "committed bureaucracy" when the Congress was in power. The Co-ordination Committee of the constituent parties worked like a super-cabinet when non-Congress parties ruled and the CM was like a show boy who converted his cabinet into a body rubberstamping what the committee barons decided or desired. Since 1990, the governor is supposed to be weak because he is the representative of the coalition government at the Centre. But as the governor of Karnataka issued notices to ministers on charges of corruption in 1990 and the Supreme Court came with the decision that governors could not be removed arbitrarily since they neither employees nor agents of the Union Government, role perception about Governor has changed. In Bihar, as the Chancellor, the governors have been asserting their independence and autonomy. The Universities bill passed by the two houses remained pending for the governor's signatures for quite sometime. The governors have

not become weak with the Coalition government at the Centre.

2. Coalition Governments represented the most unscrupulous exercises in political opportunism. Capturing power by hook or crook was the sole motive; ideology was all forgotten between 1967 and 1986. But Manmohan Singh as the head of the UPA coalition provided an ideological teeth with the pioneering of liberalization as an economic policy and with the conclusion of Indo-US Nuclear deal despite left's opposition. However, as the head of UPA-II, he had to withdraw the Bill on FDI Trade and is called the "weakest Prime Minister"or Sonia's poodle. He is not able to take decisive action in cases of many of his ministers' involvement in serious scams. Prashant Bhushan said that as PM, Manmohan Singh was like "shikhandi" and Kinar: Bed likened him to Dhritarashtra.
3. The politics of unscrupulous combinations manifested such a fluid situation that a line of demarcation between the government and the opposition lost its clarity due to large-scale shifts of political affiliations and allegiances between 1967 and 1986. Most of the constituent partners during the aforesaid period behaved like interest groups rather than political parties. It was commonly found that what the ministers belonging to one political party could not gain in the meeting of the cabinet or through the co-ordination committee, they sought to gain through making alliances with parties in opposition. So members of the coalition between 1967 and 1989 tended to stoop low for smaller gains which was glaringly reflected in their day to day behaviour. Members of the UPA Cabinet twitter and speak out of turn against the country's own ministries or a secretary on a foreign soil. This betrays lack of individual responsibility and collective working spirit.
4. Coalition experiments rehabilitated state politics in India in the eyes of people and showed that there are

possibilities for further development.[15] The rise and fall of coalition governments in states and frequently held elections made voters matured and discriminating. It was testified that the Indian voter despite low literacy level, poverty, lesser exposure to media, etc. was politically conscious and aware.

5. Cases of electoral corruption, intimidation and criminalization particularly grew since 1977 but they were effectively checked since Sheshan came to be appointed as the Chief Election Commissioner. He sent K. G. Rao as an election observer to Bihar who did a splendidly good job in stopping booth capturing to a large extent and ensuring fair voting by his frequent inspections and visits of booths in the consecutive *Vidhan Sabha* elections in Bihar.
6. The heterogeneity and diversity are being reflected in coalition governance since 1990 while a certain sense of unity and integration are also persisting. The unique party system obtaining in India is a reflection of the obtaining Indian social system.

Coalition system of pre-election alliances of political parties with similar political orientations and ideological moorings and commitments succeeds. Even if a coalition is made of political parties with divergent and heterogeneous policies and issues, a common minimum programme should be agreed upon in advance and a strong will on the part of the head to implement the agreed upon programmes is helpful for the system as a whole.[16]

We shall, however, strike a note that imperial Prime Ministerialism cuts the roots of both political modernization and democratization. The CMs since 1972, i.e. since Kedar Pandey assumed office were foisted upon the state and appointed by PM Mrs. Gandhi and her sons, Sanjay or Rajiv Gandhi as a sign of imperial Prime Ministerialism. As a consequence, the office of the CM suffered in its position and prestige heavily. The process of nomination by the PM tainted the traits of institutionalism and structuralism which are the sine qua non of political modernization. This is an aberration in the normal growth of party system in which party leaders should have equation with their constituents and electorate. The caste equations and defections (particularly before Anti-Defection Act 1985 was enforced) as determinants of the choice of CMs in the Indian federal system were also aberrations. Since 1989, at the Union level also, we have a federalised coalition system and the CMs have become strong. Regional parties and regional satraps rule the roost but sub-nationalism as a phenomenon ought to be discouraged. Many languages, many cultures, yet one nation should be the motto for India like that of Canada.

Notes and References

1. R. C. Prasad, "Bihar : Social Poliarizations and Political Instability" in Iqbal Narain (ed.), *State Politics in India*, pp. 62-63.
2. D.C. Gupta, *Indian Government and Politics*, Delhi, Vikas, 1972, Sixth edition, p. 505.
3. *Indian Nation*, 17.03.1972. The Bihar C.L.P. was directed by the central observer, G.L. Nanda to authorise Mrs. Gandhi to nominate its leader and accordingly, the C.L.P., in a specially convened meeting for the purpose, authorised her to do so. This became a precedent to be followed in all other cases between 1972 and 1977 and 1980 and 1984 except when the Centre was in a position to foist its candidate without such explicit authorisation as in the case of Jagannath Mishra in 1975.
4. *The Hindustan Times*, Patna, 16.04.2010.
5. *Ibid.*
6. *Ibid.*
7. *The Hindu*, Kolkata, 22.05.2010.
8. *Ibid.*
9. *Ibid.*
10. *The Times of India*, Patna, 23.05.2010.
11. *Hindustan* (Patna), 17.05.2010 (in Hindi).
12. *The Hindu* (Kolkata), 16.04.2010.
13. Avinash Kumar, "Illegitimacy of the State in Bihar", *Economic and Political Weekly*, October 31, 2009, pp. 8-11.
14. V.A. Pai Panandiker and Ajay K. Mehta, *The Indian Cabinet*, Delhi: Konark, 1996, pp. 5-6; and Paul R. Brass, *The Politics of India since Independence*, Delhi: Cambridge University Press, 1994, p. 119.
15. *Sunday Times* (London), 19.03.1967.
16. See Recommendations of Mizoram Regional Branch, Fortieth Annual Conference of Members of the IIPA, Indian Institute of Public Administration, October 27, 1996, p. 17.

4

The Politics of Appointment, Background and Style of CMs

In constitutional terms, the governor but in empirical terms, party politics and socio-economic contours play important roles in the appointment of CMs. Hence, appointment pattern of CMs of Bihar has varied in one party dominant system, coalition system, and upper/backward caste dominant system.

Article 164(1) of the Indian Constitution enjoins that "The Chief Minister shall be appointed by the Governor and the other Ministers shall be appointed by the Governor on the advice of the Chief Minister". The only pre-condition placed on the CMs of Bihar, Orissa and MP is that there shall be a minister in charge of tribal welfare who may in addition be in charge of welfare of the Scheduled Castes and backward classes or any other work. Like the appointment of ministers, the allocation of portfolios among ministers and their removal are the prerogatives of the CM. The CM presides over the meetings of the cabinet (the entire Council of Ministers hardly meets), brings necessary co-ordination in the working of various ministries and departments; and greatly influences the deliberations and decisions of the cabinet and over all working of ministries and departments through his "supervision" (to use Nehru's term to which Patel objected) and interventions.

An important clause in the Constitution is Article 164(2) which lays down that the Council of Ministers shall be "collectively responsible" to the Legislative Assembly of the state which implies that the CM of the Indian state has, in all times, to enjoy majority support in the Assembly; and only one who has or who is expected to show that strength can be invited by the governor to take oath as the CM of that state. A person who is not a member of the Assembly has been (Rabri Devi, for example) or can be invited to take oath as the CM of the state and form government. He or she, however, is obliged to become a member of either house of the legislature within a period of six months as stipulated in Article 164(4).

The role of the governor in the appointment of the CM is most formal when a single party commands absolute majority in the Assembly following a General Election. The single party with absolute majority in the Legislative Assembly communicates the name of its leader to head its legislative party in the government and the governor, presented with the *fait accompli*, designates him as CM. The question of governor's pleasure does not arise; he has no "discretion" in this situation, the Assembly being the "repository" of the will of the people.

The governor uses "marginal"[1] or "situational" discretion in the appointment of CM when the party position is fluid or no party singly or in coalition is in a clear majority in the Legislative Assembly or for any reason, the majority party is not able to indicate the choice of its leader. In such cases, the governors have resorted to two methods: to request the single largest party to head the government or instead, allow the formation of a coalition government,[2] depending upon their predilections, hidden command of the Centre or their personal assessment of the situation.

A point of controversy arose because governors started acting variously in the same situation or differently in different situations reflecting their bias or prejudice in the exercise of "marginal discretion" in the appointment of CMs. In 1952, the Congress party had 155 and combined opposition (called

Samyukta Vidhayak Dal) 166 out of a total of 351 seats in the then called Madras *Vidhan Sabha*. Sri Prakasa, the then governor of Madras, (now named Chennai) invited the single largest party, the Congress to form government. The same year, the Rajpramukh of PEPSU invited the leader of the Congress, the single largest party (with 26 seats out of 60) to form government. In that very year, the leader of the Congress party was invited to become the CM of Andhra Pradesh, though he had the strength of 51 in a house of 140. In November, 1967, Dharma Vira, the governor of West Bengal invited P.C. Ghosh, a defector from the UF Ministry to head a Congress supported government. In that very year, the governor of Rajasthan, Sampurnanand invited the Congress party to form government when the party had only 88 out of 183 seats in the lower house. The same pattern was repeated in most of the states. In all these precedents, benefits were reaped by the party in power at the Centre but the same precedents were not followed in 1967 itself in Bihar and West Bengal where the Congress party, though the single largest party, was not invited to form government because PM Mrs. Gandhi did not want the Congress to form government in these two states at that point of time as the leaders who were expected to become CMs under the circumstances were not of her choice. In Punjab, the *Samyukta Vidhayak Dal* (though in majority) was invited to form government only after the Congress refused the offer. The governors in all these cases used their personal judgment or acted at the behest of the Centre; they did not go by any uniform and absolute standards.

The piquant situation of absence of any viable single party or coalition between 1967-72 in the lower house in some of the Indian states provided ample opportunity for governors to play ball and they played it either at their own will or generally, at the behest of the Union government headed by Mrs. Gandhi. When conflicting claims were placed before the governor for choosing the CM among diverse coalitions, the governors either accepted one of the several claims or having concluded that the formation of no stable ministry was possible, recommended to the Union Government the imposition of President's rule.[3] Actions of some of the governors raised the question of constitutional impropriety and apart from media and the public at large, Parliament acrimoniously debated the issue. Some members of Parliament wanted the then Home Minister of the Union, Y.B. Chavan, to consider the feasibility of issuing guidelines or drawing a code of conduct for the governors in the appointment of CMs in situations where the party position in the lower house of their states was fluid.[4] The Home Minister referred the matter to an Expert Committee consisting of five eminent jurists. The Committee conclusively opined that a governor's position was analogous to that of a British monarch and therefore, he "had to act with detachment and impartiality in choosing the leader of a party for appointment as Chief Minister."[5]

The opinion of the experts did not satisfy those who were anxious with the governors acting under the direction of the Union government while exercising their constitutional "discretion" in appointing CMs taking advantage of fluidity of the situation. The governor of Rajasthan's appointment of CM in 1967 is cited as an example of Congressman by a Congressman,[6] and *ab initio* unconstitutional. Conversely, in many states where non-Congress parties had emerged as the single largest parties after the 1967 elections, their leaders were not invited by the governors to form governments. Partiality shown was much too obvious, glaring and annoying.[7]

M.C. Majahan, however, opines that it is not necessary for the governor to invite the leader of the single largest party to form government in all cases because in exceptional cases, he weighs and assesses other factors, as he should do, while inviting a leader to form government.[8] The Speaker of the Punjab Legislative Assembly, Joginder Singh Mann similarly ruled that "there was no provision that the leader of the majority party alone should be the Chief Minister. . ." The Reports of the Governors' Committee headed by Bhagwan Sahay, the then Governor of J&K, also suggested that the leader of the largest single party may not be invited to head a government if the governor is satisfied that the leader of the combination of parties is in a position to command a stable majority in the legislature.[9] The leader of the largest party has no absolute right to claim that he should be asked to form government. The relevant test is nor the size of a party but the ability to command the support of the majority in legislature.[10]

"Marginal discretion" came into play also in situations of political defection which became rampant in post-1967 scenario. Almost all the nine CMs who captured office in Bihar between 1967 and 1972 were products of defection. UP and West Bengal were experiencing similar situation. The Centre was intervening from behind but much too apparently; and the legislators of state units were dancing to make political or in some cases, even monetary gains.

It is being suggested, the governor should invite such a person for forming the government who, in the fluid situation, is in the objective judgment of the governor, capable of commanding the confidence of the majority of the lower house for a reasonable period of time. It would be incongruous if the governor's appointee either failed to face the lower house or was voted out the day he faced it. The Governor's job is to find stable government in accordance with the letter and spirit of the Constitution. While designating a CM, he has to act as the custodian of the best traditions and interests of the state and the legislature. We shall now examine the politics of appointment of the CM with particular reference to Bihar and also emphasize the role of social aggregates and primordial groups in the appointment of the CMs of Bihar.

APPOINTMENT IN THE CONGRESS'S FIRST DOMINANT PHASE (1937-67)

The appointment of the CMs of Bihar is said to have generally taken place in the backdrop of the rise and growth of caste alliances, animosity and rivalries in social as well as political arena. After the partition of West Bengal (1911) and bifurcation of Orissa from Bihar in 1936, the educationally advanced caste of *Kayasthas* was a fore-runner; they dominated the urban political scene till the late thirties. Rural scene was dominated by *Bhumihar Brahmins*. The entire political scene was dominated by elite upper caste Hindus and a few aristocratic Muslim families.

Political rivalry for state leadership among the four Hindu upper castes started by early twenties. Shyam Nandan Sahay and Ganesh Dutt Singh were mobilizing *Kayasthas* and *Bhumihars* respectively. The *Brahmins* were social status-wise at the top and the richest *zamindar* of Bihar, Kameshwar Singh who was a *Sarotri Maithil* had hold over *Zamindars,* though he lost election to the Lok Sabha to a young *Bhumihar,* Shyam Nandan Mishra *in* 1952 itself. Swami Sahajanand emerged in the 1930s both as a leader of the peasants, as a freedom fighter and as one who exhorted *Bhumihars* (called *Babhans* in rural parlance) to claim the status equal to *Brahmins,* do *yogas* and all kinds of *karmakands* by themselves and not invite *Brahmins* to undertake them on their behalf. In this cauldron, in the forties, Karyandnd Sharma and others in association with Swami Sahajanand spearheaded *Kisan* movements. Along with caste struggles for upper caste mobilization, polarization of peasantry against *zamindars* took place in the 1940s. S. K. Sinha was also a member of the *Kisan Sabha* constituted at Sonepur as we have mentioned earlier.

In the electoral battle in 1937, the chief medium of caste was used by the Congress party which was largely made up of leaders drawn from three upper castes—*Bhumihars, Rajputs* and *Brahmins* with stronghold in rural hinterland.[11] Rajendra Prased extensively refers to "jealousies and rivalries" among Congressmen before the local election in Bihar in 1920.[12] The scenario continued in the electoral politics of the post-20s and post-30s as well.

The brewing tensions in the top ranking leadership in Bihar came to the fore when the Congress was to form the First Ministry in 1937. The Congress thought it prudent to entertain the opinion of organizations of non-congress members which, too, was received in terms of caste alliances. Whereas *Kayasthas* established rapport with the Rajput leadership, other caste groups acted as supporters or opponents of *Bhumihar* or *Rajput* leadership of S.K. Sinha and A.N. Sinha respectively. A polarisation of differences of opinion was attempted to be done. Rama Dayalu Singh and Dharmaraj Sharma supported S.K. Sinha; Rajendra Prasad was said to have soft corner for A.N. Sinha. But when the time for the bell to ring came, Prasad (a *Kayastha*) exercised influence as an observer to reconcile the two groups and declared consensus in favour of S.K. Sinha who was elected leader of the CLP and, therefore, the premier of the state. Apart from caste strength, personality factor, oratorical skill and role in and contributions to the freedom struggle in favoured S.K. Sinha.

In the formation of the second ministry in 1946, conflict between the two stalwarts took place again and soundings to groups started. Defection from one group to another took place on the eve of election. K.B. Sahay, a *Kayastha* switched his loyalties from A.N. Sinha to S.K. Sinha generating a general impression in political circles that *Kayasthas* in general had switched over to *Bhumihars* which was far from true. This time also, S.K. Sinha got elected unanimously, though A.N. Sinha claims that "Rajendra Prasad was inclined to" him.[13] Factional rivalries in leadership election in 1952 intensified to the extent that it necessitated the intervention of PM and Congress President, Nehru. Central leadership took active interest[14] so that leadership election could pass smoothly; and it was conducted peacefully. The old dispensation was in office again. Only the nomenclature of the chief executive had changed under the 1950 constitution. S.K. Sinha came to be called CM; as he was no longer designated as the premier of Bihar by or under the Constitution of India.

A slight departure from the bifactional system took place following the exclusion of some of S. K. Sinha's followers from 1946 to 1952 ministries.[15] Notable among them were Kamakhya Narain Singh (a *Rajput Zamindar*) and Mahamaya Prasad Sinha (a *Kayastha*). They called themselves "centrists" within the party; they resented the inclusion of Mahesh Prasad Sinha (a casteman of the CM and close to him) in the cabinet. K.B. Sahay, too, felt disgruntled and after sometime, shifted once again to A.N. Sinha group. K.B. Sahay and Mahesh Prasad Sinha engaged themselves in fractional warfare which led to the defeat of both in the second General Election to the Bihar *Vidhan Sabha* in 1957.

In 1957, a direct contest between S.K. Sinha and A.N. Sinha for the office of the leadership of the Congress Legislature Party (CLP) took place. Nobody was willing to compromise. A.N. Sinha felt that his position had become stronger with the coming of K.B. Sahay and the centrists to his fold. But the result was unexpected for him. S.K. Sinha won once again, elected as the leader of the CLP, though the personal relationship of the rivals remained smooth. Mahesh Prasad Sinha and K.B. Sahay now emerged clearly as favourites to the two former freedom fighters and stalwarts, S.K. Sinha and A.N. Sinha respectively. Following the leadership contest, the social relationship of *Kayasthas* and *Bhumihars* became visibly strained. As senior a leader as Jayaprakash Narayan (a *Kayastha*), socialist subsequently turned a *Sarvodayi* leader and lastly, *Janata* party founder intervened by accusing S. K. Sinha of favouring Mahesh Prasad Sinha, his casteman, and discriminating against K.B. Sahay.[16] S.K. Sinha replied back in sterner terms accusing *Kayasthas* of earning even by counting the oceanic waves and clarifying his own position in the matter, steering himself clear of the accusations made by Narayan.

Like factional conflicts, caste conflicts in Bihar have also not been neatly bi-polar as is generally supposed. Both S.K. Sinha and A.N. Sinha cast their nets wide and along with the solid support of their castemen, took care to obtain support of other castes-upper, lower and middle.[17] The phenomenon of intra-caste conflicts and ultra-caste support was explicitly noted. In 1946, Karyanand Sharma of the C.P.I. contested against S. K. Sinha for a seat in the *Vidhan Sabha*, though both were *Bhumihar* leaders of standing. Nand Kishore Singh, Dip Narayan Singh and Sardar Harihar Singh remained loyal supporters of S.K. Sinha, though all the three were *Rajputs*. One may, therefore, suggest that neither Sinhas were out and out caste leaders (as it is often made out) nor Bihar politics has had been caste politics in its entirety.

The death of A.N. Sinha in 1957 and that of S.K. Sinha in 1961 replaced bi-factional politics by multi-factional one. A.N. Sinha's group broke into two- Rajput and non-Rajput with the former rallying completely around his son, S.N. Sinha. Many different castes organised under the leadership of Binodanand Jha. S.K. Sinha's faction fragmented after his death as Mahesh Prasad Sinha could not hold it together.

S.K. Sinha's death in 1961 was followed immediately by the appointment of a stop-gap CM (D.N. Singh) by the governor—a precedent which was to be followed at the Centre after the death of Nehru and the assassination of Mrs. Indira Gandhi respectively. Since D.N. Singh was the most senior member of the cabinet, the governor's choice was tangible, principled, and constitutional. Though not provided specifically in the Constitution, the situation demands that the appointment of an acting PM or CM be made by the formal head to avoid the impropriety of there being a governor without a CM or a President without a PM even transitionally (even if the outgoing Council of Ministers is provisionally retained).

After the death of S.K. Sinha, two broad sub-groups emerged in the Congress party. One sub-coalition led by Binodanand Jha, K.B. Sahay and S.N. Sinha (A.N. Sinha's son) drew support from *Brahmin, Kayastha* and *Rajput* castes respectively and the majority of lower caste Hindus among the MLAs. Another was primarily a *Bhumihar* faction with limited support among the lower castes which found itself by and large isolated. At the numbers game, B.N. Jha was superior to Mahesh Prasad Sinha and so, Jha defeated Sinha and became the second CM of Bihar. *Brahmins* felt emboldened by Jha's victory. Though the Brahmins had been the highest in the caste hierarchy of the Hindus, they had played second fiddle in the politics of Bihar so far. Now they came to form an independent group of their own.[18] But rift occurred sooner rather than later between Jha and Sahay, and then between Jha and S.N. Sinha. However, Jha maintained his mantle even after the third general elections in 1962 because of the blessings of the Central leadership. When Jha resigned under the Kamaraj Plan in 1963, S.N. Sinha and his followers deserted the Jha group and joined hands with the newly formed K.B. Sahay–Mahesh Prasad Sinha sub-coalition. The Jha faction was isolated and for the first time in Bihar, a backward caste lieutenant (of Jha), Bir Chand Patel was set up as a candidate for the CM's office who lost to Sahay maintaining the upper caste hegemony in the Congress through control over CM's post for the third time in succession. Sahay, however, could not keep S.N. Sinha and Mahesh Praasad Sinha in good humour for long. The two factions fell apart before long and Sahay was out in support of a new sub-coalition. Sahay castemen were not in sufficient numerical strength in

Bihar. In a bid, to counterbalance *Bhumihar–Rajput* power structure, he adopted the strategy of rallying the intermediate and lower castes around him. A change which had been in waiting since long came in the open. The defunct "*Tribeni Sangh*" formed in 1924 by the three intermediate castes—*Yadav, Kurmi* and *Khushwaha* was sought to be revived. Sahay's effort was not altogether novel. Even in the first cabinet in 1937, S.K. Sinha had provided adequate representation to backward castes, SCs and Muslims. But under K.B. Sahay, a marked effort in the direction of representation appeared to be in sight.However, the civil society of Bihar had come under specific political mobilization and the lollipop of co-option was not enough to arouse mobilized masses. Therefore, Sahay's efforts did not yield political dividends for him. Sahay bade time till 1967 general elections both to lose election as an MLA and to find the party reduced to minority in the Legislative Assembly. The only solace for him was that the non-Congress wave was not peculiar to Bihar; it had swept eight other states of the country as well.

APPOINTMENT OF CMs IN THE COALITION PHASE (1967-72)

Political mobilization further sharpened and assumed new dimensions during and after the fourth general elections (1967). Bihar whose roots of political affiliation under the Congress Party were the upper or "dominant" castes[19] was changing its affiliating partner. Intermediate and lower castes were aspiring to capture power on their own and not by co-option as was the case before 1967. Personal factionalism,[20] too, had raised its head high which, in turn, gave rise to two contradictory tendencies and which highly impacted the recruitment pattern within the Congress party. The first tendency arose out of the tendency felt by the contending groups of widening political support base—a widening social sub-coalition. The necessity derived contending groups to seek and win support from different caste groups. Secondly, leaders of different caste groups made endeavour to consolidate their political support base. The existence of intense competition among the leaders and the consequent move on their part to consolidate their political support base predisposed the leaders to prefer their own castemen in positions of power.

The fourth General Election of 1967 constituted a watershed in the history of party-cum caste politics in Bihar. There was explicit political mobilization of intermediate castes led by R.L. Singh Yadav whom K.B. Sahay had patronized. The debacle of the Congress party in many states in 1967 General Elections and the emergence of coalition governments in the states were symbolic of the politics of mounting frustration. In this General Election, people deserted the Congress party which had suffered the first such defeat in Bihar and other eight states. After decades of uninterrupted rule, the Congress party had been displaced from power and tasted powerlessness.

With the Congress securing 128 out of 318 seats and the non-Congress parties securing 178 and the independents 12 seats, the way had been paved for the formation of coalition governments in Bihar. Due to lack of absolute majority but more due to vacillation to become a partner in coalition government and Mrs. Gandhi's dictate, the Congress did not form the ministry in the state in 1967. Among the non-Congress parties, the largest single party in the legislature with the strength of 67, the *Samyukt Socialist Dal* (SSD) took the lead in attempting to form the alliance of six non-Congress parties. Consequently, the UF Ministry was formed under the leadership of Mahamaya Prasad Sinha, the then *Jan Kranti Dal* (JKD) President. Mahamaya Prasad Sinha had been President of the state Congress party in 1947 but turned to be a dissident leader soon and resigned from the Congress party in 1951. He came back to the Congress party in 1962 and left it again in 1966 to become the leader of the JKD. But the first UF government hardly functioned for ten months when it was voted out on January 25, 1968 on a no-confidence motion by the Congress opposition due to the defection in allied parties.

After the downfall of the first UF Ministry, B.P. Mandal claimed to form government on the support of the Congress party, though he was not qualified under Article 164(4) since he had already served as a Minister without being a legislator for about a period of six months. Therefore, a stratagem was employed to let Satish Prasad Singh, a member of *Soshit Dal* and a nominee of B.P. Mandal form a minority ministry for four days only to nominate Mandal as an M.L.C. The Satish government nominated Mandal as a member to the Legislative Council and thus paved the way for Mandal to form a ministry. Satish resigned and Mandal formed government but Mandal's government, too, could not last as B.N. Jha along with 17 other Congress party legislators crossed the floor to form *Lok Tantrik Congress*. Now Jha's nominee, B.P. Shastri became CM with the help of other opposition parties.[22]

Thereafter, a series of minority governments and governments of defectors started coming and going in the state which had brief spans of life.[23] Widely expressed fear was being aired about the instability of coalitions among parties having divergent ideologies and the consequence thereof for the governance of the backward state. The experience of coalition politics in Bihar, suggests that the conflict arising out of ideological and programmatic differences along coalescing parties are not as formidable as they could be expected to be. The main challenge to the maintenance of the coalition governments primarily came from sources other than ideological intractability. Two major factors appear to have played the crucial role in this matter: (i) lack of coherence and cohesion in the pivot parties often leading to sizeable defection, and (ii) the process of continuous fission and fusion characterising the smaller parties and transitory groupings and alliances of careerists and political entrepreneurs. The result was a quick turnover of Congress-led and non-Congress coalition governments in which almost all the parties in the system freely participated. So, the ideological differences among the parties did not prevent inter-party co-operation in coalition formation and maintenance. Paul Brass rightly observes that inter-party conflicts on matters of principle were more easily reconciled...than intraparty conflicts which related to party in power in the government.[24]

Even the mid-term poll in Bihar in 1969 did not end the recurrent instability. In fact, they unleashed fresh forces of political chaos whose ramifications unfolded gradually. The expectations of the civil society could not be fulfilled in the absence of healthy political and economic development. Various factors combined to make Bihar politics one of the murkiest in the country and prevented the growth of stable administration in the state which could end the under-development of the state and provide effective governance.

The politics in Bihar at that particular point of time had not so much been based upon parties' programmes or policies. The myriad social forces were tremendously mobilized and competition among the caste groups had been intense. All the parties which had a multi-caste membership had powerful caste-faction orientation as well. This was evident in the undivided Congress, the Congress (O), the Congress (R) as well as in other major parties. However, the fact of caste orientation of parties and groups does not mean that they were motivated by caste-interests and were not attached to the organisations; in fact, they used party labels and exploited caste loyalties to build and support political elitism. Castes got politicized and became a means to retaining power; whereas the party instrument was the means for legitimizing power. The other notable feature that characterized the political scenario in Bihar and became responsible for the collapse of as many as nine governments in quick succession during 1967-72 had been the phenomenon of a large number of migratory legislators in the state indulging in frequent marches and counter-marches from one political platform to another, largely with a view to gaining ministerial berth or other personal benefits, by helping to topple successive governments and helping put others in their places.

The sordid consequence of the nature of the 1969 elections was that the discredited faction leaders[25] in the Bihar Congress like K.B. Sahay, Mahesh Prasad Sinha, S.N. Sinha and R.L. Singh Yadav who had been kept out by being denied tickets to contest the election (as all the four were facing the Aiyar Commission of Inquiry for political corruption) raised their heads and tried to play the role of king-makers and enjoyed the vicarious pleasure of coming back to possess pelf and power. They sponsored Sardar Harihar Singh as their candidate for the leadership of the Bihar CLP after the consensus taken by Y.B. Chavan. Whereas the dissidents put up Daroga Prasad Rai as their candidate, ministerialists' candidate, Sardar Harihar Singh (a *Rajput*) was elected leader of the Bihar CLP. But Harihar Singh's ministry too could not last long as his government was defeated in the budget session. Later, he left the party as the Congress in 1969 split into two-Congress (Ruling) and Congress (Organisation); Singh joined Congress (organisation).

The CLP leadership fell the next time on the shoulders of Daroga Prasad Rai. The then All India Congress Committee General Secretary, H. N. Bahuguna reached Patna and D. P. Rai emerged in a compromise formulae with Kedar Pandey and L. N. Jha acting as Deputy leader. From Feb.16 to Dec. 22, 1970, Rai remained CM. In a no-confidence motion, Rai was defeated due to desertion of the CPI, *Jharkhand Party* and PSP. Karpoori Thakur became the next CM but having remained on the post for six and odd months, he dramatically resigned on the eve of the Assembly session on June 2, 1971 without facing it.

B.P. Shastri, till then in the *Lok Tantrik Dal* was asked for the third time to form a coalition government with the support of the Congress party. The CLP leadership went to Ram Jaipal Singh Yadav after the consensus in the party. His contestant for the CLP leadership was Budhadeo Singh, another Yadav, R.L.S. Yadav was acting as the Deputy CM in the Shastri Ministry but having remained in this position for six months, Congressmen started demanding Chief Ministership. When it was not conceded by Shastri, they left the ministry *en bloc* on 30.12.1971 and Shastri had no choice left but to resign. He again recommended dissolution of the Assembly; and President's rule came to be clamped for the third time in the state since 1967.

The situation prevailing in the end of 1971 indicated that Bihar had lost enthusiasm and idealism in a bitter struggle for survival of ministries amidst caste and subcaste rivalries. Despite the two spells of President's rule and nine experiments in minority and coalition ministries of various sorts during the four years after the 1967 general election, the governments in Bihar had remained chronically unstable. The administration under them was neither clean nor effective. Bihar experienced that political development was eclipsed by factors like sub-nationalism, factionalism, particularlism, ascriptive and affective allegiance-borne favouritism, nepotism and corruption. These factors not only made the state poorer but to use Atul Kohli's phrase for Bihar, there was "breakdown in a backward state".[26] It had several governments in between but no governance whatsoever.

To go back to 1960 and to appointment of CMs in post-split Congress, we find a new dimension. As we had noted earlier, the Congress party has had a long tradition of factionalism and in-fighting; and the former kept it alive as a dominant system. Congress (R) inherited the disease from its parents. Dissidence continued to remain organised around personal, familial, feudal and caste loyalties. But the aspirations and frustrations (arising from non-fulfilment of the former) due to denial of berth in the ministry was the insect that mostly stung. In order to fulfil this ambition, campaign for a change of CMs was launched to try luck with the next incumbent. The usual method employed before the insertion of the Tenth Schedule through amendment to the Constitution of India was to cross the floor and align with the opposition if intra-party manoeuvres did not appear to yield results. A mini-syndicate always operated within the party. Not only the Congress party but most of the parties in Bihar suffered from this chronic disease. They split more than once. Factionalism and splits were paying propositions. Every fragmentation created more leaders and every faction leader with a following of a few legislators acquired a position from which he could bargain with or bully any CM or would-be-CM.

The very nature of the post-1967 multi-party governments militated against the concepts of political stability and effective, responsible and good governance. These coalitions represented some of the most unprincipled alliances; and the most unscrupulous methods were employed to forge them. Noble causes, principles, policies and programmes were merely facades to cover the ugly realities of motivations of personal aggrandizement. It was little wonder, therefore, that the coalition governments in Bihar proved notoriously short-lived and unstable.

The politics in Bihar was characterised by the mass psyche of mounting frustration all these years. Bihar politics continued to be crazy, cynical and murky. According to a newspaper editorial, nowhere was the record of politicians "so obnoxious as in Bihar". They behaved "like children clamouring for lollipops".[27] With almost every party having had its share of innings, all failed miserably. All of them suffered from the maladies of casteism, corruption[28] and factional stiffness and splits. So, during 1967-71, level of integrity of ministers and bureaucrats was poor. It was not likely to improve even if there was another general election in which people provided a clear verdict. But when in December 1971, the last coalition led by B.P. Shastri paved the way for a general election by advising the governor to dissolve the Assembly and hold a fresh election; people of Bihar heaved a sigh of relief and hoped that things could improve.

APPOINTMENT OF CMs IN THE SECOND CONGRESS RULE : THE IMPERIAL STYLE

Between 1971-74, the country moved towards order and stability to be disturbed after a short interval by Gujarat movement, Allahabad High Court judgment unseating the PM, the JP movement and inhumanly implemented internal emergency (in north India) by Mrs. Gandhi with the support of S.S. Ray and Mrs. Gandhi's younger son, Sanjay Gandhi. Concentration of power at the Centre in the hands of the PM under the shadow of 'Garibi Hatao' politics could not make matters better. No doubt, the shaky politics of coalition was over; the 1971 election helped the Congress party to consolidate its position and to stabilise the Indian political system. A move, with far reaching consequences for the states was for the P.M. and her younger son to take over the power to appoint CMs of their choice to establish their monolithic control over the party and to eliminate the role of local politics and factionalism. The issue of state leadership was solely decided by the Congress high command between 1972 and 1989 whenever it ruled. (It did not rule between 1977 and 1980 when the *Janata* Party or *Lok Dal* came to power).

In March 1972, the Assembly elections were held and Congress (R) obtained absolute majority in Bihar after the

Congress having emerged victorious after facing five years of wilderness. The leadership issue again took momentum in the state politics. With the introduction of the new phenomenon of nomination by the Centre, the decline in the self oriented and state-bound leadership of the state CLPs, i.e. of the CMs started from thereon. There were four names pending under the consideration of the PM, Mrs. Indira Gandhi. They were A.Q. Ansari, Kedar Pandey, Mrs. R.D. Sinha and Vidyakar Kavi. Ansari had an edge over others. But dramatically, Kedar Pandey was nominated the leader of the Bihar CLP. Gulzarilal Nanda who came as an AICC observer to "conduct the leadership election" asked partymen to authorise the PM to nominate the leader which members of the CLP, like faithful and loyal servants, did.[29] After a telephonic talk with the PM at the venue of the meeting itself, Nanda announced the name of Kedar Pandey as the CLP leader. From March 19, 1972 to July 2, 1973, Pandey remained CM. But he had to quit as there was repeated demand for his ouster from the dominant group of the party. As his ouster campaign gained momentum with the reshuffling of the cabinet by him on May 26, 1973, he was instructed by the high command to reseek confidence of the CLP.[30] Ultimately, he sought vote of confidence of the CLP which he failed to get and resigned on the 24th June, 1973.

After the resignation of Kedar Pandey, the Bihar CLP again passed a resolution (moved by Kedar Pandey, the outgoing CM, and seconded by the BPCC President, Vidyakar Kavi) unanimously authorising the PM, Mrs. Gandhi to nominate a new *leader*.[31] Abdul Ghafoor was nominated as the new leader and assumed Chief Ministership on July 2, 1973 due to the blessings of the PM after due prevarication, dramatization and hesitation. V. Krishna Ananth comments that "Gafoor had earned a name as the most effete Chief Minister that Bihar had since then and was indeed the cause of the popular mobilization against the Congress a few months after he became the Chief Minister".[32] Indeed, in J.P. movement, students identified him with toddy or liquor. Ghafoor did not apply due restraint in dealing with the J.P. movement leaders; and newspaper reports and photographs showed how the police brutally lathi-charged J.P. and Nanaji

Deshmukh,[33] etc. Ghafoor, soon after his election to the Assembly from Madhubani Constituency, fell apart from the dominant group and after some time, constitutional crisis aggravated due to the movement started by Jaya Prakash Narayan to dissolve the Bihar Legislative Assembly. The demand for Ghafoor's ouster gained such a big momentum that at last in disgust, he offered to step down voluntarily. Following receipt of signal from the PM, he tendered his resignation on the 6th April, 1975.

The political drama in the state again re-started for leadership. After five days of political drama during which Kedar Pandey again announced his candidature and primarily because of "persuasions from High Command", Jagannath Mishra emerged as the unanimous leader of the CLP on 6.4.75.[34] Jagannath Mishra was the first unanimously elected leader of the CLP after S.K. Sinha in the state. But the contest could not have been ruled out without the intervention of the PM. The crucial murder of L.N. Mishra, the elder brother of Jagannath Mishra, weighed in favour of his election as a leader. Consequently, Mishra joined the Chief Ministership on 11.4.75. Mishra was a 'Sanjay man'. Power within states like Bihar had become a function of loyalty to not only the supremo but even her younger son, Sanjay. Sanjay could pick and choose CMs as he did in the case of Jagannath Mishra.

Mishra period, especially during the Emergency, is characterized by analysts as the 'dark period in state administration when corruption, favouritism and nepotism reached their zenith'.[35] Atul Kohli notes that the trend towards criminalization intensified under Mishra.[36] Government turned "ineffective" due to the decline of the police and the bureaucracy and above all, due to the deliberate decision of Mishra government to arm private caste groups (like the *Lorik Sena*, the *Bhoomi Sena*, the *Kunwar Sena*, the *Brahmrishi Sena* and the *Lal Sena*) to cope with the escalating agrarian violence.[37] The government did anything but govern because it started the new practice of appointing "loyal" ministers, civil servants and police officers leading to deprofessionalization and ineffectiveness of the state's administrative arm. One of the characteristic examples of deprofessionalization is for politicians to ask the police to render support for booth capturing or for other illegal deeds.[38] Appointment to the police or transfers and posting of SPs and DMs and even to junior rank officers were made largely on caste grounds. That made the police limp. A politico-administrative culture developed in which honest and competent people found it hard to survive. There were hoardings of 20-point programmes but policies and programmes were not implemented. What went on was: get into power, amass wealth, keep talking about removing the poverty of the poor, and figure out how to win the next election. The missing of the concept of politics as a constructive programmatic use of power or forum of action which started in full swing in the mid-70s made Bihar one of the poorest states of the country. Mishra's Ministry ruled for two years, that is, up to June, 1977. But Mishra had contributed such a great deal to criminalization of politics that the quality of elections deteriorated since 1977; criminals started entering into the electoral arena in a large number and many MLAs came from such background that they struck terror in the hearts of their constituents.[39] V. Krishna Ananth writes that Mishra turned Bihar into a "lawless land".[40] In September 1980, 31 undertrial prisoners in the Bhagalpur Central Jail were blinded by the prison authorities and police officials by putting acid into their eyes. Such cases were happening more often. Killing took place of *Dalits* in Pipra in February, 1980. Mishra government did nothing to protect the human rights of the prisoners or lives of the poorest of the poor, writes Ananath.[41]

APPOINTMENT OF THE *JANATA* CMs (1977-79)

After the 1977 *Lok Sabha* elections, the Congress (R) could not secure majority in the Lok Sabha. The *Janata* Party[42] ministry headed by Morarji Desai was formed at the Centre, The President, on the advice of the Council of Ministers, dissolved the Assemblies of nine states including Bihar on 30.4.77. Bihar was placed under President's rule. A fresh Assembly election was held in Bihar in the month of June, 1977. In this election, the Congress fared badly due to excesses done during the imposition itself of internal emergency bypassing constitutional processes and for the first time, introducing stark authoritarianism. The newly formed *Janata* Party swept almost all the states except West Bengal. After this crucial General Election in 1977, the leadership issue again got momentum. In Bihar, talks to reach unanimity over the choice of leader for the *Janata* Legislature Party (JLP) failed giving ample indication of a contest. The Central leaders of the *Janata* Party were taking keen interest in the settlement of leadership issue. All the possibilities of unanimous election of JLP having failed, ultimately, the election was held under the supervision of Nananji Deshmukh, an observer of the All India *Janata* Party on the 21st June, 1977. Karpoori Thakur and S.N. Sinha were two main contenders for leadership.[43] Karpoori Thakur's selection became a certainty after the erstwhile *Jana Sangh* bloc, which was the largest in the JLP, decided to withdraw its candidate, Kailashpati Mishra and support Thakur.[44] Consequently, the result was announced in favour of Karpoori Thakur as the leader of the JLP. Thakur got full support of erstwhile *Bhartiya Lok Dal* (BLD) and *Jana Sangh* constituents of the party and the legislators belonging to the backward castes, *Dalits* and *adivasis*. Among the legislators of forward castes, more or less all of them supported Karpoori Thakur except those of Rajput caste who were with their caste candidate, S.N. Sinha.[45]

Among the factors which weighed in the victory of Karpoori Thakur in his election as the leader, the most important factor was the unqualified support extended by the BLD-*Jana Sangh* combination which swept in the leadership contest in all the eight states[46] where leaders of the JLP were elected. There was nothing surprising about the result of the elections; the BLD-*Jan Sangh* combination got leadership of four states each.[47] The result of Bihar in the leadership contest was thus in tune with the total scheme of things.[48] A large number of *Janata* Party workers including dissidents demanded thorough probe into the alleged "highhandedness" of Deshmukh, the then General Secretary of the party, and the "manner" in which he conducted the election of the JLP leader as an observer. He was charged with playing a 'dubious rule'; and that after reaching Patna, he had held a meeting[49] of erstwhile *Jana Sangh* legislators and directed them to support Thakur. The State *Janata* Party Chief and one of the Contenders, S.N. Sinha also spoke on this occasion and all alluded to the *Jana Sangh*–BLD conspiracy to capture power in eight states and made allegations about Deshmukh's role particularly in the leadership contest in Bihar. Though elected with consensus, Karpoori Thakur followed the strategy to consolidate his power base among the backward castes. He tried to implement the policy of reservations (quotas) in both government jobs and in admissions to educational institutions in 1978. His attempt led to a considerable outburst of opposition from the forward castes to the extent that the figure of rioting in 1978 climbed back to the same high level as in 1974, the year before the Emergency was proclaimed.

Francine Frankel sees the 'backward class movement' led by Karpoori Thakur as' the organization of the poor in a double assault on the caste system and the class structure'.[50] But Atul Kohli feels that this approach overemphasizes socio-economic variables at the expense of political factors[51] Middle peasants had been in search of a political role commensurate with their improved economic standing; and the creamy layer of ruling class wanted a share in state-controlled jobs and educational opportunities for their progeny. Forward castes economically stagnated because they could neither invest in their farms nor put labour from their own hands. So they considered it imperative to continue to have access to the state's patronage resources. It is this conflict of interests that led to the rage and violence that eventually toppled the Thakur government.

Atul Kohli cites data to contradict to seeing the event as the consequence of discord between forward and backward castes.[52] 80% of the forward castes came down by the late-70s to the status of middle and small landowners. The objective economic interests of the forward caste and backward caste peasants were not distinguishable. The *Bhumihars* and the *Rajputs* supported not the Congress but the *Janata* Party in the 1977 election; whereas significant minority of *Ahirs* supported Congress party even in the post-emergency election. Caste, class, and party cleavages were far from being neat and easily identifiable during the political conflict of the late 1970s. Neither the rise nor the fall of Karpoori Thakur can be attributed to the emerging caste-class conflict. Thakur had not won the 1977 poll on the basis of his backward caste leadership rather because of anti-Indira sentiment. Having won and having become CM, he chose to consolidate his power base among the backward classes. With that intent, he loaded his ministry with members of the backward castes and sought to implement reservation policy. The anti-Thakur agitations were not socially but politically organized. They had been engineered by students fed by newspaper publicity. Rural masses were not involved. Leaders and parties provided the impetus. The threatened Congress elite allied themselves with the city-based forward castes, especially students, to mount an opposition movement that simultaneously put an end to reservation policies and toppled Thakur from power.[53]

The Karpoori Thakur Ministry faced real danger in April, 1979 and with the resignation of a large number of ministers, the defeat of Thakur Ministry became a certainity. The JLP meeting was held on the 19th April under the observership of Samar Guha, the party observer in which Thakur lost the confidence of the JLP by the margin of 30 votes.[54] It was not Karpoori Thakur but the BLD that lost the battle with the *Jan Sangh*, the Congress (O) and several other factions and groups determined to oust him. The BLD's insistence on forming ministries free from *Rashtriya Swayamsevak Sangh* (R.S.S.) elements had offended Jana Sangh. The BLD had antagonised a large section of the forward caste people and its performance on many fronts, such as public order, was disappointing.[55] The communal riots which erupted in Jamshedpur and in which a leader of the *Janata* Party was allegedly involved had tarnished the image of the party.

With the end of the Thakur Ministry, a flutter started for the election of a new JLP leader. The entire JLP was divided into two groups–dissidents and the ruling.[56] Ram Sundar Das, a *Dalit* leader, was fielded by the party legislators, though Thakur camp wanted to name another candidate for the contest. Announcing the name of Das as their agreed choice, the leading section hoped him to get elected JLP leader unanimously. Das had got the blessings of Jagjivan Ram, the then Deputy PM. But Karpoori Thakur or non-changers announced the name of Jageshwar Mandal for the contest. Leaders like Raj Narain, S.N. Mishra and S.S. Bhandari took interest in the result of this leadership contest. Raj Narain was in favour of election through contest while Bhandari wanted unanimous election of Das. After the powerful intervention of the Centre, the matter was squared up to the unanimous election of Das on the 21st April, 1979 as the JLP leader under the supervision of Samar Guha.[57] The BLD group led by Karpoori Thakur remained angry and indicated to work against this alleged RSS-dominated ministry by boycotting the oath ceremony at Raj Bhawan on 21.4.79. Later on, the dissident (i.e. Thakur) camp offered to extend support on the condition that *Jana Sangh* should not be included in the ministry but it was flatly rejected by the new elected CM, Das. He also dismissed the claim of Raj Narain that the ministry had no majority and challenged that he would prove his majority in the Assembly even without the support of the dissidents.[58] The *Janata* government under a socialist (*Dalit*) leader ruled until 1980 but it did not pursue the policy of reservations for backward castes initiated by Karpoori Thakur. However, within a short period, the constitutional crisis started at the Centre and the Lok Sabha was dissolved on the 21st June, 1979 and after the General Election in January 1980 which brought the Congress back to power at the Centre; on the 17th February, 1980, the Bihar Legislative Assembly was dissolved for seeking fresh mandate of the people under President's rule.[59] It is notable that Bihar elected *Dalits* as CMs both during the *janata* and the Congress regime before 1980 and none thereafter.

APPOINTMENT OF CMs UNDER REVIVED CONGRESS RULE (1980-85) : CONTINUED PRIME MINISTERIALISM

The election of Bihar legislative Assembly was held in June, 1980 and the result of the election returned the Congress

(I) with absolute majority.[60] Not only the states, but the Central parliamentary Board of the Congress (I) too at its meeting started discussion over the selection of the CLP leaders. A suitable candidate was being looked for in a meeting presided over by Indira Gandhi, the then PM herself. Expected contestants were Jagannath Mishra on the one hand and Kedar Pandey or his nominee on the other. But the Central pressure or persuasion paved the way for the unanimous election of Jagannath Mishra as the CLP leader.[61] On June 7, 1980, Jagannath Mishra was elected the unanimous leader of the Bihar CLP under the supervision of T. Anjaiah, the party observer of the Central Parliamentary Board.

Among the factors which contributed to the election of Mishra as the CLP leader, the most important factor again was the blessings on him of the Centre. Jagannath Mishra continued to have the blessings of Sanjay Gandhi who was by then an MP and had emerged as the most powerful personality in the power echelons of the party and the government. As General Secretary of the Congress (I), he was dealing with almost all the leadership issues of the Indian states at the instance of the PM Indira Gandhi. It was reflected also in the formation of the ministry in Bihar, when Jagannath Mishra gave unprecedented representation to Youth Congress (I),[62] a wing of the Congress organisation Sanjay Gandhi patronized. Through Sanjay Gandhi, Jagannath Mishra also enjoyed the blessings of the PM, Indira Gandhi. Apart from their combined blessings, Mishra had constructed his own image by campaigning in the constituencies vigorously for the Congress (I) during the critical days of the party in 1977 and the 1980 Lok Sabha elections. In comparison to his rival contenders, he enjoyed greater confidence of the legislators and after taking oath, he pacified most of the legislators by all means. However, he took no major policy initiative during his three-year rule.

Jagannath Mishra[63] faced a difficult situation when he was presented disgracefully and unfavourably for his "misdeeds" as CM before the high command and Rajiv Gandhi,[64] the successor General Secretary of the All India Congress Committee and holding the special charge of Bihar state. Many of his acts like being a respondent in a case of criminal misappropriation of funds of an Urban co-operative Bank, misuse of office, passing of the infamous press bill, dropping of a large number of ministers from the ministry including his henchmen in the name of removing corruption[65] and his controversial statements in regard to the Central government irritated the high command which compelled Jagannath Mishra to vacate the office. His argument that since a majority of MLAs and MLCs were with him, he was in a strong position did not go well with Delhi. It was on the 14th August, 1983, and after the meeting with Pranab Mukherjee, an observer, at *Raj Bhawan* that Jagannath Mishra submitted his resignation letter to the governor and after hectic search of a non-controversial leader, who could refurbish and improve the image of the Congress party in Bihar, a Central Minister of State was chosen by Mrs. Gandhi as the next CM.[66] The CLP meeting was held on the 14th August, 1983 at which C.S. Singh, a Union Minister of State for Energy and Delhi's nominee for Bihar CLP (I) leadership was elected uncontested for the coveted post. He possessed sophisticated disposition and impressed people by his oratory but did not possess good administrative skill. As a result he could not make much dent. The outgoing CM, Jagannath Mishra was asked to propose the name of the new leader and it was seconded by Mishra's colleague, Karamchand Bhagat, the outgoing Education Minister. In the meeting, Pranab Mukherjee, the observer, said that the change in the leadership was necessitated by "the voluntary resignation" of Jagannath Mishra and not because of his ouster or removal as erroneously reported by the newspapers. But the facts pointed to the contrary of what Mukherjee had claimed.[67]

The newly elected leader, C.S. Singh had, at he very start of his innings as CM, assured the people of Bihar to give "a fair and impartial administration". But Singh could any how run the governmental administration up to the next General Election in 1985. In this election, the Congress retained majority and for sometime, there were hectic efforts from Singh's side to retain the leadership of the Assembly. Jagannah Mishra was also making efforts to get the confidence of the central high command and that of the young PM, Rajiv Gandhi to be foisted as the CM. But the decision squared up on a third person, the BPCC President and an old labour leader and ex-minister, Bindeshwari Dubey. He took the oath of Chief Ministership steeped in a zigzag manner watching constantly to his trap master, Jagannath Mishra who was said to have favoured his nomination.

Bindeshwari Dubey who ruled between 1985 and 1988 could have reversed the growing trend towards governmental ineffectiveness. But like Jagannath Mishra, he too did not undertake any major policy initiative. Deinstitutionalisation of political parties had already led to increase in the statistics of violent incidents in the Lok Sabha elections in 1984 and Legislative Assembly elections in early 1985. Factional strife within the Congress party contributed to the growing crisis of governability in the state.

Between 1988-89, Bihar had four new CMs. Throughout the 1980s, the Congress government did not act with any amount of cohesiveness; the Congress leaders were actively engaged in internecine intrigues. None of the CMs could devote time and attention to solving state's pressing economic and political problems. Rajiv Gandhi continued the practice of changing CMs at frequent intervals during the tenure of his imperial Prime Ministerialism (1984-1989). During Bindeshwari Dubey's regime, transfer business flourished. Within the first fifteen months of his rule, he transferred nearly 300 IAS officers within the state.[68] The level of turnover of personnel was unprecedented even in Bihar and it proved the axiom that in Bihar "every new government . . . makes its predecessor look like angels".[69] Dubey's government poorly handled Arwal massacre in 1986 which led to a large protest demonstration by civil rights groups. During his dispensation, the Naxal groups spread their tentacles. A government report in 1982 suggested that nearly 200 villages were under Naxal influence and various armed leftist political groups were running 'parallel governments' in those areas.[70] The fact that private caste armies, supported by government, were organized to counter them suggests that the government failed to work. The party competition had been rendered insignificant because of elite factionalism, unusually weak political parties, agitations and mass mobilization as established modes of conducting the business of politics, extreme economic backwardness that made continued access to the state's resources a highly valued good, and the extremist appeal both attractive and counter-productive.

After Dubey, once again, the experiment of sending a Central Cabinet Minister, Bhagwat Jha Azad was tried on the grounds C.S. Singh's appointment had been made. Jha was an idealist but not pragmatic enough to turn his ideas into practice. He wanted to act against the *mafia* groups but offended the caste groups in his own party in the process. He also made the bureaucrats unhappy by trying to stop the March Loot. He toured Naxal affected areas and showed interest in, land reforms. But since he was not a practical politician, his tenure could not last for more than a year. At long last two ex-CMs tried their hands- S.N. Sinha for 9 months and Jagannath Mishra for 3 months. Since Mishra left office on 9.3.1990, the Congress had not been in power in the state again.

In retrospect, we find that from 1937 to 1967, in the first spell of the Congress rule, the CMs were leaders of their state units where they enjoyed a solid political base. But the CMs from 1967 to 1971 did not enjoy solid base as they headed unstable governments in the state. All the CMs of this period managed to be leaders only on the basis of their personal capacity of forming and managing groups for some time. The base of the CMs could not be strengthened even after the revival of the Congress party to power in 1972 and thereafter. After retaining majority after 1972, on none of the occasions, the CM was elected solely and exclusively because of his base in the Legislative Assembly. The CMs were imposed by Mrs. Gandhi or Rajiv Gandhi, the PMs during their tenure of (imperial) Prime Ministerialism. No wonder, the office of the CM suffered in its position and prestige heavily.[71] It was least cared that the CM of a state is not only the leader of the legislature party in the state, but he is the leader of the state party, the leader of the state government, the leader of the state legislature and of the people of the state. He reflects the opinion of the state and is responsible for good governance.

The period between 1990 and 2012 represents the period of empowerment of OBCs symbolized by occupying the office of CM by Laloo Prasad (a cowherd)/Rabri Devi (an *Ahir*) and Nitish Kumar (a *Kurmi*), the three representatives of the highest among the intermediate castes in Bihar. Just as Karpoori Thakur who made a bid to implement Mungeri Lal Commission Report in 1978 became CM through most enthusiastic support of upper castes in 1977, Laloo Prasad also became CM in 1990 because Raghunath Jha heeded the advice of Chandra Shekhar (a prominent Rajput leader operating from Ballia in U.P. and Delhi) to keep his fifteen supporters away from the electoral fray for Chief Ministership and thus allow Laloo Prasad (whom these fifteen MLAs did not want to vote for) to have a sway over his nearest rival in the *Janata* Party, Ram Sundar Das. Thus in the triangular contest for the CM's post, Laloo had his way. Had the three candidates been in the field, Ram Sundar Das would have captured the coveted post. Thus it can be said that Laloo Prasad became the CM because of the support he received at the hands of upper caste leaders like Chandra Shekhar and Raghunath Jha. However, once Laloo Prasad became CM, he championed the cause of OBCs and remained loyal to Devi Lal in *Janata Dal*; and emerged as a leader who enhanced the position and provided dignity to OBCs. When he was chargesheeted by the CBI and had to go to jail, it is said that Radha Nandan Jha, a former Speaker of Bihar Legislative Assembly and his next door neighbour and adviser, though a Congress man told him that he should not hand over the charge of the office of the CM to any other OBC but only to his wife. Jha's advice suited Laloo and he acted accordingly. Thus Rabri Devi ruled Bihar as a proxy CM for six to seven years a record Nitish Kumar has broken.

People of Bihar, particularly upper castes, a substantial number of Muslims, Kurmis and a segment of OBCs and EBCs got disgusted with Laloo-Rabri regime after fifteen years of their combined rule. So there was popular uprising in favour of JD (U)-BJP combine in the 2005 *Vidhan Sabha* elections and even before the election, it was agreed that in case this combination got electoral victory, Nitish Kumar would be made CM. So Nitish Kumar, belonging to the intermediate caste, Kurmi which is the second dominant caste among the intermediate castes, became the CM in 2005 and completed his first term in 2010 as the head of a coalition government. He is presently the head of the second NDA coalition which is governing Bihar (JD(U) + BJP combination) since 2010.

THE BACKGROUND OF THE CMs

The study of the background of the CMs in Bihar points to the heterogeneity of the political background they represented. There has been no uniformity in the selection or election of leaders on the basis of their personal or social background.[72] The highly relevant factors have been the caste equation, power thirst shown by defection and polarisation, and in the period since 1972, nomination by Mrs. Gandhi or either of her sons who were supposed to be bred as prospective PMs. In the twenty-first century, one is happy to note that CM's identification with or image of good governance provides the background for his selection, stability, power equation in the party and government and general reputation in the country and abroad as reflected by the media and other kinds of reports.

The standing of the incumbent's family has not been of much consequence in the recruitment of CMs. Most of the CMs have come from lower middle-class families and in those, only two enjoyed the help of their family in their appointment as CM. The ancestry of S.N. Sinha (known more for his sophisticated style of living and caste leadership) or fraternity of Jagannath Mishra may have helped them achieve the post of the CM. Most of the CMs, other than those of the Congress party, attained their office because of their personal equation or political polarisation.

Education, too, has not played a pivotal role in the selection of CMs in the period under our study. S.K. Sinha had B. A. degree from Patna College (Patna University) followed by the degree of law and started practising in Monghyr bar from

1915. But Binodanand Jha was only a matriculate. K.B. Sahay, of course, had a B.A. degree with Honours. Kedar Pandey had acquired M.Sc. and B.L. degrees; and Abdul Ghafoor had got higher education at Aligarh Muslim University. The most qualified CM of Bihar, Jagannath Mishra was an awardee of Ph.D. degree with a few published works in Economics to his credit. C.S. Singh was an M.A. in Economics and an ex-editor of Hindu Daily. Among non-Congress CMs, most of them had got education up to the college level but none except one of them was highly qualified. Mahamaya Prasad Sinha and B.P. Mandal had got education up to the B.A. level, B.P. Shastri too was a graduate and Karpoori Thakur's education was up to the I.A. level. Laloo Prasad had B.A., B.L. degrees from Patna University and Nitish Kumar possessed Bachelor of engineering degree from the same university. So, all the CMs in Bihar were more or less qualified but it cannot be argued that they got weightage in their selection as CMs on this count.

In respect of political background, barring a few, almost all the CMs had long political experience. S.K. Sinha had been a member of the Constituent Assembly of India and earlier, in 1940, he was declared the first *Satyagrahi* of Bihar by Mahatma Gandhi. He remained in jails for a total of eight years (2,920 days) in the struggle for India's freedom. Binodanand Jha, Sardar Harihar Singh, D.P. Roy and K.B. Sahay too were freedom fighters. Non-Congress CMs like Mahamaya Prasad Sinha, B.P. Mandal, B.P. Shastri, Karpoori Thakur and R.S. Das had old affiliation with politics. Jagannath Mishra became CM after a comparatively short span of political life. C.S. Singh, an old freedom fighter, had joined politics in his early life and had dedicated himself to the service of the people. Bindeshwari Dubey had been a tried leader of trade unions of coal fields but his tete-e-tete with J. Mishra made his tenure as CM a failure. Among non-Congress CMs, Mahamaya Prasad Sinha was a former president of the Congress party in 1947. Later on, he joined as the president of several newly formed parties like the PSP, JKD, etc. B.P. Mandal and B.P. Shastri had been primarily members of the Congress party. B.P. Mandal was primarily a caste leader and after he was expelled from the Congress Party in 1965, joined the SSP under the leadership of Ram Manohar

Lohia. B.P. Shastri became a member of the Bihar Legislature in 1952 and also joined the Council of Ministers of the state in 1952. He held some other important posts in the political sphere. Later on, he became the Chairman of the *Loktantrik Party*. D.P. Roy was also a veteran leader of Bihar politics. He joined politics in the late forties and was first elected to the Assembly in 1952. He was a dissident in the Congress party in 1963. He had made name as a fighter for the independence of India. Sardar Harihar Singh had started his political career as an independent leader and joined the Congress party later on and rejoined it in 1968. He, too, was a past-master in the politics of defection as he, no less than three times, shifted from one party to another. Karpoori Thakur, the most notable CM of the non-Congress party, had entered into active politics in 1942. Primarily, a member of the Congress Socialist Party (which after 1948 became the Socialist Party of India), he rose to be the Chairman of All India SSP. He had been a popular leader in Bihar and became CM twice-once in the capacity of a SSP leader and another time in that of a *Janata* party leader. R.S. Das had also been a man of political stature. A socialist leader in the beginning, he subsequently became the leader of the *Janata* Party. Laloo Prasad and Nitish Kumar had been the products of the J.P. Movement and became prominent after serving as President and General Secretary of Patna University Students' Union respectively. Laloo had been an office–bearer of the *Janata* party and of JD and an M.P. before being CM. Nitish Kumar, too, had been an office–bearer of the *Janata* party, and of *Janata Dal* party and an M.P. and a Minister of Railways in the Union Government before becoming CM. Almost all the CMs except Satish Prasad Singh (was the youngest politician aged about 32 years at the time of becoming CM and a member of *Soshit Dal*, a newly formed party) and Rabri Devi (who had no political experience) thus had long political experience.

As regards prior parliamentary or administrative experience, gaining such experiences was not possible for all before independence. S.K. Sinha became the premier of Bihar province when the Congress party came to power under the Government of India Act, 1935. He formed the cabinet at Patna on the 20th July, 1937. He and his cabinet resigned on the issue of disagreement with the Governor on the issue of the release of political prisoners and over passage of Bihar Tenancy Act which was in favour of peasants. The governor acceded to the demands but the cabinet resigned again in 1939, as did all the then Congress premiers, over the question of involving India in World War II without the consent of the Indian people.

Mahamaya Prasad Sinha changed his parties and principles now and then. Before becoming CM, he had only organisational experience but little governmental experience. He had the reputation of being a giant, having defeated the most powerful Congress stalwarts like Mahesh Prasad Sinha in 1957 and K.B. Sahay in 1967. B.P. Mandal had legislative experience, too. But it cannot be said that most of the CMs of coalition period had insignificant legislative or administrative experience; some of them had good hold over the parties they were in.

Kedar Pandy had past experience of both legislative and executive administration. Ghafoor had been a deputy minister in Binodanand Jha's ministry, a minister in Shastri's ministry and Chairman of the State Council. In *Janata* party rule, Karpoori Thakur had the longest legislative experience than all other CMs of Bihar. He had been a member of Bihar Legislative Assembly right from the first General Election. Like Bhola Paswan Shastri, Thakur was the Deputy Chief Minister in Mahamaya Prasad Sinha's ministry. Later, Thakur became CM during the U.F. Government. He maintained strong hold over any party to whichever he belonged. Although he faced contest for leadership; his modest and courteous behaviour was appreciated by all factions and he was agreeably a man of national political calibre.[73] He could be compared in stature to Bhola Paswan Shastri alone who too started as a legislator and a minister in 1952 and rose to be CM more than once. Though Shastri was a *Dalit* and Thakur belonged to an extremely backward caste, their stature was such that they commanded both respect and affection. Ram Sundar Das, also a *Dalit*, had comparatively lesser legislative and administrative experience. After revival of the Congress party in 1980, Jagannath Mishra, an ex-minister and CM maintained hold in the party as a legislator. Although his length of legislative experience was not much, he built himself up in a short span of political life. He had a vivid personality and maintained solid loyalty patterns among MLAs. He has been criticised severely by Atul Kohli, V.K. Ananth and others for abetting corruption in the state and also for maladministration. C.S. Singh had long experience of legislature and short span of governmental experience. His recruitment as CM was due to his reputation for administrative efficiency and good character. He wanted to place his heart on developmental cart from where Bihar had derailed. His appointment as the CM was hailed, on that account, by the people of the state but the expectations could not be fulfilled by him due to various reasons. Bindeshwari Dubey, a veteran trade union leader had long parliamentary and governmental experience. He was famous for his mild and sober nature even in the political field. Azad, too, was a man of long political standing who wanted land reforms, end of *Mafias* and control over March *Loot* but he lacked the necessary grip over administration to achieve the desired results. Both Laloo Prasad and Nitish Kumar began as the symbols of empowerment of OBCs and leaders of their own caste in particular. They believed in cobbling up an arrangement of OBCs, EBCs and Muslims so as to make a strong winning electoral arithmetic. They differed in style and mannerisms, Nitish identified himself with people' aspiration for good governance since the beginning as CM and created an image of a leader who could provide good governance in an extremely backward state while Laloo saw his role in securing respect for the OBCs in the society and self-respect to them and other weaker sections.

Finally, it may be noted that the office of the CM has not been the exclusive domain of any caste or class or any combination of castes. There has been circulation of elites and counter-elites. Sub-elites have also got the chance to occupy the office of the CM. This has kept different sections satiated from the point of view of access to political power or political participation when they felt that they needed to be in power. Persons belonging to all layers of Hindu castes: forward (who exclusively ruled between 1947-67), backward, S.C., as well as Muslims got the chance to head the government of Bihar. But so far as ideology is concerned, no CM has shown inclination for a distinct political ideology. Identification of the CM with particular schemes or programmes has also not been notable. However, S.K. Sinha was a centrist, pro-Nehru and pro-*kisan* in ideology while Nitish Kumar is identified with women's empowerment, Pasmanda Muslim's EBC's or Mahadalit's uplift and in general, good governance. The Congress CMs since 1972 were duty bound to seek identification with twenty or twenty-five points programme of the Central unit of the party to remain in office. A distinct personality structure and programmatic base have been mostly a casualty; this may particularly explain lag of political and economic development of Bihar.

The three CMs of Bihar from 1947 to 1967: S.K. Sinha, Binodanand Jha and K.B. Sahay enjoyed seemingly stable political order because it was a narrow elitist small political order that ruled the state during that period. Another cause for their stability was that they were sensitive to the progress of the state and good administration. S.K. Sinha with the help of K.B. Sahay pioneered the first legislation in the country to abolish the Zamindari system in 1952. The legislation on land ceilings was introduced in the *Vidhan Sabha* in 1955. A watered down version was passed in 1959 and got Presidential assent in 1962. There was political mobilization of social forces in 1967 and caste-class conflict over reservations in 1978 resulting in considerable turmoil. Challenges to the power of the forward castes have grown on since 1967 in both the civil society and the state. But the most glaring factors of Bihar are: squabbling politicians (CM *v.* anti-CM groups), massive leakages of public funds through corruption by Minister-civil servant nexus, dysfunctional governance for many long years (unresponsive to the poor and to state's development in general), failing agricultural productivity and industrial production, declining standards of education and the increase in agrarian conflict in the civil society. Undisciplined power struggles among the competing political elite is an important cause of all these factors. We agree with Atul Kohli's thesis that the disintegration of the state (for which succeeding CMs are[74] most responsible) and growing (unrestrained) socio-economic

List of Chief Ministers Indicating their Castes

Sl. No.	*Name of the Chief Minister*	*Parties*	*From*	*To*	*No. of Days*	*Caste (By birth)*
(1)	(2)	(3)	(4)	(5)	(6)	(7)
1.	Mohammed Yunus as premier	Muslim Independent Party supported by Congress Party	1.4.1937	19.7.1937		Muslim
2.	S. K. Sinha as Premier	Congress Party	20.07.1937	31.10.1939		Bhumihar
3.	S. K. Sinha	Congress Party	02.04.1946	31.01.1961		Bhumihar
4.	Deep Narain Singh	Congress Party	01.01.1961	18.01.1961		Rajput
5.	Binodanad Jha	Congress Party	18.02.1961	02.10.1963		Brahmin
6.	K. B. Sahay	Congress Party	03.10.1963	05.03.1967		Kayastha
7.	Mahamaya Prasad Sinha	SSP, PSP, JS, CPI, JKD	05.03.1967	28.01.1968	297	Kayastha
8.	Satish Prasad Singh	Minority Ministry backed by Congress	28.01.1968	01.02.1968	4	Kushwaha
9.	Bindeshwari Prasad Mandal	Soshit Dal backed by Congress	01.02.1968	22.03.1968	47	Ahir
10.	Bhola Paswan Shastri	LTC, CPI, Janata, JS	23.03.1968	28.06.1968	96	*Dalit* (Paswan)
FIRST PRESIDENT's RULE			29.06.1968	26.02.1969		
11.	Sardar Harihar Singh	Cong, Janata, Soshit Dal	26.02.1969	20.06.1969	115	Rajput

12.	Bhola Paswan Shastri	LCD, Soshit Dal, BKD, Jharkhand, backed by SSP, JS, CPI	21.06.1969	04.07.1969	11	*Dalit* (Paswan)
SECOND PRESIDENT's RULE			04.07.1969	16.02.1970		
13.	Daroga Prasad Rai	Cong (R) Jharkhand, Soshit Dal backed by CPI, PSP	16.02.1970	22.12.1970	306	Ahir
14.	Karpoori Thakur	SSP, Cong (O), JS, SWT, Janata, BKD, Soshit A section of PSP	22.12.1970	02.06.1971	163	Nai or barber (EBC)
15.	B. P. Shastri	Cong (R), CPI, PSP, Soshit Jharkhand (HORO)	02.06.1971	09.11.1972	217	Dalit (Paswan)
THIRD PRESIDENT's RULE			09.01.1972	19.03.1972		
16.	Kedar Pandey	Cong (R)	19.03.1972	02.07.1973		Brahmin
17.	Abdul Ghafoor	Cong (R)	02.07.1973	11.04.1975		Muslim
18.	Jagannath Mishra	Cong (R)	11.04.1975	30.04.1977		Brahmin
FOURTH PRESIDENT's RULE			01.05.1977	24.06.1977		
19.	Karpoori Thakur	Janata	24.06.1977	21.04.1979		Nai or barber (EBC)

(Contd.)

TABLE (*Contd.*)

(1)	(2)	(3)	(4)	(5)	(6)	(7)
20.	Ram Sundar Das	Janata	21.04.1979	18.02.1980		*Dalit* (Ravidas)
FIFTH PRESIDENT's RULE		18.02.1980	08.06.1980			
21.	Jagannath Mishra	Cong (I)	09.06.1980	14.08.1983		Brahmin
22.	Chandra Shekhar Singh	Cong (I)	14.08.1983	12.03.1985		Rajput
23.	Bindeshwari Dubey	Cong (I)	12.03.1985	14.02.1988		Brahmin
24.	Bhagwat Jha Azad	Cong (I)	14.02.1988	11.03.1989		Brahmin
25.	S. N. Sinha	Cong (I)	11.03.1989	05.12.1989		Rajput
26.	Jagannath Mishra	Cong (I)	06.12.1989	09.03.1990		Brahmin
27.	Laloo Prasad	Janata Dal	10.03.1990	30.07.1997		Gareria
28.	Rabri Devi	Rastriya Janata Dal	30.07.1997	23.11.2005		Ahir
29.	Nitish Kumar	JD (U)	24.11.05			Kurmi

conflict combined to produce a crisis of governability in Bihar.[75] On the other hand, civil movement even of the magnitude of J.P. movement of 1974 did not impact the large society of Bihar as the *Nav Nirman* movement of Gujarat impacted Gujarat. So the society of Bihar is governed without programmes and without prospects of reforms; and for this, style of governance of CMs is a causative factor. However, the regimes of S.K. Sinha and Nitish Kumar may be exceptions to our disparaging comments.

Notes and References

1. In the case of Varadarajan vs. State of Travancor-Cochin High Court (1953. T.C.49), the court used the word "marginal discretion" to characterize such cases.
2. Sir Ivor Jennings envisages three possibilities for the use of "marginal discretion"; (i) a coalition government may be allowed to be formed; (ii) one party may form a minority government which can advise the dissolution of the house as and when warranted to do so; and (iii) a minority government may be formed which can maintain itself in office in spite of lack of absolute majority by a single party. See Sir Ivor Jennings, *Cabinet Government*, Cambride University Press, Reprinted in 1961, pp.29-30
3. Ashok Chanda, "Controversial Decision by the Governors' Conference", *The Statesman* (Calcutta), 7.3.1970.
4. Cited in D.C. Pavate, *My Days as Governor*, Delhi; Vikas, 1974, p.16.
5. *Ibid.*
6. *The Hindustan Times* (Delhi), 7.3.1969.
7. *The Statesman* (Delhi) made it the theme of debate in the issues of 16.3.1971 and 25.3.1971. See Whne Wilcox, "Madhya Pradesh" in Myron Weiner (ed.), *State Politics in India*, New Jersey: Princeton University Press, p. 150
8. *The Indian Express* (Delhi), 25.3.1967; for Mann's ruling, see D.C. Pavate, *My Days as Governor*, Delhi: Vikas, 1974, pp.35.
9. *The Report of the Committee of the Governors*, New Delhi: President Secretariat, 1971, p.29.
10. *Ibid*
11. For details, see Ramashray Roy, "Congress Party in Bihar" in Iqbal Narain (ed.), *State Politics in India*, Meerut: Meenakshi, 1967.
12. Rajendra Prasad, *Autobiography*, Bombay: Asia Publishing House, 1957, p. 212.
13. A. N. Sinha, *Mere Sansamaran*.

14. *Ibid.* He writes that L. N. Singh 'Sudhanshu', the then Congress President of Bihar was called to Delhi for guidelines
15. Ramashray Roy, "Dynamics of One Party Dominance in an Indian State", *Asian Survey,* 8.7.1967, p.564.
16. The correspondence between J. P. and S. K. Sinha is published in *The Indian Nation, 8.8.1959.*
17. *Ibid.*
18. Jawaharlal Pandey, *State Politics in India,* Delhi: Uppal Publishing House
19. Iqbal Narain (ed.), *State Politics in India,* Meerut: Meenakshi, 1967. We are using the words "dominant castes" in the sense M. N. Srinivas uses it in *Social Change in Modern India,* Orient Longman, 1972, pp. 10-11.
20. Paul R. Brass has studied the role of factions in U. P. Politics extensively. Their role is not less extensive in Bihar.
21. Mrs. Gandhi, the PM in her Patna speech did not explicitly request the electorate of Patna to support the CM, K. B. Sahay. See Iqbal Narain (ed.), *op.cit.*
22. Subash C. Kashyap, *The Politics of Power: the Defections and State Politics in India,* Delhi: National Publishing House, 1974, pp. 305-308.
23. *List of Coalition Governments' CMs (67-71) with caste and education.* (see Table on the next page)
24. Paul. R. Brass, "Coalition Politics in North India", *American Political Science Review,* LXII, December, 1968, pp. 1174-1191.
25. They were referred to as the multi-syndicate of Bihar.
26. Atul Kohli, "Breakdown in a 'Backward' State: Bihar" in *Democracy and Development in India: From Pro-Socialism to Pro-Business,* Delhi: Oxford University Press, 2009, pp.253-286.
27. *National Herald,* 2.10.1969.
28. The Mudholkar Commission, constituted against the First U. F. Ministry led by Mahamya Prasad Sinha, confirmed the corruption charges against 13 ministers on November 19, 1967.
29. *The Indian Nation* 17.3.1972. The one-sentence Bihar CLP resolution said that "this meeting authorizes the P. M., Mrs. Indira Gandhi to nominate the party leader".
30. As Kedar Pandey dropped many senior ministers from the cabinet, the dissidents started an ouster campaign under the leadership of L. N. Mishra, a Union minister, close to the PM, Mrs. Gandhi, See *Ibid.,* 25.6.1971
31. *Ibid.,* 25.6.1973.
32. V. Krishna Ananth, *India Since Independence: Making Sense of Indian Politics,* Longman, Delhi, 2009, p. 114.
33. *Ibid.*
34. The Indian Nation, 7.4.1975.

Sl. No.	Name of the Chief Minister	Parties	From	Uptil	No. of Days	Caste (By birth)	Education
(1)	(2)	(3)	(4)	(5)	(6)	(7)	(8)
1	Mahamaya Prasad Sinha	SSP, PSP, JS, CPI, JKD	05.03.1967	28.01.1968	297	Kayastha	B.A.
2	Satish Prasad Singh	Minority Ministry backed by Congress	28.01.1968	01.02.1968	4	Kushwaha	
3	Bindeshwari Prasad Mandal	Soshit Dal backed by Congress	01.02.1968	22.03.1968	47	Ahir	B.A.
4	Bhola Paswan Shastri	LTC, CPI, Janta, JS	23.03.1968	28.06.1968	96	Dalit (Paswan)	B.A.
5	Sardar Harihar Singh	Cong, Janata, Soshit Dal	26.02.1969	20.06.1969	115	Rajput	
6	Bhola Paswan Shastri	LCD, Soshit Dal, BKD, Jharkhand, backed by SSP, JS, CPI	21.06.1969	04.07.1969	11	Dalit (Paswan)	B.A.
7	Daroga Prasad Rai	Cong (R) Jharkhand, Soshit Dal backed by CPI, PSP	16.02.1970	22.12.1970	306	Ahir	
8	Karpoori Thakur	SSP, Cong (O), JS, SWT, Janata, BKD, Soshit A section of PSP	22.12.1970	01.06.1971	163	Nai or Barber (EBC)	I.A.
9	B.P. Shastri	Cong (R), CPI, PSP, Soshit Jharkhand(HORO)	02.06.1971	27.12.1971	205	Dalit (Paswan)	B.A.

35. See the analysis in *The Hindustan Times*, 15.8.1986, p. 12.
36. Atul Kohli, *op. cit.*, p. 264.
37. *Ibid.*
38. Cited in *Ibid.*, p. 265.
39. Report of The Times of India cited in *Ibid.*, p. 266.
40. Ananth, *op. cit.*, p. 253.
41. *Ibid.*, p. 254.
42. The *Janata* Party was formed following the merger of four units of parties viz. Cong (O), *Jan Sangh, Lok Dal* and Socialist.
43. Sumitra Devi was also a contender for the post but she got negligible support.
44. *The Indian Nation*, 22.6.1977.
45. *Ibid.*
46. The eight states were : Bihar, Orissa, U.P., M.P., Himachal Pradesh, Rajasthan, Haryana and Delhi Union.
47. Whereas Rajasthan, M.P., H.P. and Delhi Union were in the hands of *Jana Sangh*: Bihar, U.P., Orissa and Haryana were in the hands of B.L.D.
48. *Ibid.*
49. *The Indian Nation*, 23.06.1977.
50. Cited in Kohli, *op. cit.*, p. 268, footnote.
51. *Ibid.*
52. *Ibid.* p. 269.
53. *Ibid.*, pp. 269-71.
54. Dissidents got 135 votes and the ruiling 105.
55. The Indian Nation, 20.04.1979.
56. The dissidents were Jan Sangh, Cong (O) and Socialist Constituents; ruiling was the B. L. D. faction led by Thakur.
57. *The Indian Nation*, 22.04.1979.
58. *The Indian Nation*, 22.04.1979.
59. *The Indian Nation*, 18.02.1980.
60. After unexpected defeat in the 1977 general elections, the Congress (R) was divided into two factions ushering in a new trend to form the party on the individual names: (i) Congress (Urs) after the name of Devraj Urs, the party president of Karnataka.
61. Kedar Pandey clarified that he is not in the run. See *The Indian Nation*, 6.6.1980.
62. *Ibid.*
63. Jagannath Mishra dropped his surname 'Mishra' to obliterate the tinge of caste identification in March, 1982. But that hardly made any difference.
64. The eldest son of Indira Gandhi, the then PM and Congress party president, Rajiv Gandhi who said that he would not join politics did

so after the death of his younger brother, Sanjay Gandhi who was believed to be the natural successor of the dynasty, had he been alive.

65. *The Indian Nation,* 12.08.1983.
66. *Ibid.,* 11.08.1983.
67. *Ibid.,* 13.08.1983.
68. *The Times of India* (Patna), 23.8.1986.
69. Cited in Kohli, *op. cit.,* p. 271.
70. Government of Bihar, Notes on 'Extremist Activities-Affected Areas', mimeographed, May 1982.
71. S.R. Maheshwari, *State Governments in India,* Delhi: Macmillan, 1979, p. 55.
72. In the U.K., the PMs are usually well-educated, aged and politically matured.
73. In the late part of his political career as CM, Karpoori Thakur was criticized for laxity in maintaining public order.
74. List of CMs in the period of our study is appended.
75. Kohli, *op. cit.,* p. 286.

5

The CM vis-a-vis The Governor

Both the CM and the governor function in the parliamentary–federal constitutional matrix, multi-party political dynamics; and their functional interrelated role performance has a personal or behavioural dimension, too. We shall take up the constitutional position first.

CONSTITUTIONAL POSITION

Article 163(1) of the Indian Constitution enjoins that:

> There shall be a Council of Ministes with the Chief Minister at its head to aid and advise the Governor in the exercise of his function, except in so far as he is by or under this Constitution required to exercise his functions or any of them in his discretion.

The sixth schedule appended to the Indian Constitution specifies the specific areas in which the governors of Assam,

Meghalaya, Tripura and some other tribal areas have discretionary powers. Administrators of UTs under Article 239(2) have discretionary powers in the specified areas.[1] The governor of Bihar does not possess discretionary powers of that kind. Like other nominal and constitutional heads of parliamentary executives, he exercises (and of course, on several occasions, has exercised) "situational" or "marginal" discretion in the appointment or dismissal of CMs, dissolution of Assembly, etc. particularly in the phase of coalition governance. We shall cite specific instances after presenting how courts and constitutional experts view the position of the governor *vis-à-vis* the CM. Suffice to note here is the fact that the Constitution bars judicial intervention in the specific areas of governor's discretion. Article 163(2) provides that:

> If any question arises where the Governor is required by or under this Constitution to act in his discretion his decision shall be final.

The validity of authority of anything done by the governor shall not be called in question on the ground that he ought or ought not to have acted in his discretion. Article 163(3) provides that the question whether any, and if so, what advice was tendered by ministers to the governor shall not be inquired into by any Court.

The crucial question is whether the governor has the power to act in his individual capacity or in his discretion at all. The Chairman of the Drafting Committee of the Constitution, B.R. Ambedkar categorically stated in the Constituent Assembly that "The Governor has no function which he is required to exercise either in his discretion or in his individual judgment".[2] He cannot disregard the advice of the ministry and act in any other manner that is act in consultation with any agency other than the Council of Ministers headed by the CM. A prominent member of the Drafting committee of the Constitution, T.T. Krishnamachari clarified that "There is no discretionary power at all vested in the governor and... he will be taking the advice of the Ministries in all matters".[3] The Drafting Committee had originally planned to make the formal head, i.e. the governor to be elected by direct vote but abandoned the idea on the ground that in that case, the governor might consider himself superior to the CM. This would be in violation of norms of parliamentary governance.[4] It would also look improper to make the second best available man of the party, governor and the supreme party leader, CM. After long debate, the Constituent Assembly settled the matter in favour of having President's appointees as governors. In other words, governors were designed to be nominees of the Union government headed by the PM. The Supreme Court now has made clear that the governors are neither employees nor agents of the Centre under ordinary circumstances.

The issue of the governor's powers was decided at the judicial level for the first time in 1950 before the Calcutta High Court which unambiguously held that the present Constitution had taken away the governor's power to act in his discretion or in his individual capacity which he had under the Government of India Act, 1935 and "The Governor, therefore, must act on the advice of his Ministers".[5] Following this verdict, it came to be widely expected that the governor has to act only after consulting or on the advice of the Council of Ministers headed by the CM unless the constitution provides otherwise.[6] Five years later, the Supreme Court confirmed in an often quoted judgment (Ram Jawaya *V.* State of Punjab) that "The Governor occupies the position of the head of the executive in the State but it is virtually the Council of Ministers in each State that carries on the executive government".[7] The Supreme Court in a subsequent judgment drew attention to the significance of the use of the word "shall" in Article 163(1) and opined that it meant that the governor must keep the Council of Ministers in office except in the case of President's Rule in the state under Article 356 because he has to act on the advice of ministers except in cases where the Constitution specifically provided the use of discretion by the governor. In U.N.R. Rao *v.* Indira Gandhi and in Karunanidhi cases, the Supreme Court reiterated this position.[8]

Legal, academic and political luminaries have expressed divergent opinions on this issue. P. Govinda Menon who held the office of Union Law Minister expressed the view that the governor had the power to exercise his discretion in relation to three matters – appointment of CM, dismissal of the ministry and reservation of bills for consideration of the President.[9] According to the then Union Home Minister, Y. B. Chavan, the governor can act in his discretion only under Articles 200, 239(2) and 356.[10] We have referred to the last two articles earlier. Article 200 refers to the governor's right to reserve a bill passed by the legislature of the state for the President's assent. The Setalvad Study Team, appointed by the First Administrative Reforms Commission (1967) identified the following areas of governor's discretion:[11]

1. Appointment of the C. M.;
2. Dismissal of the ministry;
3. Dissolution of the Assembly;
4. Right to encourage, warn and advice;
5. Withholding assent to a bill;
6. Statutory functions; and
7. Discretionary powers of the governor of Assam.

M.C. Setalvad and Alladi Krishnaswami Aiyar had negatived President R. Prasad's interpretation of the Constitution that as President, he had the right to withhold assent to a bill and some other powers in legislative matters. Prasad had expressed his wish to exercise those powers on his own i.e. in his individual capacity. President Prasad budged in the matter and did not use any discretionary power. He never withheld any bill. Much later, President Zail Singh withheld Postal Bill which was defective on many counts) which President R. Venkataraman forced the cabinet to withdraw. But it has been an exceptional case. Normally speaking, if the President cannot withhold assent to a bill, so the governor, too, cannot withhold it as a matter of "discretion". The Union cabinet forced President Kalam to sign the Office of Profit Bill which he had returned at the first instance for the cabinet's reconsideration–a right the cabinet has got through the 44th Amendment of the Constitution to Art. 74.

The governor's power to address the legislature or send message to it is also not discretionary. He is merely the mouthpiece of his government in reading out the address prepared by the state government. He can neither add nor alter nor omit a single word. The governor of West Bengal, Dharma Vira (1967-

69) learnt this constitutional mandate the hard way. He advised the UF Ministry headed by Ajoy Kumar Mukherjee to omit those portions from the prepared draft of the governor's address (to be delivered on 6.3.1969) which were "critical" of his own conduct in 1967 in dismissing the UF Ministry headed by Mukherjee and setting up a minority government which adopted repressive measures. The CM refused to omit those "critical" portions and insisted that the address be read in full.[12] The governor did not heed to the advice of the ministry. While reading out the address, he did not read out the portions to which Mukherjee had raised objections. This act of the governor resulted in severe attack on him by the Mukherjee government forcing him to proceed on leave and ultimately, to tender resignation. To ward off such embarrassments, Sri Prakasa had suggested that it was better to amend the Constitution to do away with the holding of ceremonial address by the governor. The CM himself in the lower house and a senior minister in the Upper House may read out this speech, telling the members what their policies and proposals are likely to be. But for more than six decades, we are maintaining the façade of dual and decorous parliamentary executives and retaining the Constitution's language in which the President and governors, although nominal constitutional functionaries, are named per se as repository of power. So the façade persists.

Academicians have stressed that the governor may at times act as an umpire and resolve conflicts if he scrupulously keeps off from groups and factional politics of the state. Iqbal Narain talked of "situational" and Shiviah of "marginal" discretion of the governor,[13] everybody is agreed that the exercise of his discretion is a hidden one and is purely constitutional. If governor's action smacks of arbitrariness or partiality, he is blamed to be an agent of the Union– a dangerous proposition for "co-operative federalism". The governor has to respond to the political situation in a dignified and normative manner adhering always to the Constitution. It was deemed essential to amend Article 74 of the Constitution through the 44th amendment making the re-considered decision of the Union Council of Ministers binding on the President. Article 163 has not been amended to say so because there is a check on the governor who holds office during the pleasure of the President. He can be removed in the mid-term, if he goes beserk but as the present judicial pronouncement says, not ordinarily or "arbitrarily". However, for any self-respecting governor, it is better to maintain norms than to invite undue criticism or recall.

GOVERNOR'S SELF-PERCEPTION OF THEIR POSITION

Ideally speaking, the governor and the CM should respect each other. National interest demands that working and functional interrelationship at all times should exist between them. A clear understanding of respective status, powers and functions based on judicial pronouncements and interpretations of the intelligentsia and reactions of the media and the public should have led by now to institutionalisation and functional inter-relationship of the two offices. But there is something amiss even now in the role identification and the role delineation of their inter-related roles. Personality clashes, ego conflicts apart, different party belongingness of the two functionaries and particularistic demands made by CMs and resistance by governors on the ground that they impinge upon the Constitution or the existing Acts, Statutes, Ordinances (or the hidden will of the Union they have to carry out) stand in the way of smooth relationship till to-day. Some CMs vent feelings of grievances, level charges and make open criticisms in the public. What is worse, situations of acrimonious relationships between the two functionaries are sometimes created, catching public eye. Some of them are not even at times seen exchanging greetings. The relations between governor G.N. Singh and C.M. Bhagwat Jha Azad were strained and those between Governor S.S. Bhandari and Rabri Devi were so strained that the latter used unparliamentary language with reference to the then governor in public. But in other cases, the relations have been smooth and working relationship existed. Even when the governors acted at the behest of the Centre during coalition era or during imperious Prime Ministerial era, the political dynamics dictated that political groups led by CMs should neither appeal to the Union nor to the public. Therefore, they acquiesced in mostly and made little noise. However, there were times when Parliament, state legislature, media, public meetings, lobbies, etc. were used as fora to vent feelings of grievances against petty matters such as misuse of equipments of Raj Bhawan by a governor or the elaborate arrangements asked to be made by the governor when he went out on tour or the CM complained of instances of ostentatious behaviour on the part of governors at the cost of taxpayers' money. Such criticisms have come generally from the mouths of the ex-governors or at times from the mouth of an incumbent CM.

Vijaya Laxmi Pandit, after resigning from the governorship of Maharashtra published an article in which she argued that the office of the governor was useless.[14] She added that the only thing that can induce a person to accept governorship is the salary that it carries.[15] K.M. Munshi said, "his only job as governor was to run a hotel and entertain guests".[16] Pavate who had been governor of Punjab remarked that he felt like Alice in Wonderland in Raj Bhawan. "The difficulty with the Governors", according to him, "is to find work or create some. His engagements were confined to occasional addresses to educational institutions, inaugurating conferences, presiding at prize giving to winners in Sports Competition".[17]

Two of the former governors, K.N. Katju and N.V. Gadgil, however, disfavour the suggestion of granting more powers to governors. Katju opines that a governor being dependent upon the President's support cannot have "full power to deal with the Ministers individually and collectively".[18] Whereas Gadgil opines that since people have no power to dismiss the governor, it is only proper that the governor exercises only advisory functions,[19] Sri Prakasa said that governors are like "defeated Generals... least concerned with their duties and responsibilities" and hence, they "readily surrender themselves to the domineering Chief Minister in their respective states or to their benefactors in New Delhi".

A few CMs have expressed similar opinions.An incumbent CM called governor "nothing but an expensive irritant". M. Karunanidhi, the then CM of Madras (now called Chennai) said that the present system was "unsatisfactory"; that all the parties and the CMs are agreed that the office of the governor should be abolished;[20] his functions may be performed by the President or the Chief Justice of the High Court of the state concerned.

President Zail Singh had complaints that the PM was not keeping him informed about the affairs of the nation and partaking such information he asked for which the PM was constitutionally obliged to do under Article 78. Stung by personal criticisms levelled by a Minister of State (MoS) in the Lok Sabha, he threatened that he would not take the ceremonial farewell salute by the army unless the said MoS was made to resign. Previously, Zail Singh was even contemplating (and consulting experts) if he had the power to dismiss the then PM for his failure to fulfil constitutional obligations under Article 78. So the nominal executives in our parliamentary system, though nominated, feel uneasy and disrespectful in their "august" offices. Nehru performed his obligations under Article 78 perfectly well; Rajiv Gandhi faltered in this matter and allowed the matters to go below standards for which he bears responsibility. CMs of Indian states also bear the responsibility to keep the governors informed but at times, they, too, have faltered in performing this constitutional obligation.

ACTUAL ROLE PERFORMANCE

The CM has been designated by Article 167 of the Constitution to be the Chief link of communication between the governor and the Council of Ministers. He is duty-bound to supply to the governor information on matters relating to the administration of state or proposals for legislation as the governor may call for. What is communicated to the governor in terms of this Article is the decision and not the recommendation of the Council of Ministers since the cabinet is the decision maker. But CM's specific obligation is listed as duty of the CM under Article 167.

CMs do not want the governor to have any dealing with any state official even in most ordinary matters except through them. Even if the matters relate to draining out accumulated rainwater from the streets on the ground floors of city dwellers, clearance of garbage or distribution of loan to Self-Help Groups (SHGs), the CMs do not like the governor to meet and issue directions to officials to help the adversely affected citizens. This kills time particularly if the CM is out of the state. But the CM would like to avoid an impression gaining ground that since the CM was not efficient enough to act or not available in time, it called for exigent intervention of the head of the state.

The CM or the Union cannot, on the other hand, combine to by-pass the rules of conduct of official business which is a written law. A category of notifications is earmarked which is to be issued by the state government in the name of the governor with his seal and signature and after duly informing him. Some matters like the appointment of the Chairman and members of the Public Service Commission require the signature and seal of the governor. If the cabinet takes a decision about it, it should hold the communiqué to the media and notification back till the formal signature and seal of the governor is obtained. President Prasad had complained to ministers of the Union that he heard about the appointment of governors and ambassadors from the media before the communication of the government reached his desk. The Union government, thereafter, instructed the Cabinet Secretariat to send their relevant communications first to the President and only thereafter, make the news public. In the same manner, the despatch of mercy petitions by the state government to the Union government should be routed through the governor.

The CM of one of the states directly sent to the President mercy petitions of condemned prisoners without obtaining the opinion of the governor on them or even informing him about or without performing the paraphernalia of obtaining the governor's signature on the papers.[21] The CM went in direct touch with the Union Home Ministry; and the latter did not deem it necessary to obtain the governor's formal signature, or opinion in the technical sense. Thus the Union as well as the CM both were parties to the scheme to by-pass the governor; and it was an administrative lapse which violated the Constitution.

Article 271(1) of the Constitution makes a provision for "consultation" of the governor by the President in the matter of the appointment of judges of the state High Court. The A.R.C. in a Memorandum of Procedure prescribed the route thus: the Chief Justice (CJ) would communicate to the CM for his view as to the person or persons to be selected as judges.[22] The CM, *in consultation with the governor* (emphasis added with the question if this consultation is formal information to the governor or exchange of information and views about persons concerned?) forwards his recommendation to the Union Home Minister along with full details of the name of the persons in the panel. The CM consults the governor (the governor's name has been used independently of the CM as if to imply that he were an active consultant), the CJ is informed accordingly and his comments are invited. The comments of both the CM and the CJ are then forwarded by the CM to the Union Home Minister where the final selection takes place in consultation with the CJ of the Supreme Court of India. The Council of Ministers communicates the decision to the President who makes the appointment. The same procedure is followed with regard to the appointment of the CJ except that the recommendation originates from the CM and communication between the CM and the governor is made in writing and copies of the recommendation are forwarded to the Union Home Minister along with the CM's recommendation.[23] Thus the role of the governor in the appointment of the CJ and other judges of the High Court of his state appears to be advisory. The requirement of consultation as required by the Constitution and convention may not permit this interpretation in toto. But "consultation" denotes effective deliberation and exchange of views, opinion and information at the command of the two consulting parties unless it is deemed to be a "formal" consultation. In the selection of Judges, the CM and CJ are enjoined to send joint comments after "consulting" the governor. So far as the power of appointment of high state officials, their postings, transfers and redressal of grievances is concerned, there are relevant institutions for the purpose to advise the CM; and the governor is not consulted.

Making a departure from other judgments, the Supreme Court in the case of Jayantilal Amritlal *v.* F.N. Rao vested the authority of promulgating ordinances in governor and not in state government.[24] Article 154(1) and 163 deal with the executive power of the governor, whereas article 154(1) deals with his legislative power. The governor is a part of the legislature and his ordinance-making power emanates from his legislative power where, according to a minority opinion, he may not be bound by the aid and advice of the ministry. Y. B. Chavan pointed out that legally, a governor was bound to promulgate an ordinance if so advised by the Council of Ministers[25] and that appears to be the right position and it has been so in practice as well. President Shankar Dayal Sharma did not assent to two ordinances sent to him by the cabinet on the eve of 1996 *Lok Sabha* elections probably to influence the electoral outcome. But that is an exceptional case. The standing legal opinion is that the President or the governor has to sign the ordinances sent to them by the cabinet.

The power to summon or prorogue the Assembly lies in the domain of the CM and even if he advises the governor to do so with the intention to strengthen his position or bypassing an impasse created by an adjournment of the Assembly by the Speaker, the Governor has no right to sit in judgment over or assess what his intentions are;[26] he has to sign on the dotted lines.

POWER TO SUMMON THE ASSEMBLY

Article 174(1) of the Constitution empowers the governor to summon the legislature from time to time within a period of six months. According to parliamentary convention, the governor exercises this power on the advice of the CM of his state. But the governors have acted differently with regard to summoning of the house. For instance, the governor of Bihar did not press the UF ministry headed by Mahamaya Prasad Sinha to convene the Assembly session to test its strength in the wake of mass defections from his party; whereas the governor of West Bengal insisted that Ajoy Kumar Mukherjee-led ministry summon the Assembly as in the Governor's assessment, the ministry had lost majority in the Assembly and when Mukherjee did not accept the advice of summoning of the Assembly, the Governor dismissed Mukherjee Ministry and installed P.C. Ghosh Ministry which, however, did not solve the problem in view of the Speaker's ruling against it.

As per Constitutional propriety, under a situation of mass defection or a split in the party leading to doubt about the CM having lost majority in the lower house, the governor may ask him to call the session of the house to test his strength in the ministry. The strength, however, must be tested on the floor of the house and not in the *Raj Bhawan* or elsewhere. If the no-confidence motion is pending in the lower house and the majority of the members of the Assembly request the governor in writing to summon the house for discussion on it, the governor may advise the CM to summon the Assembly within the shortest possible time and the CM has to comply with the advice. Thus the CM has not got the sole power to summon the Assembly when his or her majority is in doubt; and if he or she neither resigns nor faces the lower house, the governor is within his right to request him to summon the house to prove his majority. If the CM goes on avoiding, he may invite the dismissal of his ministry by the governor.

POWER TO PROROGUE THE ASSEMBLY

Similarly, the CM has the power to prorogue the Assembly but the advice to prorogue the Assembly by a CM in an eventuality when no-confidence motion against the Speaker or the ministry is pending before the lower house which is in session and the units of the coalition group have withdrawn their support from the government, reducing the government to minority may not be accepted by a governor. The governor in such cases uses "marginal" discretion to ensure that the CM may not use the prorogation as a political weapon to bypass the will of the Legislative Assemblies. Governor's action of prorogation of Madhya Pradesh, Punjab and Tamil Nadu Legislative Assemblies in 1967 came to be widely criticized in the Lok Sabha in 1967. The role of the governor in proroguing the Haryana Assembly after its *sine die* adjournment by the Speaker came in for severe criticism by opposition members in both the houses of Parliament on March 4 and 5, 1970.

Upholding the action of the Haryana governor, the Union Home Minister, Y.B. Chavan told the Lok Sabha that the governor had no other alternative but to accept the advice of the CM. He stressed that the governor was the head of the state and not an agent of the Centre or the Parliament and as the constitutional head of the state, he was bound to accept the advice of the CM.

Nehru remarked in the Constituent Assembly that he favoured the scheme of nominated governorship partly because it would keep the Centre in touch with the units and moreover, would remove a source of possible separatist tendencies.[27] Many members including T.T. Krishnamachri asserted that in no sense, the governor would be an agent of the Central government. We had examined in the last chapter that the Governors did not adopt uniform standards in the appointment of the CMs and in several cases, acted at the behest of the Centre. The Governors who were like "birds in the golden cage" became active during coalition era. Their action at the behest of the Centre either in the formation or dismissal of the ministry, dissolution of the house or promulgation of the President's Rule came to be marked. Some examples were much too glaring. In Rajasthan in 1967, the governor did not permit the coalition government of non-coalition parties to be formed whose 93 out of 184 members of the Assembly were physically presented to the President of India to request the President to impress upon the governor to allow them to form government. The governor instead created favourable situation for the Congress party to secure majority by recommending the imposition of President's Rule. The Governors of West Bengal and Punjab invited the leaders of the minority parties to form Government with Congress support in November, 1967 in undue haste. In 1970, the governor, on the other hand, refrained from asking the CM, Rao Birendra Singh to summon an early session of the Assembly, though he knew that he had lost majority in the lower house and was liable to be removed from office. During 1967-72, almost every state ruled by a party other than that of the party at the Centre attributed political motives to the governor's actions and suggested that their actions were dictated by the Union government. These unsavoury actions contributed to regionalisation in India's political process, and this led to Assam coming under the bandwagon of a non-Congress regime. Had the governors acted as a custodian of the Constitution and by the oath they took and acted in the best interests of the state which they headed,[28] sub-nationalism or regionalism would not have raised its head high. President Narayanan used his powers under the amended Article 74 to return to the Union Cabinet its decision for reconsideration the invocation of President's Rule in U. P. which was a majority government, though the governor had recommended imposition of emergency under Article 356. The Union cabinet did not send back the proposal and acquiesced. But governors even now act at the behest of the Centre, though Bommai judgment (1994) has restricted the misuse of Article 356.

POWER TO DISMISS CMs

The controversy relates to governor's power to dismiss a CM and it is often pointed out that since the Council of Ministers is collectively responsible to the Legislative Assembly, the Assembly alone can remove him after passing a no-confidence motion against him. But we have seen that if a CM does not summon the legislature to test his strength in the Assembly when according to the memorandum of the opposition parties duly checked by the governor, his majority is in doubt and needs to be tested on the floor of the Assembly or if the CM does not resign even after a no-confidence motion has been passed against him, the governor may exercise his power under Article 164(1) which makes the continuance of the CM contingent on the pleasure of the house to which the Council of Ministers is collectively responsible. Since Sarkaria Commission Report and the Supreme Court in Bommai Judgment (1994) have stipulated that the appropriate place to test majority support of the CM is the floor of the Assembly alone; governors are restrained to act arbitrarily in the matter. Dismissal of ministries by governor Dharma Vira (West Bengal) in 1967 and by governor Gopala Reddy (UP) had been done in haste. They ought to have sounded the Assembly before taking the extreme step.

In contrast, the governors of Bihar and Haryana did not compel their CMs to face the Assembly. M.A. Ayyangar, the governor of Bihar, in response to the demand of B.P. Mandal, said, "you want to verify the list. I have no machinery to verify. It is only the Assembly which can do under the Constitution on a properly moved motion in a duly convened House".[29] According to some experts, even when the house is not in session, it cannot be compelled to meet to test the strength of majority in lower house. The Advocate General of West Bengal opined that no Assembly could be summoned just to test the majority of the CM, the legislature is summoned for normal purposes.[30] According to A. B. Vajpayee, there is permissible limit of six months and nothing can be imposed on the CM during this period.[31] Ambedkar, however, had opined in the Constituent Assembly that the ministry is liable to be removed if it had lost the confidence of the house and if it was not pure. The latter ground is much too controversial and the governors have chosen not to invoke this ground for dismissal. Kairon was neither dismissed by the governor of Punjab nor asked to resign despite several charges of corruption against him. In Bihar, in October 1973, the Governor R.D. Bhandare said at some of the meetings in Maharashtra that he had "sufficient documentary evidence and intelligence reports" which are sufficient to "summarily dismiss four ministers and eighteen officials and send a few legislators in jails".[32] He did not make it clear whether the incumbent CM was one of them. However, he did not take any step against any of them. There were a large number of allegations of bribery, malpractices against Jagannath Mishra. He dropped eleven ministers on the alleged charges of corruption and some of the ministers had been closest to him and there were reported charges by the CBI and IB against them. Probably, he dropped them to save his own skin. But there was no attempt by the governor's side to remove the CM or even obliquely suggest that the CM initiate action against the currupt ministers. Since the number had risen to about a dozen, it was certainly formidable enough to eat into the vitals of the government and administration. Laloo Prasad had clear majority in the *Vidhan Sabha* but he had to step down from office when the governor gave consent to the CBI to prosecute him on the basis of charges prepared after due investigations by the CBI under the supervision of the Patna High Court. A minister of Bihar was dismissed by the governor in 1999 on the ground that he was under age (below twenty-five) and hence, unfit to hold the office of an M.L.A. or a Minister. Ministers act under individual and collective responsibility. It is not for the governor to take action against them to enforce responsibility; CM and ultimately, people are to ensure individual or collective responsibility. However, the action of governor of Karnataka in issuing notices to two ministers on charges of corruption and misuse of office to serve their business interests in 2010 appeared to be a new development in the constitutional history of the country. The Governor pursued the matter further by recommending the imposition of President's Rule which had by then become an uncommon practice. The Karnataka government proved its majority and the Governor lay low till he got new opportunity to ask the CM to resign with *Lokayukta* of the state submitting detailed report listing charges of involvement of the CM (Yeddyurappa) and two of his ministers in earning huge wealth through giving mines on lease and putting the government to big losses.

All defeats on the floor of the Assembly do not and need not result in a Ministry's resignation. Mahamaya Prasad Sinha and B.P. Mandal in Bihar and others in several states resigned soon after they were defeated on the floor of the Assembly but governor D.C. Pavate of Punjab had to dismiss the CM, Gurnam Singh when he did not resign after his defeat in the Assembly on a major issue. Earlier, some CMs were not dismissed or they did not resign when they were defeated. The governor of Orissa, peculiarly enough, requested the CM to continue after he was defeated in the Assembly. The most glaring instances of *en masse* dismissal of CMs by governors came to the national glare when the CMs of Sikkim, J&K and Andhra Pradesh in 1984 came to be dismissed one by one by their respective governors of the states concerned. This was widely held to be an arbitrary exercise of power in view of the affinity of the governors to the ruling party at the Centre and their action was widely held to be taken at the behest of the then young and immatured General Secretary of the Congress party, Rajiv Gandhi. The Congress party tendered its support to the successive governments in J&K and A.P. governors, however, felt discomfiture and the Congress party, embarrassment when the ousted CMs were returned to power in the elections that followed.

After the removal of the ministry, the governor can explore the possible opportunity to forming an alternative ministry in the state. He has to report to the President under Article 356 if such a possibility does not appear feasible. The governor of Bihar, M.A. Ayyangar said on 28.11.1967 that the governor should install an alternative ministry, if possible but should not make the existing ministry fall by dragging its feet; that would not be in consonance with the constitution.[33] The phenomenon of defections became very common in India after 1967 which ultimately made the coalition governments unstable and the problem of dissolution occurred on a large scale.

POWER TO DISSOLVE THE ASSEMBLY

Dissolution of assembly is held to be one of the prerogatives of the governors. Mahamaya Prasad Sinha-led coalition government, formed in Bihar in 1967, was defeated within a year when no-confidence motion was passed against the government. He resigned and recommended the dissolution of the Assembly.[34] But his advice was not accepted and Satish Prasad Singh was appointed interim CM to keep the chair warm for four days within which the only act he undertook was to nominate B.P. Mandal to the Legislative Council.[35] The appointment of an interim CM and acceptance of his advice to nominate B. P. Mandal as an MLC made a mockery of the constitutional process. It would have been more proper to grant Satish Prasad Singh twenty or thirty days' time to prove his strength in the *Vidhan Sabha* before accepting his confirmation as CM and before accepting his advice to nominate B.P. Mandal as an MLC. This case was analogous to the nomination of C. Rajagopalachari, a defeated MLA in Madras (now called Chennai) in 1952, as an MLC on the advice of an outgoing CM and then appointing Rajaji as CM. Such cases are avoidable.

After sometime, B.P. Shastri joined as CM but he too tendered his resignation and advised the governor to dissolve the Assembly. In his letter of resignation, he said "the position of my government has become unstable as one of our constituent parties has put such impossible conditions before me as are unacceptable in the interest of the state. I have, therefore, decided to resign in order to have a stable Government".[36] The governor did not accede to the demand of Shastri[37] and invited Mahesh Prasad Sinha to form the government but Sinha demanded four days to explore the possibilities of an alternative government.[38] In the meantime, the constituent parties of the UF had resolved their differences and communicated to the governor that their leader be invited to form the government.[39] Ultimately, the governor, Nityanand Kanungo, recommended President's Rule to be followed by mid-term-poll. The governor justified his action on the ground that the period of vote on account was expiring on June 30, 1968, and unless some method had been devised to sanction expenditure beyond the date, all administrative work would have come to a standstill from July 1. In 1971, the governor, Dev Kant Barooah, rejected the advice of the CM, Karpoori Thakur, when he was reduced to minority through the instrumentality of defections in the wake of 'Indira wave'[40] and invited B. P. Shastri to form the Government on June 2, 1971. But the same governor, D.K. Barooah, dissolved the Assembly on the 27th of December, 1971, on the advice of the CM, B.P. Shastri.[41] This was widely criticised in the press and elsewhere. He was said to have received the resignation of all the thirty-four ministers. He did send an "Urgent Report" to President V.V. Giri "and while awaiting Central orders" took the drastic step of dissolving the Assembly due to meet the next day "and accepted the resignation of all Ministers except those of the Chief Minister and another..."[42] The surprising element in his act was that the governor could not follow normal and decent behaviour in conducting constitutional business. But Barooah had previously declared ignominiously in public that 'Indira is India' and "India is Indira'. So much surprise did not spring from his indecent conduct as governor. Successive governors did not conduct themselves in such a manner. In many other states, e.g. U.P., Haryana, Madhya Pradesh and Punjab, under similar situations , the governors had acted in different manners leading each time to controversy and accusations. One common thread in all these instances, however, was that the governors of the states did not follow the advice of the defeated CMs of the respective states.

The governors have adopted no criteria with regard to the power of dissolution. For instance, in Haryana, the Legislative Assembly was dissolved to punish the defectors but in Punjab, the governor, D.C. Pavate, rewarded the defectors by appointing Lachman Singh Gill, the CM. There has been no consistency in the opinion tendered by the Union government either. According to the opinion of the Union government, the advice of the defeated CM was not obligatory in Punjab but the defeated CM had legal and acceptable right to advise dissolution in Madhya Pradesh, Mrs. Gandhi declared.[43]

The consensus of opinion in the country appears to be that the governor can dissolve the Legislative Assembly only on the advice of the CM. But the right to refuse the CM's request to dissolve the Assembly rests with the governor.[44] It is therefore, essential that certain conventions develop which regulate the role of the governor with regard to the prerogative of dissolving the state Assembly like Commonwealth countries for the maintenance of parliamentary propriety. Ambedkar had stated in the Constituent Assembly on 18.5.1949 that the right of the dissolution would be exercised by "convention".[45] In his opinion, the House of the People would generally be dissolved on the advice of the PM or the CM according to the conventions but the head of the state was not necessarily bound to accept the advice of the PM or the CM who wanted dissolution of Parliament or legislature in a situation when the opposition leader was prepared to form a Government; and he could take charge of the affairs of the state administration with the existing Parliament or legislature without being dissolved.[46]

There are two kinds of dissolution. Firstly, the governor dissolves the Assembly and keeps the outgoing ministry in power as a care-taker ministry till fresh elections are over. Secondly, the house is dissolved, President's Rule is clamped, ministry resigns and the governor administers the state as a representative of the Centre.

Following the dynamics of parliamentary democracy, dissolution of the Assembly by the governor is normally done on the advice of the CM unless it is the case of dissolution advised by a CM immediately after the General Election to the Assembly. If a CM is defeated in the Assembly or loses his majority at any time while he is in office, he is within his rights to advise dissolution without resigning and the governor ought to follow this advice. It is open for the governor to search for an alternative ministry to be formed but he loses his face if the old CM (whose request to dissolve Assembly is refused by him) returns back to power. So it is constitutionally proper for the governor to dissolve the house. The governor's power to dissolve the Assembly is thus not discretionary except in a formal sense. It has become atrophied by disuse (not used since 1783) in the U.K. whose practice we follow.

In the states in India, the governors have exercised their power for dissolution in different ways and therefore, no uniform practice has grown. The following episodes which occurred between 1952 and 1967 are illustrative:

(1) In Travancore-Cochin, CM P.A. Tharupillai suffered defeat in the Assembly in February 1952 and advised the *Rajpramukh* to dissolve the Legislative Assembly; the advice was not accepted.

(2) When T. Prakasham Ministry in Andhra Pradesh resigned in 1954 and advised the governor to dissolve, the Assembly was dissolved.

(3) In 1958, the Orissa CM, H.K. Krushna Mahatab resigned and advised the governor to dissolve the Assembly. The governor, instead prevailed over the CM to withdraw his resignation and the CM was made to continue in office.

(4) In July, 1967, after his defeat, the CM of Madhya Pradesh, D.P. Mishra sought the permission of the Congress high command to advise dissolution of the Legislative Assembly. The permission was not granted and Mishra continued as the CM.

(5) In November, 1967, the CM of Punjab, apprehending defeat in the Assembly, advised governor D.C. Pavate

> to dissolve the Assembly but the governor did not accept the advice, claiming that he was not bound by the advice of the outgoing CM to dissolve the Assembly.

The role of the governors in the above-mentioned cases sprung surprise and they came under attack. After the 1967 elections, this became a situation of everyday battle belittling the position of the CM and confirming governor's role as an agent of the Centre. To tackle political chaos in many states, the Centre was expected to take measures to ensure so that democratic institutions functioned in a reasonably smooth way. The Centre's first reprehensible act was to suspend the Rajasthan Legislative Assembly and proclaim President's Rule because no single party had emerged with absolute majority and the legislative party was not able to elect its leader. A series of deadlocks followed thereafter. Stability was restored in Bihar since 1990. However, the UPA-I and UPA-II Governors have not acted strictly according to the aid and advice of the Council of Ministers. The Governor of Bihar, D. Konwar kept many bills passed by the legislature pending for long. He has chosen to appoint Vice-chancellors generally without consulting the state government which the Universities Act do not entitle him to do and for this reason, two of his appointments of VCs have been undone by the Patna High Court and he is facing trial for the appointment of several VCs and pro-VCs without consulting the state government in PIL cases.

APPOINTMENT OF GOVERNORS

Performance in office of the governor is dependent upon the process of appointment of governors. The discussion on the role of the governor *vis-à-vis* CM will remain incomplete without examining who appoints whom. Articles 155 and 156 of the Constitution of India provide that the governor shall be appointed by the President and shall hold office during the pleasure of the President. But the convention has developed over the years that the appointment of a person as governor of a state has to be concurred by the CM of the state concerned.

The CM of West Bengal headed by Ajoy Kumar Mukherjee sent a panel of three names for the choice of governorship.[47] But the Centre did not agree with his point of view. It at best agreed to consult the states which sometimes means only to inform the state beforehand about the name of the person the Centre purposes to appoint as governor of the particular state. D.C. Pavate as governor of Punjab in 1967, Nityanand Kanungo as governor of Bihar in 1967 and governor of West Bengal in 1969 were appointed in spite of the opinion of the CMs of the states concerned to the contrary.

In Kanungo's appointment, there was wrangle between the ministry of Bihar and the Centre. The term of office of the governor, M.A. Ayyangar was due to expire in December, 1967. The Centre appointed Nityanand Kanungo in his place. The cabinet of Bihar sent strong protests against Kanungo's appointment. The then Local Self Government Minister of Bihar, Bhola Prasad Singh accused the Union Government of conspiring to topple the UF Government by appointing a diehard Congressman. Similarly, the CM of Punjab (Gurnam Singh) was not inclined to accept a Congressman or a civil servant or anybody connected with the Government of India in the past as the governor of Punjab.

Such wrangles did not arise before 1967 because the Congress party was in power at the Centre and in all the states except Kerala (since 1957) and therefore, the writ of the Centre ran without let or hindrance almost throughout the country. But the situation underwent a sea-change in 1967 and hence, Centre-state wrangles started over the issue of the appointment of governors also. The Centre took the stand in the case of Bihar that "consultation" does not mean that states have the right to veto. Chavan forced the CM of Bihar to accept Kanungo as the governor of Bihar in 1967. However, in order to soothe the feelings of the UF Government of Bihar, Kanungo assured the coalition government in Bihar that he would perform his duties as governor like the three proverbial monkeys. "I would not see, hear or speak anything without being advised by the Chief Minister", he assured.

There was a time when Nehru or Patel could not send a non-Bengali governor to West Bengal against the wishes of the then CM of the state, B.C. Roy. Both B.C. Roy and S.K. Sinha were so confident of their position and stand that they laid an example for their counterparts in other states. There were other strong CMs as well; and as a consequence, men of standing were chosen as governors. Now, with the exception of one or two ex-officials, all the governors have been chosen from the ranks of the political party in power; not unoften, politicians who had lost at elections or were otherwise considered inconvenient are appointed as governors.[48]

Arguments have been put forward that prior consultation with the CM in the appointment of governor has no constitutional sanction and it ends up by enabling powerful CMs to get suitable domiciles for themselves as governors. "Consultation with the person who happens to be the CM at a particular time and might change while governor stays does not tend to have much meaning". All these arguments notwithstanding, Administrative Reforms Commission I observed, "There is merit in consulting the Chief Minister beforehand, because otherwise the governor's delicate task would be rendered even more difficult. We do not therefore recommend a change in the present practice by which the Chief Minister is consulted. We would nevertheless stress that the primary responsibility to appoint competent and suitable men as governors rests with the Centre and that consultation with the Chief Ministers must not be allowed to dilute this responsibility or lower the quality of these appointments".

Governor Dharam Vira did not like the 'dull life' of Raj Bhavan, governor M.A. Ayyangar (Bihar) had no respect for the Bihar politicians; and Governor K.C. Reddy, B. Gopala Reddy and D.C. Pavate acted in their own ways on account of their personal dispositions and capabilities. Ayyangar, the then governor of Bihar, never cared for any "person" at the Centre because he was not after extension. Though he was favourably inclined towards the first non-Congress government headed by Mahamaya Prasad Sinha in Bihar, he took every decision independently. The way he functioned in those critical days, while the governors were inclined to please the Central bosses, straightaway proved that he was free from the clutches of political compulsions. Instead of pleasing the Central government, he took every such step which annoyed the Central bosses to a large extent. This resulted in his departure, though he was the popular choice of the state. To the contrary, K.C. Reddy and B. Gopala Reddy always tried to please the Centre to get further extension, though both these persons failed in their mission. Thus it can be said that the relationship between the two functionaries of the state is based on mutual understanding, co-operation and constitutional propriety but for the fact that the attempt of governors to play a mediatory role between the Centre and states usually lands them in becoming partial and partisan. The fine distinction between the role of a governor as a mediator and as an agent of the Centre; and that of a CM as the leader of the state as the nominee of the Central party leader must be played delicately.

GOVERNORS OF BIHAR SINCE INDEPENDENCE

1.	**Sri Jai Ram Das Daulat Ram**	15.08.1947	11.01.1948
2.	**Sri Madhav Shri Hari Anne**	12.01.1948	14.06.1952
3.	**Sri Rangnath Ramchandra Diwakar**	15.06.1952	05.07.1957
4.	**Dr. Zakir Hussain**	06.07.1957	11.05.1962
5.	**Sri Madbhushi Anant Sayanam Ayyangar**	12.05.1962	06.12.1967
6.	**Sri Nityanand Kanungo**	07.12.1967	20.01.1971
7.	**Sri Justice Ujjawal Narayan Sinha** (Acting)	21.01.1971	31.01.1971
8.	**Sri Dev Kant Barooah**	01.02.1971	04.02.1973
9.	**Sri Ram Chandra Dhondhwa Bhandare**	04.02.1973	15.06.1979
10.	**Sri Jagannath Kaushal**	16.06.1976	27.05.1978
11.	**Sri Justice K. B. N. Singh** (Officiating)	27.05.1978	26.06.1978
12.	**Sri Jagannath Kaushal**	26.06.1978	31.01.1979
13.	**Sri Justice K. B. N. Singh** (Acting)	31.01.1979	20.09.1979
14.	**Sri Akhalak-ur-Rahman Kidwai**	20.09.1979	14.03.1985
15.	**Sri Venkat Subbaiah**	15.03.1985	25.02.1988
16.	**Sri Govind Narain Singh**	26.02.1988	24.01.1989

17.	**Sri Justice Dipak Kumar Sen**	24.01.1989	28.01.1989
18.	**Sri R. C. D. Pradhan** (Officiating)	29.01.1989	02.02.1989
19.	**Sri Jagannath Pahadia**	03.02.1989	02.02.1990
20.	**Sri Justice G. G. Sohani** (Officiating)	02.02.1990	16.02.1990
21.	**Sri Md. Yunus Salim**	16.02.1990	13.02.1991
22.	**Sri B. Satya Narain Reddy** (Officiating)	14.02.1991	18.03.1991
23.	**Sri Md. Shafi Qureshi**	09.03.1991	13.08.1993
24.	**Dr. Akhalek-ur-Rahman Kidwai**	14.08.1993	26.04.1998
25.	**Sri Sundar Singh Bhandari**	27.04.1998	15.03.1999
26.	**Sri Justice B. M. Lal** (Officiating)	15.03.1999	05.10.1999
27.	**Sri Surajbhan** (Officiating)	06.10.1999	22.11.1999
28.	**Sri B. C. Pandey**	23.11.1999	12.06.2003
29.	**Sri M. Rama Jois**	12.06.2003	31.10.2004
30.	**Sri Ved Prakash Marvah** (Officiating)	01.11.2004	04.11.2004
31.	**Sri Sardar Buta Singh**	05.11.2004	29.01.2006
32.	**Sri Gopal Krishna Gandhi**	31.01.2006	21.06.2006
33.	**Sri R. S. Gavai**	22.06.2006	09.07.2008
34.	**Sri R. L. Bhatia**	10.07.2008	28.06.2009
35.	**Sri Devanand Konwar**	29.06.2009	

Notes and References

1. Durga Das Basu, *Introduction to the Constitution of India,* Delhi: Prentice Hall, 1966. Basu discusses in detail the situation in which governors of certain states have been specifically granted 'discretionary' power by the constitution.
2. *C.A.D.*, Vol. II, p. 469; for his collaborative statements, *see ibid.*, Vol. IX, pp. 41 and 61.
3. *ibid.*, Vol. XI, p. 957.
4. See Basu, *op. cit.*, p. 200 for a good discussion.
5. Sunil Kumar Bose *vs.* The Secretary to the Government of West Bengal, AIR, 1950, Calcutta, p. 799; the issue was also examined in

detail and clarified in the state of Travancore-Cochine, AIR, 1953, p. 140.

6. See M.M. Singh, the *Constitution of India (Situation in Perspective)*, The World Press, 1975, pp. 782 and 791.
7. Ram Jawaya *v.* State of Punjab, 2 SCR, p. 225.
8. Reported in *The Times of India* (Delhi), 18.03.1971.
9. Report of the *Centre-State Relation Inquiry Committee*, Government of Tamil Nadu, 1971, pp. 126.27.
10. *The Times of India* (Delhi), 13.3.1969.
11. *Rajya Sabha Debates*, Vol. LXXI, 1970, Col. 210.
12. Subhas, C. Kashyap, *The Politics of Power; Defections and State Politics in India*, Delhi: National, 1974, pp. 556-57.
13. Iqbal Narain, "Office of the Governor: Problem of Role Identification", *Journal of African and Asian Study*, New Delhi University, Vol. I, No. 2, Spring Issue, 1968, p. 175; and Shiviah, "The Governor in the Indian Political System", *Journal of Constitutional and Parliamentary Studies*, Delhi, Vol. 2, No. 4, October-December, 1968, p. 92.
14. Cited in Sri Prakasa, *State Governors in India*, Meerut: Meenakshi, p. 7.
15. Cited in D. C. Pavate, *My Days as Governor*, Delhi Vikas, 1974, p. 9.
16. *Ibid.*, p. 14.
17. *Ibid.*
18. *The Tribune (Ambala)*, 1.10.1962.
19. *Ibid.*, 2.10.1962
20. M. Karunanidhi, "You can't Run India from Delhi", *The Illustrated Weekly of India*, Vol. XCIX, No. 13, March 26-April 1, 1978, p. 14.
21. *The Tribune* (Chandigarh), 17.3.1969.
22. Anup Chand Kapur, *Constitutional History of India (1765-1970)*, New Delhi: Niraj Prakashan, 170, p. 781.
23. A.R.C., *Report of the State Team on Centre-State Relation*, Vol. 1, 1968, pp. 182-83.
24. *Ibid.*
25. Cited in D.C. Pavate, *op. cit*, p. 154.
26. *Ibid.*, p. 157
27. M.M. Singh, *op. cit.*, p. 797.
28. *C.A.D.* Vol. VIII, p. 454.
29. *Ibid.*, p. 535.
30. M.M. Ismail, *The President and Governors in the Indian Constitution*, Madras: Orient Longman, 1972, pp. 93-94.
31. *The Hindustan Times*, (Delhi), 13.9.1967.
32. *Lok Sabha Debates*, Vol. IX, 1969, Col. 847.
33. *Ibid.* Col. 833.

34. *Link*, 21.10.1973, p. 19.
35. *Lok Sabha Debates*, Vol. X, 1967, Col. 4289.
36. *The Tribune* (Chandigarh), 26.1.1968.
37. *The Searchlight* (Patna). 29.1.1968.
38. *The Hindustan Times* (Delhi), 26.6.1968
39. *The Tribune* (Chandigarh), 26.6.1968.
40. *The Hindustan Times* (Delhi), 27.6.1968
41. *The Statesman* (Delhi), 28.6.1968.
42. *The Hindustan Times* (Delhi), 13.6.1971.
43. *Ibid*. 29.12.1971.
44. *The Statesman* (Delhi), 10.12.1971 and *The Hindustan Times* (Delhi), 10.12.1971
45. *Rajya Sabha Debates*, Vol. XI, 1967, Col. 1436.
46. Report of the Study Team on Centre-State Relations, *op. cit.*, p. 281.
47. *The Statesman* (Calcutta), 20.3.1969.
48. Ashok Chanda, *Federalism in India: A Study of Union-State Relations*, London: George Allen and Unwin, 1965, p. 99.

6

The CM and the Cabinet[1]

The appointment of ministers and distribution of portfolios among them is a prerogative[2] of the CM. Constitutionally, ministers "shall be appointed by the governor on the advice of the Chief Minister".[3] Following the dynamics of parliamentary system, cabinet-making is considered to be the exclusive domain of the CM—a duty to be performed by him or her in the way he or she considers proper or expedient. However, in the matter of formation of Council of Ministers in the states, the role of the high command of the party and its intervention in this regard had come to be reckoned with by the CMs particularly of the Congress-ruled states till the era of coalition or minority governments started at the union government level since 1990 bringing federalism in focus and making CMs masters in their fields. CMs like Laloo Prasad, Nitish Kumar, Narendra Modi, Mayawati, Karunanidhi or now Mamata Banarjee and Jayalalithaa are masters of their states and they are high command of their party dominating decision-making even in party matters.

FREEDOM AND CONSTRAINTS IN CABINET-MAKING

Certain conventions and political compulsions inhibit the CM's freedom in the choice of his or her colleagues. Cabinet-making in parliamentary government is generally preceded by consultation, mutual accommodation and bargaining with and among senior party leaders. A CM inherits a number of colleagues whose inclusion in the cabinet is essential. They are there because of their standing in the party and if left out, they can be a potential danger to the CM. Those who have been in the previous cabinet and had unsullied political image against the possible charges of corruption, inefficiency and lack of legislative or popular support are to be included and some of them may be influential enough to dictate even the choice of their portfolios.

Right from the first Congress government[4] in 1937 through the second in 1946, the third in 1952 and the fourth in 1957, A.N. Sinha (though after he openly contested S.K. Sinha for leadership postion in 1957 was, for the first time, not consulted in ministry-making), virtually appointed himself and also chose his portfolios. S.K. Sinha had to concede second position to A.N. Sinha with the portfolio of finance marked for him in all his ministries.

Feuds existed in the Congress party during the premiership or Chief Ministership of S.K. Sinha itself. By the 1920s, *Bhumihar-Kayastha* rivalry had started at the levels of social, educational and employment opportunities. By 1937, it turned to *Bhumihar-Rajput* rivalry, particularly to capture the office of the premier of the state. However, this feud did not go to the extent of constraining, limiting and binding the hands of the then premier in cabinet-making or in any other sphere of decision-making. A potent example of this is that S.K. Sinha was able to retain K.B. Sahay in his cabinet even though, as S.K. Sinha mentions in his letter to J.P., "revered Gandhiji" advised him to remove K.B. from the ministry. S.K. Sinha had sternly replied to Gandhiji's advice, "I was prepared to bow down to his orders but I would have to go out along with him." This strong reaction on the part of S.K. Sinha prevented K.B.'s exit. After 1952 election when ministry was being formed, S.K. Sinha was again pressed not to include K.B. Sahay but he refused point blank. This shows that a premier (called CM since 1952) like S.K. Sinha could resist even strong pressure and act independently in cabinet-making.

In selecting candidates for MLA seats in 1952, S.K. Sinha reportedly managed that his men or women were allotted tickets. In this way, he was able to thwart the ambition of L.N. Singh 'Sudhanshu' who wanted to contest as CM or to seal the machinations of a few leaders to foist Rajendra Prasad as CM were also sealed. In the First General Election, keeping in view the tradition of the struggle of Indian freedom, the recommendations of *Thana* Congress Committees, District Congress Committees and Bihar *Pradesh* Congress Committee had been asked for but ultimately, the views of the CM and the high command prevailed. In 1957 and 1962 elections, the Central Election Committee took upon itself the right to decide to distribute tickets but the CM continued to have a voice in finalising the list.

S.K. Sinha was politically astute enough to provide representation to members of backward castes, *Dalits* and Muslims in the Congress Ministry formed by him in 1937. However, these ministers were not grassroot members or leaders of their caste and hence, were treated as having been co-opted or imposed from above.

The Congress Ministry headed by S.K. Sinha formed on 2.4.1946 had nine cabinet ministers but among the nine, there was no one from the backward castes or tribal community. The cabinet consisted of two *Bhumihars*, one *Rajput*, one *Brahmin*, two *Kayasthas*, two Muslims and one *Dalit*. K.B. Sahay, a Parliamentary Secretary of the 1937 Ministry was elevated to the cabinet rank in 1946 after he moved away from A.N. Sinha camp to S.K. Sinha camp and one more Parliamentary Secretary of the 1937 Ministry was elevated to the cabinet rank.

S.K. Sinha maintained his hegemony in ministry-making in 1952. But in 1957, the Congress share of seats declined and S.K. Sinha's position comparatively weakened. He brought in Kumar Ganganand Singh (a representative of the Maharaja of Darbhanga properties elsewhere), a person who had been closely connected with the *Hindu Mahasabha* (he had been

President of *Bihar Hindu Mahasabha* for ten years) into the cabinet. In the 1957 Cabinet, there were two *Bhumihars*: S.K. Sinha and Mahesh Prasad Sinha, two *Rajputs*: A.N. Sinha and D.N. Singh, two *Kayasthas*, one *Brahmin*, two Muslims, one *Dalit* and one backward caste member. In place of Kumar Ganganand Singh, Krishna Kant Singh, Deputy Minister, Education was virtually handling the portfolio. Another *Bhumihar*, L.P. Shahi had joined as Deputy Minister with important portfolio and yet, another *Bhumihar*, Nawal Kishore Singh was acting as the Chief whip of the CLP. Though Smt. Krishna Shahi did not hold a political position till then, her being the adopted daughter of the CM gave her an aura in the political arena. Preponderance of *Bhumihars* was an eye-sore for many non-*Bhumihars* and they openly resented and gave vent to it even during the debates of the *Vidhan Sabha*. An old general of the Congress, Ramcharitra Singh had revolted against the Congress Party on being denied the MLA ticket. He had won as independent candidate and his presence on the opposition benches strengthened the opposition. A point that ignited resentment was also that there was no tribal in the 1957 cabinet. S.K. Sinha had erred in his matured years in tilting the cabinet towards upper castes. Backward castes and tribals suffered from a sense of alienation and anomie.

After S.K. Sinha's death in 1961 (a year before the third General Election was due), Binodanand Jha, a *Brahmin* formed a cabinet of nine members consisting of two Muslims, one *Kurmi*, one *Dalit* and five persons from upper caste. There was neither a tribal nor a woman in the cabinet. This cabinet, too, was dominated by upper caste Hindus and continued to ignore the emerging socio–economic realities. Even after the 1962 elections when Jha formed his second cabinet, the number of upper castes was six out of a total strength of 9. No tribal was included in the cabinet, though S.C. Tubid was made a Deputy Minister and was later elevated to cabinet rank. Daroga Prasad Rai, an *Ahir*, was appointed a Minister of State. K.B. Sahay was also included in the cabinet later, raising the number of upper castes in the cabinet to 7 out of 11.

After Jha's exit in the Kamaraj Plan in October 1963, there was a contest between K.B. Sahay and Bir Chand Patel (a

Kurmi) for the Chief Ministerial *gaddi* in which the former was victorious. The presence of backward castes and tribals followed by contest for the leadership of the CLP by a member of the backward caste signalled that backward castes were arriving in the political horizon of Bihar.

The composition of Sahay's 11-member cabinet in October, 1963 further confirmed the fact of arrival of backward castes and the attitude of K.B. Sahay to them. For the first time, upper castes did not have a majority in the cabinet. They had only four members representing each upper caste. Second, there were three members from backward castes, one each from three "dominant" intermediate castes: *Ahir*, *Kurmi* and *Kushwaha* (in the descending order of dominance). Third, a woman (mother-in-law of the present Speaker of the Lok Sabha, Meira Kumar and *samadhin* of Jagjivan Ram), Sumitra Devi (who was also simultaneously a representative of the *Kushwaha* community) was included for the first time in the cabinet. Fourth, a tribal leader—S.K. Bage was inducted as a cabinet minister. Fifthly, Sahay took care to induct two Muslims– one belonging to the upper strata among them and erstwhile leader of the Muslim League (Jafar Imam) and the other to the lower strata and a staunch nationalist. Thus Sahay formed a composite cabinet with an eye to the socio-economic realities.

Sahay thus put all his efforts in applying tactics for curbing the hitherto prevailing monopoly of upper castes (his own caste has been numerically meagre in number and resides mostly in towns and cities) and providing representation to backward castes. He also tried to enlist the support of backward castes by organizing or helping them organize their caste organisations. In August, 1965, he addressed the All-India *Yadav* Conference at Patna and later, attended a conference of *Dusadhs*. He backed the revival of *Tribeni Sangh*, an old organization of *Ahirs*, *Kurmis* and *Kushwahas* which was started in 1924 but had been defunct since then.

It may, however, be pointed out that that the effects of Binodanand Jha and K.B. Sahay to fight the dominance of landowning castes—*Bhumihars* and *Rajputs*—through the monetary support of the rich backward peasants reinforced by physical and emotional mobilization of their barefooted brethren ended in creating reaction among the backward castes to unite among themselves (on their own) and not under any upper caste leader's umbrella. Secondly, they could appreciate even in the 1960s that what would help them was a radical restructuring of Bihar's socio-economic structure while political leaders both before and after 1967 were not at it. The CMs of Bihar including the champions of OBCs (Karpoori Thakur, Laloo Prasad and Nitish Kumar) to this day have not realized that genuine land reforms (even if initiated in limited amount) against the background of capitalist economic development initiated by five-year plans had destabilized Bihar's age-old static society. With the change in socio-economic balance of forces, the CM and his party colleagues or cohorts ought to become agents of the change of this balance of forces if they really have interest in the creation of a resurgent Bihar.

The formation of cabinets after 1967 had one marked negative feature. They represented feuds which were more naked and exhibited unbalanced pursuit of power. All the nine coalition governments that came to exist (beginning from Mahamaya Prasad Sinha to Bhola Paswan Shastri) were based on multi-partism. Names of ministers were demanded from different political parties constituting the coalition who were in turn inducted as ministers. The first CM, Mahamaya Prasad Sinha was sworn in on the fifth March, 1967 with fourteen ministers to begin with but this small number did not satisfy the aspirations of an unusually large number of aspirants who had for the first time tasted power on their own. *Ahirs* who had emerged as the largest caste group after the *Rajputs* got only one post of minister in the cabinet and that seat, too, went to a woman, Premlata Rai. Only 20% backward castes got ministerial positions as against 67% captured by the upper castes. Subsequently, on March 16, four ministers and three Ministers of State were added to the ministry raising the total strength of the ministry to twenty-one. This ministry was constituted on party–quota basis[5] and even then, left many desires unfulfilled and wrangles continued for berths in the ministry.[6] This ministry was expanded again in order to patch up the demands of the aspirants to be included in the ministry.[7] But a number of allegations, counter-allegations and day-to-day defections ultimately brought the ministry in minority and finally, the coalition ministry failed to survive.

One reason for the downfall of Mahamaya Prasad Sinha-led *Samyukt Vidhayak Dal* ministry was that there was no collective functioning of the government from the very beginning. Ministers tried to advance the programmes and policies of their respective parties but Mahamaya Prasad Sinha as CM lacked the strength to enforce the Common Minimum Programme (CMP). While the *Jana Sangh* wooed landholders and rich peasants and opposed land reform measures including the abolition of Tata's *zamandari* rights in Jamshedpur; the then Revenue Minister belonging to the CPI, Indradeep Sinha got a circular issued on October 3, 1967 which laid down that no sharecropper would be evicted without an order of the court; no landowner would be entitled to more than $7/20^{th}$ of the total produce from him, and the sharecropper was entitled to demand a proper receipt for the share of the produce given to the landowner. The *Jana Sangh* faction opposed the circular tooth and nail forcing the CPI's proposed progressive measure to remain on paper alone.

The virus of ambition and opportunism stung the confidants of Lohia as well- B. P. Mandal was not ready to resign from Mahamaya Prasad Sinha's cabinet. Following Lohia's explicit wish expressed to him to do so, Jagdev Prasad (who claimed to be Lenin of Bihar) defected to Mandal to become a minister. Mandal Government dispensed with the team of lawyers which was scheduled to appear before the Aiyar Commission; Tata's *zamindari* rights were continued and laws concerning sharecropping were also not enforced. Mandal himself was one of the biggest landlords of Saharsa district, so his class interest lay with big landholders. His ministry had a good number of big landlords in it. During his 47 days in office, a series of caste riots took place at Jehanabad, Siwan, Muzaffarpur, Gaya and Hazipur which brought a bad name to his government.

All the non-Congress, Congress-supported or Congress-ruled coalition governments met the fate that Mahamaya Prasad Sinha-led government had faced. After a spell of four days, the ministry, headed by Satish Prasad Singh, resigned,[8] after completing the single job of nominating B.P. Mandal as a member of the Legislative Council; and the Congress-supported ministry was installed with Mandal as the CM. He, too, constituted his team on the basis of reconciling different fractions and groups. Although this was a *Soshit Dal* Ministry, it enjoyed the support of the Congress for some time.

The most notable feature of cabinet-making by Mandal was that most of members of the legislature (including defectors) were made ministers. The Congress supported the ministry but did not join the ministry formally, so the government was a minority government. The ministry, by its very nature, was short-lived and soon gave way to another ministry led by B. P. Shastri. B. P. Shastri constituted his ministry twice but could not show his talent of long experience of legislature and administration to bear upon cabinet-making. He, too, formed both his ministries on the basis of providing factional representation and by promising to cater to their myriad interests.

Both the CMs, Sardar Harihar Singh and Daroga Prasad Rai represented Congress factions. Harihar Singh was supported by the Bihar triumvirate, K.B. Sahay, Mahesh Prasad Sinha and S.N. Sinha but was opposed by Congress leaders like Kedar Pandey and Abdul Ghafoor; and internecine quarrels came to such a pitch that Harihar Singh, 'a pro-syndicate' leader[9] was expelled from the party. Though a veteran freedom fighter, Sardar had been a constant champion of landed interests. His ministry was heavily tilted in favour of upper castes who held 42 per cent of the positions while the backward castes secured only 24 per cent. This aggravated intra-caste conflicts in the main constituent of the coalition. Sardar was branded as a rightist who wanted only to retain power. The inclusion of the Raja of Ramgarh[10] and the refusal of the dissident leader, D.P. Rai to join the cabinet provoked intense feelings of discord and the differences came to the fore in the Congress Working Committee of Bihar. The then dissident leader, D.P. Rai was not even consulted in cabinet-making; whereas Rai was claiming a sizeable share in the cabinet on the ground of his strength in the CLP. To begin with, Rai did not join the cabinet but after sometime, Rai himself got elected as the CM of Bihar. In the Congress (R)-led ministry of

Rai, most of the ministers were from the two coalition partners—B.K.D, and *Jharkhand* Party in addition to those from Congress (R). It may be noted here that factional politics dominated cabinet-making in these two Congress-led governments, too, as had been the case with the non-Congress governments. Rai antagonised upper castes by reducing their representation in his ministry to 33 per cent while increasing those of *Dalits* and tribals. He also antagonised the neo-rich among the backward castes by resisting the pressure to increase their representation from the existing 20 per cent.

With the fall of the Congress governments, Karpoori Thakur (the S.S.P. Chairman) constituted a S.V.D. ministry in December, 1970. His Ministry, too, was an embodiment of factional politics; and the members of the ministry were drawn from each group and also on individual basis. Surpassing all previous records; in seven weeks, Karpoori ministry was expanded five times and the number of ministers, finally, rose up to 41. Equitable partywise distribution of ministerial position was the *sine qua non* of the survival of this ministry for six months. *The Hindustan Times* commented that ministry-making in Bihar was assuming the grotesque pattern of rival claims based on the dubious support of persons who had cynically pledged their support to both sides. During 1967-71, Bihar did not get any government that really governed.

CABINET-MAKING UNDER IMPERIAL PRIME MINISTERIAL ERA

The period of unstable governments in Bihar, ended with the General Election in Bihar in 1972. Kedar Pandey, the then leader of the Congress (R) legislature party constituted his team on the advice of the then PM and party high command, Mrs. Gandhi, who had emerged as "strong man" of the new Congress or her Congress. Kedar Pandey, a nominee of Mrs. Gandhi as the Congress (R) legislature party leader, himself said that he would not personally take any action independently about the composition of the cabinet. The personnel of the ministry would be decided by the Congress high command and he would not like to do anything on his own.[11] So no question of CM's choice arose in cabinet-making arose. A composite cabinet was formed by him. Young blood was given adequate representation but senior members of the party and old experienced men were also duly taken in. The Administrative Reforms Commission had drawn attention to the desirability of fixing the size of ministries, if possible within 10% of the total number of legislature. For the Council of Ministers in Bihar also, the question of a fixed number of ministers was, therefore, under the consideration of the Congress high command. 11% quota was fixed for bicameral legislatures by the Congress Parliamentary Board.[12] But in the meantime, on 28th May, 1973, Pandey suddenly reshuffled his ministry by dropping eleven ministers at his own instance. After the expansion, Pandey had a 40 members' team in a three-tier structure. This led, among other causes, to Pandey's own fall from the Chief Ministership.

Abdul Ghafoor who succeeded Pandey also finalised a list of his team with the consultation of central leaders led by Mrs. Gandhi.[13] He was an ardent advocate of revoking groupism in the formation of the cabinet. But he had to grapple with the strong demand of group representation by the outgoing CM, Kedar Pandey. Kedar Pandey was claiming that one third representation should be given to his faction. Although Kedar Pandey was included in Ghafoor's list for a berth in his Ministry but some senior supporters of kedar Pandey had been dropped.[14] Kedar Pandey explained the untenability of this position[15] to the high command and after the intervention of central leaders including the PM, Mrs. Indira Gandhi; Pandey joined Ghafoor's cabinet after twenty days of its formation with his (Pandey's) supporters. With the joining of Kedar Pandey's supporters, the ministry became a composite one. Adequate representation was given to backwards, *Dalits*, Muslims and *adivasis*. Some new entrants like Vidyakar Kavi and Shatrughan Sharan Singh were taken in. A 37 members' (21 Cabinet, 16 states) ministry started functioning with two tiers. People belonging to upper castes and ex-zamindars were in dominant position in Ghafoor's ministry. Ghafoor did not possess hold over his colleagues. Factional squabbles plagued the ministry and team spirit was completely lacking. Initially, it was functioning well but J.P.'s movement highlighting inefficiency of Ghafoor's ministry in tackling the problems of rising prices, unemployment and corruption caused the resignation of Ghafoor after trying to tackle the movement for sometime but yielding to it at last.

In 1975, Jagannath Mishra, a minister in the past two ministries, was elevated to the position of leader of the C.L.P. Mishra received the list of his team from the Centre. But his was the shortest ministry in the state since 1952 that is since the First General Election. Most of the old figures were retained, yet Mishra's cabinet lacked coherence and was rogued by groupism and factionalism. It was known to all that Mishra had got the blessings of the high command; and that Mrs. Gandhi was trying to end the influence of infra-reds of her party. Mishra constituted a 12-men ministry (11 Cabinet and one state rank) which was a composite but not a coherent ministry. This ministry continued till the state legislatures were dissolved by the *Janata* Party in 1977 and fresh elections were ordered to gauge peoples' views after the Congress party had been completely routed in the Parliamentary elections held in 1977.

CABINET-MAKING UNDER THE *JANATA* RULE

After a spell of President's rule in the state, when the JLP leader, Karpoori Thakur, was invited to form the cabinet by the governor in 1977, the formation of cabinet would have been a difficult task for anybody since the *Janata* Party was a merger of its four constituents[16] and the reflection of differences among its constituents was looming large. Therefore, the choice of the CM in ministry-making was not free under the circumstances obtaining at that time. Karpoori Thakur had to give convincing numerical share to all its constituents. Secondly, groupism was rampant in the *Janata* Party. The group led by the contender for Bihar legislative party adequate *Janata* leadership,[17] Satyendra Narain Sinha was demanding the representation of his party and faction. Ultimately, the list was prepared with the consultation of senior leaders of all the constituents of the *Janata Party* and Central leadership. It was approved by the Central parliamentary Board of *Janata Party*. But no unanimity over the final list could be achieved and it did not appear possible to achieve it. So the Thakur Ministry was not fated to be either composite or coherent. Although this ministry admitted the largest number of ministers since 1937 in order to pacify all the constituents, factions, groups and interests, the policy of including a large number of ministers to pacify divergent interests did not yield fruitful results.

With the taking over the Chief Ministership of Bihar by Ram Sundar Das, another *Janata* leader on April 21, 1979, the question of choice of ministers became all the more difficult due to claims coming up from diverse constituents of the *Janata* party. The friction against the *Janata* Party's constituents was increasing day by day. The high command was trying to resolve the deadlock, though replying to a question of newsmen at Patna airport on his arrival in Patna, *Janata* Party President, Chandrashekhar said, "First of all I don't know, what is the deadlock in the expansion of Ram Sundar Das ministry. If there is any deadlock, the party high command will not intervene".[18] It meant that no person was available in the *Janata* Party whose word carried weight as did in the case of Mrs. Gandhi in the Congress Party. Ultimately, Das finalised a list of his team by consulting some senior state and Central leaders. But the outgoing CM was not consulted and a dissatisfied group was on rampage campaigning for its representation. Most of the ministers of the outgoing ministry (including senior one like Kapildeo Singh and Ram Chander singh Yadav) were dropped. A ministry of "balanced size" took oath but the aim of creating a composite cabinet was not achieved. Even the party chief too was not taken into confidence while announcing the team. The party chief remarked, "I had no grudge that Mr. Das did not consult me. It is up to the CM to include anybody in his ministry or to leave out anybody.[19] This was in striking contrast to the Congress political culture.

CABINET-MAKING UNDER THE SECOND SPELL OF IMPERIAL PRIME MINISTERIALISM

The Congress (labelled Congress (I) then) with its leader, the ex-CM, Jagannath Mishra formed the ministry once again in 1980. Since he had the blessings of the then PM, Mrs. Gandhi and her son, Sanjay Gandhi,[20] an MP, General Secretary of the party and the emerging political heavy weight of the Congress (I), he did not face much difficulty in the formation of the ministry. However, he, too, like his predecessors, countered dissidence and consulted the dissident group of the party led by Kedar Pandey who then was also B.P.C.C. President. It shows the political management acumen of Mishra that he satisfied all the groups, factions and classes by giving them adequate representation. It was presumed that he got guidelines in the formation of ministry from Sanjay Gandhi. It was corroborated by the fact that he had given enormous representation to the youth Congress of the state. In the three tiers of the ministry; one tier, that of the Deputy ministers was totally filled up by members of the youth Congress (I). More than 50% new faces were inducted in the ministry to concretize the advice of Sanjay Gandhi that "old politicians should retire from active politics". So a balanced and composite, though not a talented, ministry was in office.

Chandra Shekhar Singh who took the charge of the state as the new CLP leader on the 14th August, 1983 startled everybody by the fact that the day on which he was elected leader, he presented a list of ten members of his team to the governor. Before being elected leader, Singh had replied to the pressmen that "there is no question of taking advice of the outgoing CM in connection with the formation of ministry. Only the wishes of the High Command will prevail in this regard".[21] He had also hinted that a man with a clean image would not be debarred only because he happened to be pro-Jagannath Mishra.[22] In his first list, he retained seven members of the outgoing ministry. Two were new, but old political careerists and having long ministerial experience—Rafiq Alam and Nagendra Jha, the then B.P.C.C. President and a dissident leader respectively were retained. Clearly, Singh went in for a composite ministry to give representation to all sections of the party which was a good augury. But in his first ministry, he had not included any lady (later on, he included one). He expanded his ministry twice till May, 1984, the last expansion having turned the structure of the Ministry from two tier to a three-tier one. However, his ministry was out of tune with

Bihar's social realities. It was dominated by upper castes with 44 per cent representation. Backward castes had 24 per cent representation, whereas tribals and *Dalits* merely 12 per cent. But much time did not lapse before dissident activities, never far from the limelight in the faction-ridden political structure of Bihar, reared its head indicating alignment with Jagannath Mishra. With few hours of the announcement of the first expansion of the ministry, disgruntled members of the Congress (I) legislature were up in arms against Singh's selection[23] of new faces. Those who expected a clean ministry were in for shock. Umeshwar Prasad Verma and Budhadeo Singh had been involved in scandals.[24] Several ministers were introduced because they had the old parental or familiar background behind them. Bandi Shankar Singh and Krishna Nand Jha were sons of the former Chief Ministers—S.K. Sinha and B.N. Jha respectively. B.K. Singh was a relative of former Union Minister, Bhisma Narain Singh; K.R. Sahu happened to be the son of a former minister and freedom fighter, Madan Prasad Singh, a known follower of Sitaram Kesari, treasurer AICC(I); and Awadh Behari Singh was the nominee of another Central Minister. *Dalit* legislators were under-represented and they raised demand for more berths in the ministery.

Some of the disappointed persons who were waiting for the next expansion (which took place on the 31st May, 1984) got satisfaction. Shiv Chandra Jha, long awaitee for cabinet Ministership was included among two others on the awaited day. Some Deputy Ministers, too, were appointed. In protest against this expansion and as a mark of disappointment, a legislator of the party threatened that he would burn himself to death if he was not included in the ministry.[25] These facts bring out the role of affective politics as well as the aggrandized individual emotive ambition to secure a ministerial berth by hook or by crook.

After General Elections held in 1985, Bindeshwari Dubey was made the leader of the Bihar CLP and it was widely proclaimed that he had the support of Jagannath Mishra behind him. In the formation of his ministry, he did not appear to act on his own. A list of ministers was prepared by the then political elites of state politics and was carried by Dubey to New Delhi. There, certain changes were made. The two ministers were nominated at the behest of the Centre. Ramashray Prasad Singh and Mahavir Choudhary had been deprived of party tickets in the last General Election and were not members of the legislature but later on, both were made members of the Legislative Council and appointed ministers. They could not have been included without the Centre's expressed wish. In those days of Rajiv Gandhi's Prime Ministership, sudden appointments and dismissals were the order of the day. Dubey was, in this way, able to cobble up a small-sized ministry. Subsequently, the CM asked for and got PM's green signal for the expansion of his team. Dubey expanded his ministry in the second spell by dropping three ministers (two cabinet rank and one state minister), inducted Amrendra Mishra who was called Jagannath Mishra's man, and in addition, inducted 12 new ministers.

Dubey was reportedly advised by the Centre to be bold enough and not to work in a hesitating manner as he had been doing thus far. Directly or indirectly, he was given a word that he need not be overtly indebted and inclined to the former CM, Jagannath Mishra. Dubey, however, had to make a tight rope dancing even for the sake of denying his allegiance to Jagannath Mishra, not knowing how to pull without Mishra who had substantial following in the Congress and even among the ex-congressmen who had been elected after being denied Congress tickets. But unlike C.S. Singh, Dubey gave brave fight to Mishra but his old age and weakness for his relatives proved harmful for him. Dubey, finally, had to act to keep up his face. The ex-masse dismissal of Mishra-appointed Vice-Chancellors under widely publicized clean up operation scheme, and the sudden takeover of L.N. Mishra Institute of Economic Development and Social Change were acts calculated to show down Mishra. Through Dubey, the Congress high command wanted to size up Mishra but in the process, Dubey appeared to act at the behest of the Centre and not on his own.

Dubey ministry, like that of C.S. Singh, was also dominated by upper castes. At one time, out of the twelve Cabinet-rank ministers, 5 belonged to the upper castes and 4 to the backward castes while the representation of tribals, *Dalits* and Muslims was nominal.

Dubey failed to bring peace and public order in rural areas. Agrarian violence could not to be contained by the police and administration under his dispensation. In North Bihar; particularly in Champaran, kidnappings, dacoities and murders were rampant. The killing of fifty persons (mostly Rajputs) in villages of Dalel Chak and Baghaura in the district of Aurangabad shocked people. It brought the developmental work to a halt and encouraged corruption. Like his predecessors, Dubey failed to attend to the problem of inequitable land relations and this became responsible for the fact that the poor nursed grievances against him for neglecting their cause.

Bhagwat Jha Azad's ministry was also oriented towards upper castes and vested interests. He was foisted from above like C.S. Singh. So ministers did not feel that they were responsible to him.

RETROSPECT

In the period between 1937 to 1961, the CMs of the state consulted the leaders of the state as well as the Centre in Cabinet-making but the C.M.'s own choice was important in the formation of the ministry and allocation of portfolios. The CMs from 1961 to 1967 were handicapped in the matter and leaned heavily on the high command and the Central leadership of the party. They could not afford to use their prerogative in the selection of ministers. The period between 1967 to 1971 when the coalition governments ruled was a period of coalescing party chiefs of both the state and the Centre with the CMs who did not have an independent role to play. CMs of coalition governments had to act under heavy pressure and constraints of plural leadership of constituent or supporting parties in the formation of ministry and allocation of portfolios. Since 1972, the Congress political culture institutionalized the practice of nomination of the CM by the PM. During the *Janata* rule (1977-80), both the CMs had to form the ministries on the basis of their constituent units. They too, were not free from Central control. Their leaders of all the four constituents, the PM and the Party President were kept in confidence. Although both the ministries were composite and well-represented, they could not last long. The responsibility for governmental instability did not live with the state leaders; the ambitions and the jealousies of Central chieftains of the *Janata* party could be blamed among other factors.

After the restoration of the Congress party to power in 1980's General Election, the Congress party in Bihar had one leader (Jagannath Mishra) who was appointed CM thrice not so much on account of his following in the Assembly as on account of the favour he commanded of the high command of the party. But he started building "men" to the chagrin of the Congress high command and also to the dislike of his critics in the CLP and this fact of political management was brought to the public gaze both through the press and through public gossip. As a result of these factors, J. Mishra was ordered by New Delhi to drop some of his lieutenants against his presumed will; and he dropped as many as eleven ministers of his team at one instance. But this did not suffice and the Congress high command pushed him out of office, though till the time of his ouster, he reportedly commanded confidence of the majority of the legislators in Bihar.

Chandrashekhar Singh and Bindeshwari Dubey both were the nominees or choices of the Centre– the old or the new PM (Mrs. Gandhi and Rajiv Gandhi) respectively—both of whom constituted one-man high command of the Congress party. Following the policy of his predecessor and his mother, late Indira Gandhi, Rajiv Gandhi in 1985 nominated all the CMs of Congress (I) party in the states where elections were held and Congress regained majority. He not only finalised the names of their team but also finalised the cases of any inclusion, exclusion or expansion in the concerned ministries. This points to decreasing devaluation of the office of the CMs due to the very manner of their appointments and in the matter of constituting their team and allocating officers to ministers. The fact of centralization changed CMs' allegiance to the public or legislature to the Central leadership and the overall governance by the CM became a function and a condition of governance of the Centre.

In 1990-2005, under Laloo-Rabri regime, OBCs got fair representation in the cabinet and in comparison, upper castes were relegated to the background. Laloo Prasad was the supreme leader of *Janata Dal* which was later called *Rashtriya Janata Dal* (RJD). So he had not to face constraints in cabinet-making. He gave undue favour to his kins who surrounded him, demanded their due share and got it. Laloo Prasad was conscious of the caste composition of the state. So he did not disregard this factor. Nitish Kumar while forming Cabinet in 2005 formed a small cabinet of 27 members, keeping 9 seats vacant for three years. But his first cabinet was more compact. It was a wonder that coalition cabinet could be so small and function effectively. But some JD (U) MLAs particularly of *Kushwaha* community and some BJP members belonging to the *Bhumihar* community started clamouring for seats in the ministry and ostensibly for starting consultative process between the constituents of the coalition. In the process, two BJP ministers named Janardan Singh Sigriwal and Chandra Mohan Rai were replaced by other members of their caste from the ministry in the cabinet reshuffle without having a word with them. Nitish Kumar reportedly consulted Deputy CM, Sushil Kumar Modi in the cabinet-reshuffle. Nitish Kumar showed signs of pregmatism in cabinet-reshuffle which is evidenced by the fact that some *Kushwahas* who had abused Nitish Kumar in the past were accommodated and Nitish Kumar replaced each member of the ministry by his or her casteman. However, Nitish Kumar used freedom in appointing nine new members. This was a composite team but no word of appreciation is due for its efficient functioning. The CM and not the cabinet remained the sole decision-maker as in the past. Collective responsibility was lacking. Bureaucacy thrived because of cabinet impotence and Chief Ministerial overlordism.

CONSIDERATIONS AND COMPULSIONS

In a pluralistic and diverse community of Bihar, the CM, whether more powerful or less, is limited by the compulsions of geography, religion, caste and community. In the favour-seeking political culture that Bihar has, political and personal pulls and pressures influence more increasingly the formation of governments. Even Nehru had said that in cabinet-making, various consideration apart from quality or merit is some kind of geographical distribution.[26] One wonders what is the merit that qualifies one to become a minister in the eye of the cabinet maker. Some members of the Constituent Assembly who had apprehended that the diverse groups and sectional groups (especially the biggest minority, the Muslims) may suffer at the hands of the 'brute majority' while forming responsible governments at the Centre and the states and felt that it should be necessary to mention in the Constitution as to how the cabinet will be formed, felt reassured, after seeing the working of the constitution that even without such provisions in the Constitution, political culture of the parties evolved over the years in a way so as to make separate political identities viable enough to demand due and proportionate demands and get their demands fulfilled each time a ministry is constituted. Not only Muslims, upper castes and also major backward castes, *Dalits* and tribes demand proportionate and even tire-wise representation and generally, CMs accommodate them. In the lists prepared by CMs and considered by the high command, the first consideration is whether they have balanced castes, communities and groups to the satisfaction of the groups concerned. No doubt, such considerations affect the size of the ministries and usually make them too large and unwieldy before the size was stipulated to be 15% of the total strength.

So far as factions are concerned, they are too much of a political necessity to be ignored. One-party dominance, in fact, thrived much due to condescending attitude toward factionalism in the states, corruption among ministers and ideological vagueness. The Congress high command at a very early stage held the view that CM should recognise two groups in the state party—the ministerialist (majority group) of his own and minority group led by the dissidents led by his opponents inside the party. The Central high command explicitly advised the CM of Bihar in 1963, K. B. Sahay, to have an agreement with the minority group leader in preparing the list.[27] This practice has been strictly observed since 1963. Irrespective of administrative needs, CM has to accommodate communal and regional claims and satisfy personal ambitions in cabinet-making. Opportunistic claims are accepted and administrative needs are ignored. In Bihar, the practice has been in favour of forming broad-based cabinets particularly in one-party governments. Right from 1937 to this day (excluding coalition governments), it was emphasized that cabinets should be formed keeping all possible considerations and compulsions in mind; thus preferring compositeness over coherence of the executive. There is a policy decision binding on CMs of Congress-ruled states that whenever there are groups within the CLP, the party leaders must form broad-based and composite cabinets in order to achieve unity within the party.[28] So far as coalition governments are concerned, there are some extra compulsions and considerations in forming the ministry. The governor of the UP, while making a statement on October 7, 1970, said: "The CM of a coalition is not supreme in the parliamentary sense because he does not have a free hand in the choice of his ministers and has simply to accept the names given by respective party leader".[29] So the CM of a coalition government is all the more a captive of the heterogeneous wills of the coalescing parties.

The CM makes and unmakes cabinets and allocates portfolios, though it is doubtful if in affecting them, he is governed by administrative compulsions alone. It is found that "ministries and departments are treated like so many pieces of cloth in an absentminded tailor's shop; they are cut and recut, sewn together and torn asunder, and often stitched into garments without any regard whatever to texture, colour-scheme or even measurement".[30] This practice has been continuing for long and several suggestions made by commissions of administrative reforms to regulate the distribution of portfolios have not been implemented. The second generation economic reforms require that in choosing colleagues, CMs should look for their political stature, maturity, sagacity, integrity, intellectual ability, decision making capacity and sustained application to work. It is a pity that the Centre, while interfering and arrogationg to itself the right to nominate CMs and even taking active hand in approving list of ministers in the Congress-ruled states takes into account political equations and not national and administrative considerations and perspectives. This creates developmental lag that plagues Bihar in particular.

CM's RIGHT TO DISMISS MINISTERS

Constitutionally, Art. 164(1) and (2) enjoin that the Ministers shall hold office during the pleasure of the governor; and the Council of Ministers shall be collectively responsible to the Legislative Assembly of the state. They are interpreted to mean that individual ministers are liable to be removed on the advice of the CM, though he himself can be removed by the governor only on the evidence of loss of confidence in his government in the Assembly.[31] If it is the right of the CM to appoint, promote and reshuffle ministers, then it is also his right to dismiss them. It is expected that if the CM wishes that anyone of his ministers or a number of ministers resign, they will do so because individual responsibility is covered by the provision that ministers hold office during the pleasure of the governor and the pleasure of the governor means the pleasure of the CM.

Now the question arises: what are other grounds on which ministers are usually dismissed or asked to resign? They resign in the observance of the principles of "collective" or "individual" responsibility. If a Minister differs from the collective decision of the cabinet, he has either to reconcile to the majority decision of the cabinet or quit the cabinet. Besides, a minister owes individual responsibility for the running of his department.[32] The Administrative Reforms Commission I[33] recommended that a minister should be held accountable:

(i) When he fails to formulate policy in respect of a major problem or when the policy formulated is found erroneous or suffers from major weakness;

(ii) When he neglects to pay personal attention on important issues other than that of policy where such attention is expected of him or wrongly handles such issues;

(iii) When there is general or major mismanagement or maladministration in his department/ministry and;

(iv) When he commits some act of impropriety; when the minister's own actions are found to blameworthy, e.g. are found to abuse their powers for peronal ends or are known to have committed corrupt practices.

In Bihar, there have been cases of resignation on the basis of individual responsibility and policy differences. But most of the cases of resignation are due to personal differences or due to Central intervention. Only one case of resignation of a minister (Harinath Mishra in August, 1956 over firing on students) took place as a matter of policy before 1967. From 1967 to 1971, there had been a chain of resignations every year, not on account of individual responsibility but in a broad sense, on account of spurious policy differences between and among partners of the coalition governments. In other words, they were not resignations but defections to get power or to topple one ministry to try luck with the next one.

In 1973, Kedar Pandey asked some of his ministers to resign but many of them refused to do so. Consequently, Pandey himself resigned and reconstituted his ministry by dropping eleven members of his previous cabinet.[34] This was on account of policy differences among members of the cabinet. In *Janata* rule, too, there were resignations on account of political differences, abuse of power and allegations of involvement in malpractices. Baidyanath Mehta, excise minister in Karpoori Thakur's Ministry, was the first man of the *Janata* Ministry in Bihar who resigned from his office on the 1st of March, 1979 on the ground of policy differences. He resigned following differences with the then CM over the issue of suspension of some excise officials for the alleged lapses on their part.[35] One parliamentary secretary resigned or was virtually dismissed for indulging in corrupt practice.[36] On the 17th of April 1979, 13 ministers, 10 cabinet ministers and 3 ministers of state and three parliamentary secretaries submitted their resignations. These ministers declared that they had lost their faith in the existing leadership.[37] In Ram Sundar Das Ministry under *Janata* rule, Ram Jatan Sinha, the then minister of state of Industries resigned just after the formation of the ministry following differences with the CM.

After restoration of the Congress party to power with Jagannath Mishra as the CM in 1980, the CM suddenly dropped 11 ministers of his ministry after two years of the working of the ministry in August, 1983. It included dismissal of the seniormost Minister of his Ministry, L.P. Sahi, who had refused to submit resignation. The background of dismissal was that the CM was being alleged to be the leader of a corrupt ministry. In order to save his skin, he dropped three of his most important strong lieutenants from his ministry. The CM himself justified it by giving statement that the operation was conducted to remove corruption from his ministry.[38] Thus, the CM had publicly admitted that many of the ministers he had appointed in June, 1980 were corrupt. The lieutenants of the CM, on the other hand, grudged that they should not have been dropped in view of the fact that they were always loyal to the CM, acted in collusion with him and were efficient. But it was said that the three ministers were dropped because the CBI had reported against them to the PM who had asked the CM to drop the three of them all at once. But the fact that the CM could drop such a large number of ministers together and yet continue as the CM made his political standing stronger. Bindeshwari Dubey, too, dropped three of his colleagues in the first expansion of his ministry. It had been done to show his clean image in the eyes of the party high command and to get a further lease of ministerial life which was flickering because of allegations of inefficiency against him.

We have discussed about the removal of Chandra Mohan Rai and Janardhan Singh Sigriwal and some others from Nitish Kumar-led Ministry. Ministers resented it, protested against their party leader and for weeks together, BJP dissidents opposing Sushil Kumar Modi on that account agitated for change in the leadership within the party. Cracks appeared to develop in the coalition but they were managed by the leadership of both the coalescing parties.

The instances of resignation and dismissals, discussed above, show that ministers can be removed when the CM or the Central high command lose their faith in them. It is difficult for a CM to save a minister if he is under bitter attack from the party, the press, the house and the people. The CM may think a minister to be unfit for a job and ask for his resignation. But the effective exercise of the Chief Ministerial power of dismissal, depends, in a large measure, upon his own position and standing in the party. No CM in Bihar has dismissed one of his senior colleagues on his own except on rare occasions. Resignations are either the result of minister's differences with the CM or for any reason, the CM indicates that the minister should resign on his own. The CMs between 1967 to 1971 did not enjoy the right of dismissal or to ask for resignation in an unfettered manner. From 1972 to 1989, it was hardly used by the CMs barring Jagannath Mishra who dropped as many as eleven ministers which included dismissal of some of the seniormost colleagues of his team. Nitish Kumar also asked for the resignation of a minister soon after his appointment after the General Election in 2005 when he came to know that there were charges against the concerned minister. He asked for the resignation of another minister against whom it was discovered that a case was pending in a court. When the court absolved him of the charge, he was again re-inducted in the cabinet. His cabinet reshuffle was also a major operation.

INSTITUTIONAL SUPPORT TO THE CM

Bihar's first Chief Secretary, L.P. Singh had a high reputation for integrity and administrative capability. P.P. Agarwal, I.C.S., Additional Secretary to the Government was made in-charge of the work of re-organisation of the Bihar Secretariat with effect from the 27th of June, 1949. Secretariat was re-organised by 1952 and the new scheme was adopted on a permanent basis w.e.f. 1.1.1956. Cabinet Secretariat departments were re-organised in 1961 following the recommendations of P.S. Appu, Joint Secretary to the Finance Department. The first CM, S.K. Sinha maintained good working relations with the secretariat officials and protected police from demoralization because police, having done away with pre-independence legacy no longer symbolized tyranny, domination, intimidation and oppression. S.K. Sinha emphasized that in democratic India, policemen symbolized efficiency, service, protection and help to the people. Caste played no role in promotion, transfer, posting and in working relationship of police officials with ministers or the CM in the fifties.

Minister-civil service relationship changed during the sixties. CMs started transferring, promoting and even appointing officers to have favourable personnel. K.B. Sahay was a respondent before the Aiyar Commission for favouritism in the appointment of G.K. Kohli (as Registrar in 1965), Bajrang Sahay (a casteman, as a lawyer in 1965) and the promotion of two Ministerial officers (Girija Shankar Sahai and Udai Narain Singh in 1967) and for some other changes. In post-K.B. Sahay period, many successive CMs have been accused of favouritism in the appointment, transfers and promotion of senior officials. The Aiyar Commission of inquiry discussed the responsibility and relationship of ministers and their subordinates and held quite a few ministers responsible for omissions and commissions in the departments concerned in the course of their work.

The CM as the Chairman of the cabinet influences cabinet decisions which are made by consensus. It is for the CM to sum up the sense of the meeting and declare the consensus. But there is scope for exaggerating this role of the CM. An Indian Journalist writes, 'whoever presides over the meeting of the cabinet can substitute his preference for that of his colleagues'.[39] CMs like S.K. Sinha, K.B. Sahay and Jagannath Mishra influenced the Cabinet, although they too consulted or sought advice of their seniormost colleagues. Both A.N. Sinha and K.B. Sahay had been the members of the policy cabinet of S.K. Sinha till 1952, A.N. Sinha continued to be in that position till his death. Mahesh Prasad Sinha replaced K.B. Sahay in 1952 as a member of the inner or policy Cabinet and some others were also included. When K.B. Sahay was the CM, he included S.N. Sinha and Mahesh Prasad Sinha in his 'inner Cabinet'. Jagdanand Singh, Raghuvansh Prasad Singh and Ramchandra Purve were in the inner cabinets of Laloo-Rabri governments. Sushil Kumar Modi is the only cabinet minister who is consulted by Nitish Kumar in policy matters and therefore, he can be said to be a member of his policy cabinet. But after 2010 elections, Nitish Kumar is not found consulting even Sushil Kumar Modi so much. He relies more on the secretaries and principal secretaries of the Departments and has some trusted lientenants who are not members of the formal cabinet but have his ears and confidence. But most of the CMs keep some of their close and reliable members of the cabinet for important and confidential advice.

However, the CM, as a co-ordinator of all departments, has a pre-eminent position in the cabinet. CM's functions are so enormous and burdensome that the CM has to share them with his trusted colleagues. The CM is not only Chairman, coordinator, presiding officer and the arch of the cabinet but he is also the head of the government. With vast responsibility that he has to carry, through myriad roles he plays and through the cabinet unity and integrity, prosperity of the state can be achieved. He has to look after all the departments beyond his limited jurisdiction as an observer and supervisor to trace out the defects and to instruct to remove it. His first and foremost duty is to establish public order within the state. If public order deteriorates, crimes statistics are on increase and people of the state do not feel safe, discredit goes to the CM. Secondly, the quality of his governance is judged by the pace of economic development in the state. For this, he remains regularly in touch with the Finance Minister and there is also state planning Board to advise him on technical economic matters. Even if he is not the Finance Minister himself, the budget bears his imprint. However, the increase in GDP sometimes does not indicate increase in human development index. For instance, in 2011, Bihar has reported growth rate of 14.15 per cent and in 2012, it has reported growth rate of 13.1% during Nitish Kumar's stewardship of the government but this is not reflected in the increase of literacy rate, health opportunities and other aspects of human well-being.

At the head of the government, the CM has to be concerned with some important appointments. Appointments of Advocate General Chairmen of various boards and commissions are made by him in the cabinet. In addition to providing compact and competent Council of Ministers, the CM has to provide a purposeful government in the state and it is this which seems to be sadly lacking in Bihar in most of the years. The functioning of the ministers in general discloses that (i) the members chosen as ministers are not necessarily best in the party; (ii) the considerations in their selection as ministers have been influenced by casteism, factionalism and communalism; (iii) the departments are not rationally distributed; (iv) ministers misuse funds, do not supervise works of their departments and abuse their powers for personal ends; (v) lack unity and homogeneity due to ideological incoherence and also lack commitment or issue-orientation and adopt old planning methods; (vi) ministers sometimes waste too much time on meeting their constituents, castemen and favourites in a large number and exercise undue influence on service personnel through *chits* and now through telephone or broadband connections to avoid the hazards of facing Aiyar or Mudholkar Commission which had passed adverse remarks against some ministers, though the recommendations of the commission were not given due heed; and (vii) several ministers and even CMs are accused of irregularities in maintaining accounts or indulging in corruption or possessing assets disproportionate to their known sources of income. The old proverb that Caesar's wife should be above suspicion no longer stands in practice in Bihar; it stands in the reverse order. Democracy and corruption seem to be siblings in Bihar. Aspiration for good governance, in order to be realized, requires a check on corruption which is being attempted to be placed to some extent in the recent past.

The problem is how to help the CM in bearing the heavy burden of acting as the chief co-ordinator of policies and programmes, how to fill in the responsibility of keeping the ministerial team together and ensuring smooth functioning of the cabinet as well as administrative machinery. Lack of integrity and co-operation among the members of the Council of Ministers and between ministers and civil servants has already affected the morale of administration in the state. Nitish Kumar's administration generated hope for three and half years but both statistics of law and order, electoral result in by-elections to the eighteen seats held in 2009 and charges of irregularities revealed by the two reports of the C. A. G. have led to a stage where people's scepticism was generated and the amount of hope at least did not remain to the extent it was generated in the beginning of the formation of the government in 2005. Nitish's electoral triumph in 2010 made his image go high again. In 2011-12 with the introduction and implementation of anti-corruption measures, passage of legislation concerning land records and successful crrying out of the Right to Services Act buttressed by his *Janata Durbars* and *Seva Yatras*, his popularity index rose high. But the statistics of bad lów and order, rising corruption, accummulation of black money, rise of consumptive culture resulting in the construction of high rise buildings, hotels and malls in a large number tremendous rise in the prices of real estate and rent of houses and rising miseries of BPL families also because of governmental negligence towards their food security and health needs have brought the image of good governance down in 2012. It is a fact that the CM's strength in the cabinet increases or decreases in direct proportion to people's perception of his role in responding to their aspiration to receive good governance. Since people's aspirations have been aroused frustration will mount proportionately if the aspirations are not fulfilled in time.

Notes and References

1. The constitution uses the term 'Council Ministers' which includes usually three, but at times, four categories of officers: the Cabinet Ministers, Ministers of State, Deputy Ministers and Parliamentary Secretaries. The cabinet is the highest policy-making body, each cabinet minister being in independent charge of exclusive portfolios. Ministers of state attend the cabinet meeting when invited to do so to take part in discussion concerning the portfolios. Deputy Ministers are attached to the cabinet ministers and ministers of state. Parliamentary secretaries, as the name suggests, are expected to help the ministers in legislative works. All these categories of persons combined constitute the Council of Ministers. The cabinet is a composite body (about one-third of the entire strength), technically denoting only the first category in the Council who meet to decide policies and to make other decisions. But in wide political usages, the term 'cabinet' is a popular substitute for the Council. Here also, 'cabinet' is sometimes used, in the widely accepted sense. It is ordained now that the number of members of the Council of Ministers will not exceed 15% of members of the legislature.
2. The term is used by Shastri and Mrs. Gandhi.
3. Article 164(1).

4. The first Congress government was formed in 1937 with S. K. Sinha as its premier on the recommendation of the AICC.
5. A.N. sinha died in July, 1957 after a direct contest for the office of the leader of the Bihar CLP but never failed to hold the previous portfolio, Finance, in S.K. Sinha's Cabinet.
6. Subhash, C. Kashyap. *The Politics of Power; Defection and State Politics in India,* National Publishing House, New Delhi, 1974, pp. 305-8.
7. Party-wise break-up of the S.V.D. Ministry, 1967:

Party	*No. of Cabinet Ministers*	*No. of Ministers of State*	*Total*
J.K.D.	3	1	4
S.S.P.	6	2	8
CPI (R)	2	1	3
Jana Sangh	2	1	3
P.S.P.	2	1	3

8. *The Indian Nation,* January 29, 1968.
9. In 1969, the Central Congress party came to be divided into two groups: Syndicate (comprising S.K. Patil, Sanjeeva Reddy and Morarji Desai) and others who were known as indicate because they supported Indira Gandhi.
10. Kolkata High Court had passed strictures against the Raja of Ram Garh immediately before his inclusion in the ministry.
11. *The Indian Nation,* (Patna) March 18, 1972.
12. *Ibid.*
13. *The Indian Nation,* September 5, 1973.
14. L.P. Shahi, Bindeshwari Dubey and T. Bodra were to be dropped but they were, later on, included.
15. *The Indian Nation,* September 26, 1973.
16. B.L.D., Jana Sangh, Socialist Party and Congress (O).
17. *The Indian Nation,* June 22, 1977.
18. *Ibid.,* March 13, 1979.
19. *Ibid.,* March 29, 1979.
20. The younger son of Mrs. Indira Gandhi had such influence on the Party's activities that he appeared not only the groomed but the rightful choice of the Prime Ministership after Mrs. Gandhi.
21. *The Indian Nation,* 14.8.1983.
22. Jagannath Mishra had deleted his surname as noted earlier.
23. *India Today,* November 30, 1983, p. 55.
24. *Ibid.*

25. *Aryavarta*, Patna, June 1, 1984. (in Hindi)
26. *The Hindustan Times*, June 13, 1962.
27. *The Indian Nation*, October 3, 1963.
28. The Decision of the CPB was reported in *The Hindustan Times*, March 9, 1962.
29. *Op. cit.*, p. 669.
30. Cited in Michel Brecher, *Succession in India*, Oxford University press, London, 1960, p. 104.
31. Discussed in the earlier Chapter.
32. For a good analysis of the Concepts of 'Collective' and 'individual responsibility', see R.K. Alderman and J.A. Cross, *The tactics of Resignation*, Routledge and Kegan Paul, London, 1967, pp. 2-3.
33. *Administrative Reforms Commission Report*, p. 28.
34. *The Indian Nation, June 25, 1973.*
35. *The Searchlight*, (Patna) March 2, 1979
36. Rajesh Kumar, Parliamentary Secretary was alleged to misbehave with a Nurse of Lady Alegin Hospital, Gaya.
37. *The Indian Nation*, April 20, 1979.
38. *The Indian Nation*, 5 August, 1983. The three lieutenants of the Chief Minister to be dropped were Rajo Singh, Prabhunath Singh and Raghunath Jha, Ministers of State in his ministry.
39. *Asian Recorder, op. cit.*, 1969, p. 9268.

7

The CM vis-a-vis The Legislature

The CM is supposed to work in close co-operation with the legislature in a parliamentary form of government. Constitutionally speaking, the C.M. and his cabinet constitute a small body of persons selected from among the members of the majority party or parties of the legislature, holding office and exercising power as long as and in the measure the legislature permits.[1] After every General Election, every legislature party meets to elect its leader and the leader of the majority is designated by the governor as the CM of the state.

The legislature is virtually the mother of the CM in a parliamentary form of government. But as we have seen in the earlier chapters, legislature did not have a substantial role in electing S.K. Sinha. S.K. Sinha was the leader of the legislature as a matter of right because of his standing, his sacrifices during the freedom struggle, his manifold contributions, his relationships with the party elites in Patna and Delhi, his personal popularity among the MLAs and the electorate. Since he dominated the mass party and had considerable mass appeal, he campaigned not for himself but for other candidates of his party also during elections and had a substantive role in securing party tickets for them. His popularity helped the party consolidate its electoral base. So, S.K. Sinha was always unanimously elected by the CLP except in 1957 when he faced contest in which he emerged victorious because he commanded majority. in the CLP. Binodanand Jha and K.B. Sahay were appointed CMs after they defeated their rivals, Mahesh Prasad Sinha and Bir Chand Patel respectively in the contests of the CLP leadership they faced. They were formally elected leaders of the CLP after which the governor invited them to form governments as CMs.

During the coalition era, CMs were chosen by agreement among the constituent parties. Resignations and defections often led to loss of confidence of the lower house of the legislature in the particular CM; and this led to quick changes of CMs and sometimes, imposition of President's rule leading to another spell of coalition governments till the Congress rule was restored and imperial Prime Ministerial system began under Mrs. Gandhi in 1972. Between 1972 and 1977, the CLP had no role in the selection of CMs since the CMs were the nominees of the PM or either of her sons. Between 1977 and 1980 also, the CMs were not selected by the JP legislature party but came through an agreement between leaders of the two constituent parties at the national level. Between 1980 and 1984 again, Mrs. Gandhi came back as PM and continued with her practice of nominating the CMs or in some cases, her younger son did so. Between 1984-89, Rajiv Gandhi as P.M. continued the practice of his mother. Between 1990 and 2010, the three "leaders" who became CMs were "regionally" accepted leaders and one of them, Rabri Devi was imposed by the family. Rabri Devi was the choice of Laloo Prasad or his nominee. The writ of Laloo Prasad ran in the RJD, so his choice went unquestioned. The leadership of Nitish Kumar in JD (U) was unquestioned as the accepted leader of JD (U)-BJP combine and he has been holding the office of the CM since 2005. Thus we can conclude that legislature as such has not only been the creator or the destroyer of the CMs in most cases. Leaders appoint themselves by dint of their control over the legislative party, the party and the electorate in general.

In chapter V, we have examined governor's power to summon, prorogue and dissolve the Assembly. When the CM commands majority in the lower house of the legislature, the CM's aid and advice is almost binding on the governor in these matters and the governor acts according to such advice, But when the CM is in minority, when an election to the *Vidhan Sabha* is impending and an alternative machinery can be formed, CM's advice is not binding.

In a parliamentary system, there is fusion between CM, his cabinet and the legislature. The powers of the legislature are, in actual practice, exercised by the cabinet in cabinet system of government. The CM is not only the key stone of the cabinet arch but the leader of the legislature as well. The agenda of both the Legislative Assembly and the Legislative Council is determined by the Speaker and the Chairman of the respective houses in close consultation with the CM. The CM makes all important policy statements on the floor of the houses when they are in session. He defines government policies and programmes as the chief spokesman of the party. He speaks on behalf of the state government authoritatively and faces the opposition as the chief defender of the government's policies and actions taken or advances reasons for actions not taken in cases of wrong policies of administration or unsavoury happenings in the state. Whenever he feels that his cabinet colleagues are not up to the mark in satisfying the house, he himself stands up to satisfy them. He communicates the views of the cabinet and the legislature to the governor and as such, acts as a channel between them.

As a matter of fact, there has been decline of legislatures in Bihar as in parliamentary democracies all over the world. When we turn the pages of Legislative Assembly Debates or Legislative Council Debates in Bihar from 1952 to 1967, we come across speeches marked by eloquence, facts, data, wit, irony and wise suggestions for planning and implementation. There were investigative questions and attempts to put the governments in the dock only in emergent situations through adjournment motions, etc. But as time passed by and the coalition era started, the emphasis of legislators shifted from debate to defection, from holding governments under control to capturing office by hook and crook and replacing government by using any means whatsoever. This changed the genuine role of the legislature and that resulted in their decline. Since 1967, the role of the legislature in Bihar as in other states and even in the *Lok Sabha* is not so much to legislate as to stop legislative work, stage walkouts, show wraths, express grievances through making noises, going to the well of the house and sometimes even throwing chairs or tearing papers and throwing them towards the treasury benches; and so on. The non-congress parties led by Lohia, Raj Narain and Karpoori Thakur showed more interest in using the fora of Legislative Assembly for non-legislative purposes. Incidents of hooliganism, walkouts, pressure on the Speaker for accepting adjournment motions even by suspending question hour, etc. became most common practices particularly in Bihar and U. P. legislatures.

As a result, the CM and his cabinet lost initiative, vigilance and leadership qualities. Bills, resolutions, etc. that are moved in the house have prior approval of the CM as a matter of course. But weak CMs did not hold the floor to face the onslaught of the opposition and to save their government from being hackled and to maintain party discipline. The cabinet, too, did not show interest in encouraging long and detailed discussions over bills presented by it. In fact, ministers were not well-prepared to answer questions in the question hour; and bold CMs were few who made their presence felt and intervened to save the faltering ministers. The usual scene has been to see that bills were passed perfunctorily in utter haste without legislators caring to know what they contained. Ministers were not well-prepared to pilotbills and resolutions. The very fact that a barely literate and politically novice person, Rabri Devi, was made CM and hence, leader of the lower house in 1997 showed the regard leaders were prepared to pay to the proceedings of the houses. For months together, the incumbent CM was not able to make meaningful and effective interventions in the houses, she fumbled when the occasion came for her to intervene. Legislators also lacked interest in the proceedings of the houses. Under the circumstances, legislative control and vigilance over the administrative machinery became a casualty. Legislators generally did not have access to the necessary data to control the administrative machinery since 1997. Even Nitish Kumar has not given power to the legislators or even to the ministers to intervene effectively in administrative matters.

Yet, legislature plays important sustaining role in respect of CMs in cases of economic crisis, governability crisis, etc. Legislature is ultimately sounded to clinch the issue under grim situations. In a formal, legal sense, the CM can be persuaded or forced in the interim to resign or retire by the legislature to which the Council of Ministers is collectively responsible. S.K. Sinha faced no-confidence motion five times, though all the motions were defeated in the house.[2] Three CMs of Bihar have become victims of no-confidence motions brought against them in the house so far.

A strong CM (with absolute majority in the lower house) needs not bother for the voice (hurly burly) of the weak and meek opposition in the lower house. He takes for granted that the opposition cannot unseat him. The rigorous control of the whips throttles the voice of his party MLAs having any degree of difference with his official policy. The pleasure of the Assembly cannot decide the fate of "strong" CMs. The CM has to fear the *Vidhan Sabha* when there are forceful dissident elements in his party who are in a position to challenge his majority as was the case with coalition CMs. The CMs of coalition governments always had a sword hanging against them. They also acted under limitations because the co-ordination committees acted like super-cabinets. Between 1967 and 1989, in Bihar, the CMs were fearful that there might develop crises and if some MLAs walked out of the government, his government might fall. Crises management ate all their time and energy. The spectacular scenes of CM's interventions in the proceedings of the houses were witnessed in the fifties in the case of S.K. Sinha or have been seen after the fifties in the cases of K.B. Sahay, C.S. Singh, J. Mishra, Bhagwat Jha Azad, Laloo Prasad and Nitish Kumar as CMs.

Notes and References

1. Herman Finer, *Theory and Practice of Modern Governments*, Methuen and Co., London, 1956, p. 576.
2. The first no-confidence motion was moved by S.K. Bage in the Bihar *Vidhan Sabha* against S.K. Sinha ministry on April 13-14, 1955 but the motion was defeated.

8

The CM, The People, The Party and The Media

People being the ultimate sovereign; they legitimize or disapprove governmental actions and decisions through periodical elections, results of by-elections and mid-term presence showing elections in mass meetings, expressing general reactions through mass media, gossiping in street or corner meetings, or in trains and buses (which are most common in India with tropical climate). Poll surveys conducted by journals on the eve of elections take into account the opinions expressed by the residents in the metropolitan areas (most of whom are non-voters). The more affected and most effective from electoral point of view are the rural voters who vote, mobilize, campaign and till Sheshan and K.J. Rao did their best to stop the practice, captured booths in rural Bihar.

The party is both part of the whole and also acts as one of those organizational structures who in both their roles of governance and opposition aggregate mass interests and mediate between people and the ruling apparatus. Besides parties, NGOs also play the mediating role and make lives of the people worth living. Of late, media had come to play a big role with its poll forecasts and interviews of party leaders but making poll forecasts by media has been banned by the judiciary now. Yet, media with its broadcasts of who said what, where and how influences public opinion and creates a link between the electorate and the leaders. The important point is that public opinion does not manifest only during elections. Enlightened people use right to information; rural folk meet leaders with their complaints and grievances and if resentments or frustrations mount on one score or the other, the government starts losing legitimacy much before the D-day. The electorate in India have not performed the constituent, the legislative or the plebiscitary functions but they have exercised their influence through voting sensibly in spite of the fact that many of them are still illiterate or poor. The only problem that belies solution by both the government and the people is corruption; and the mighty among the people, being beneficiaries, either do not consider it to be a problem or do not want it to be solved. But if one goes by the slogans raised in *bandhs*, marches, demonstrations, mass meetings or protest meetings, the most general complaints are against price rise, unemployment and corruption. In any case, unlike other countries of South Asia, South East Asia and Africa, we have had regular elections in India, press has been comparatively free except in nineteen months of internal emergency and democracy has taken strides.

THE CM AND THE PEOPLE

Ordinarily, the CM sees at least one hundred to five hundred or even more persons on an average daily. More often, people come to meet to seek particularistic favours and not for public work or to demand interventions to check maladministration or misuse of public funds. Only sometimes, they come for getting public utility service for their areas. Leaders of the state including the CM try to create personal rapport with the people by tours, inaugurations, visits to different places including the countryside. They make it a point to make personal visits to elites' personal functions particularly in towns because it creates CM-elite bond. We shall like to note that in spite of the poor level of literacy, economic status, exposure to mass media, etc., Indian electorate is discerning. An imperious PM like Mrs. Gandhi was unseated by the Court in 1975 and when she wanted to fight back by imposing internal emergency, she lost all but one seat of the *Lok Sabha* from the entire North India in 1977 and her party had to sit in the opposition and face charges of excesses during emergency. She had even to face one day's imprisonment. Similarly, when the *Janata Party* suffered from internal squabbles and turned a divided and disorderly organisation, people had no compunction in bringing Mrs. Gandhi back to power in 1980.

Coming to Bihar, S.K. Sinha's mass meetings brought hordes of people to hear him. He was known as 'Bihar Kesari' for his lion like roars when he rose to speak. He made visits to distant places in Bihar to make mass contact in spite of his bulky body.

A few years before the first fall of the Congress party in Bihar, K.B. Sahay made efforts to satisfy men belonging to the minority communities and backward classes. He wanted to save his crown from the onslaught of other upper class factions and therefore, strategically responded to the demands of the newly mobilized and aspirant sectors of the society. But he was the first CM to face public inquiry (among some other Congress ministers, he faced the Aiyyar Commission) for indulging in corruption and misuse of power for personal ends. In the fourth General Election held during his tenure (1967), he was the symbol of corruption rampant in the Congress and people, particularly children, chanted slogans in the streets saying that:

"Gali Gali men Shore Hai,
K.B. Sahay Chore Hai".

A very serious situation arose when during the last months of K.B. Sahay's Chief Ministership and just before the election, a serious incident took place in Patna in which firing on Patna University students was made on January 5, 1967 causing many deaths and injuries. This was the second time students were fired upon, the first being in 1955 during S.K.

Sinha's regime which too had created great furore. K. B. Sahay, the then C.M., determined to maintain law and order, sternly declared that no enquiry (either official or judicial) in the police firing will be made. Sahay declared that the agitation was politically engineered and that *goondas* and anti-social elements were behind the incident. During the agitation, the CM's residence was also attacked while Sahay was on tour to Nawada. Following this incident, Sahay became the target of people's anger and in particular, he became the butt of students' ire. Bihar Teachers' convention urged dismissal of his ministry. Students signed pledges in their blood to defeat K.B. Sahay and all the Congress candidates in the forthcoming general election.[1] A victim of popular anger in the fourth General Election, he lost both the seats for the *Vidhan Sabha* from Patna West and Hazaribagh from where he contested. People's discontent was also evident when his car, carrying Morarji Desai, was stoned by a mob at Dhanbad on January 16, 1967. In his election campaign while addressing the people of his constituency in south Mandiri in Patna West, he said that the electorate was his '*malik*' (master) but masses were chanting slogans:

> *"K. B. Harao,*
> *Bihar Bachao"*

It is a fact, however, that people's anger was not against K.B. Sahay alone rather he was the symbol of the dissatisfaction and frustration with the performance of the Congress government ruling in the sixties or till then and the rampant corruption that had sprung in the body politic by the last few years of the Congress rule.

Mahamaya Prasad Sinha defeated K.B. Sahay in Patna West Constituency in the fourth General Election by giving a call that it was a fight between dictator (K.B. Sahay) and people (Mahamaya Prasad Sinha). Sinha was symbolised as the representative and symbol of the people. In this election, the Congress was for the first time dislodged from power in the state leading to a spell of coalition governments. The most "popular", among all the nine coalition CMs was Mahamaya Prasad Sinha (a *Jana Kranti Dal* President) because of his oratory which was full of *Urdu* couplets. Addressing his first public meeting at Gandhi Maidan, Patna, he said that this is the government of the people and he was the "chief servant". He assured the people that his government will resign if he failed to serve the people. He assured that the police would not enter into educational institutions any more; and there would be no more firings on students. This government had to tackle the worst famine situation of the state in which he assured that none would die of starvation. Over-conscious of the problems of the people of Bihar and particularly of its students, his government was said to be a government of the students, by the students and for the students. Once, addressing a largely attended public meeting, Sinha told the students that police would enter into the educational compound only to save the life of a professor or a student, and for no other reason. At the same time, he warned the *goondas* against misusing the educational campuses. Beginning his speech in a highly emotional tone, Sinha warned that if anti-social elements tried to create disturbance in the society, if a *goonda* tried to outrage the modesty of a girl and if a criminal wanted to loot and usurp the wealth and property of others, his government would be a government of *lathis* and bullets.[2] Mahamaya Prasad Sinha's emotional and sentimental appeals made him popular initially among the people of Bihar. His speeches had such a dramatic tinge that he was often compared to an actor of the celluloid and was said to surpass even them in shedding tears in the public in exhibiting his anguish and pain in wearing a convincing look while partaking a volley of assurances.

All the CMs of the coalition period employed chair saving devices in their own way. Karpoori Thakur, though a suave and modest socialist and popular among a large section of the people, got identified with controversial issues. He vernacularzed education and got a law enacted that students who failed in English would be promoted as "pass without English". Such students were jocularly said to have passed in 'Karpoori Division'. Karpoori, however, emerged as the symbol of the downtrodden, the vernacular and the have-nots in Bihar and his symbolisms were also cast on caste-lines, following Lohia's thesis. This made him controversial among the upper caste people at a later stage, though he was initially loved by several people of forward castes because of his cultural disposition..

After the restoration of the Congress party to power in March, 1972, Kedar Pandey, a man of fair image, took some drastic actions to improve the condition of the state as the CM. We have seen that in order to raise the standard of education, he drastically eradicated the use of unfair means in all examinations. He did this job thoroughly and got success in achieving the aim. Because of this achievement, Pandey still occupies an important place in the heart of the education loving people of Bihar. Being in favour of a clean image of the government, he dropped some of his colleagues out of his ministry but this action proved costly for him and led to his own loss of the office of the Chief Ministership.

The period which followed was a period of processions and demonstrations, trials and turbulations, conflicts and confrontations due to J.P. movement. Many lives were lost and many careers were ruined. Developmental activities slowed down and expenditure shot up on the maintenance of law and order. Money that ought to have been spent on the development of the downtrodden had to be spent over the construction of barricades and on the deployment of Border Security Force. But neither the Assembly was dissolved nor the then CM, Ghafoor resigned at the earliest in pursuance of the demand of the agitationists. Trying his best to resolve the situation, in a mammoth public meeting in Patna West, Ghafoor said that he was the most unfortunate CM[3] because since his assumption of office, he had to contend with attacks from within and outside with the result that he could not do many good things he wanted to do. Having the reputation of being meek, mild and humble in personal manners but tough, strong and determined in political conduct and implementation, he met J.P. and sought his co-operation and help in eradicating corruption. But he could not receive J.P.'s co-operation. J.P. and his followers were adamant that the Assembly be dissolved—a demand which could not have been met by the Congress party. Growing complications in the situation compelled the CM to threaten J.P. with drastic actions if he continued the agitation.[4] Ghafoor charged J.P. with creating an atmosphere of violence and came out with a stern warning that "a stage has reached when something drastic has to be done". He said that limit had been reached of his patience.[5] Ultimately, J.P. while leading a mass demonstration was *lathi-* charged making the situation more complicated and explosive. After this incident, Ghafoor went to New Delhi and offered his resignation to the PM, Indira Gandhi. Ghafoor was so much pre-occupied with the worsening law and order situation that he hardly got time either for welfare administration or for providing good governance. But P.V.N. Rao, the then General Secretary, AICC (who subsequently became the PM of India) addressing the party men closed his speech by eulogising the services of Abdul Ghafoor and recited a couplet of Kabir:

> *"Dass Ghafoora Jatan Se Orhi,*
> *Jas Ke Tas Dhar Dinni Chadariya".*[6]

(It was to the credit of Ghafoor that he returned the crown of leadership spotless to the legislature and had no stigma attached to him personally.)

With the installation of a new ministry headed by Jagannath Mishra, a new chapter opened in the political history of Bihar. It was a ministry with a difference. The decision to set free all prisoners, arrested in connection with the agitation led by J.P. within a week revealed Mishra's intention to open his innings with confidence and impressive hits on a favourable pitch. He assured that people's life and property would be protected; and government was ready to talk to end the movement. But nothing could help him in controlling the situation and ultimately, the situation rolled on to a point when national emergency was proclaimed by the Centre which culminated in the defeat of the Congress party in the General Election of 1977.

The emergence of a new party, *Janata* party, and formation of governments led by Karpoori Thakur and later on by Ram Sundar Das stand in striking contrast to the Congress or the coalition ministries of the earlier period. People expected much from the *Janata* Party CMs in consonance with the promises enthusiastically made in the election manifesto of the party. But the CM, Karpoori Thakur, after one year of being in office consolingly told the people that Rome was not built in a day. He stated that expectations had been raised with their mere coming to power and when all expectations were not being fulfilled, frustration had started growing among the people. Thakur boasted that despite all opposition from the vested interests, whatever the *Janata* Government had done in one year was more than what was done by the previous governments in thirty years. Facts, however, did not favour Thakur's tall claim. Neither state developed so much nor the people had been benefited by the policies of the state. Thakur, had, in fact, thrown the state into fire by intensifying the division of the society into backward and forward castes on the issue of reservation of seats for the former in the services. Although it was not only the programme of *Janata* party government but its predecessor government had also brought such a bill in the house but the way in which the *Janata* Party government and Karpoori Thakur adopted this bill and made speeches to get popularity among the numerically strong backward classes agitated the forward classes no end who were not prepared to accept it. Thakur as the CM, however, took some popular measures such as giving appointment letters to thousands as engineers and junior engineers at the Gandhi Maidan, Patna, exempting students from tuition fees up to matriculation, and appointing an efficient officer like Brigadier S.P. Kochar as the Chairman of the Bihar State Electricity Board with the hope that he would improve the generation and supply of electricity to consumers.

Ram Sundar Das, a *Dalit* who replaced Karpoori Thakur, had comparatively soft relations with the people. The *Janata* rule under him, however, was blamed for deteriorating law and order in the state. Heinous carnages at Parasbigha and Pipra took place under his regime. Das's personal reputation among people, however, was unsullied.

Jagannath Mishra who was restored to the leadership of the Bihar CLP in 1980 started with promises to serve the people with a big bang but an incident occurred which took place in Bhagalpur Jail involving blinding of many undertrial prisoners by the police officials in December, 1980. Jagannath Mishra was blamed morally for the incident and his resignation was demanded. Mishra tried to gain sympathy by accepting his moral responsibility[7] for the blinding episode which had no sanction of law behind it and was inhumane to the core but refused to resign on the issue. He tried to gain popularity among the Muslims by passing the Bihar Language (Amendment) Bill, 1980, with some minor amendments to make *Urdu* the second official language of the state.[8] This decision of the Government was opposed in the houses as well as in the state from many corners. But Mishra, justifying his stand blamed the opposition parties, particularly the B.J.P. and the R.S.S. of creating confusion and misleading the people over language issue. He assured the people to provide similar opportunity to other languages also for their development. But *Janata* Party President, Chandrasekhar, blamed him for anti-Urdu stir. Chandrashekhar pointed out that the manner in which Urdu had been declared as the second official language of the state gave an impression that it had been done only to get cheap popularity. If the CM was sincere, quick decision should have been made about its implementation, Chandrashekhar opined. Mishra wanted to make bridge with the people and with this view, urged the Congress (I) legislators and party workers of all ranks in Bihar to go to remote *panchayats* and villages to hold camps at the levels of villages, *panchayats* and blocks to fulfil the target of enrolling two lakh new old-age pensioners. Mishra also tried to universalize education by converting many affiliated colleges into constituent ones, by allowing the opening of non-aided colleges; and made generous deals with the teachers by improving their pay scales, etc. He also initiated democratisation of the university set-up, ensured prompt release of grants paved the way for cleaning up mess of the educational system and for making them truly autonomous. He also tried to satisfy the employees of the state by implementing the report of the fourth pay commission and by accepting to pay salaries and Dearness Allowances (D.A.) to them at Central rates. But these monetary grants could not extricate Mishra from the endless agitations of unemployed engineers, graduates and others. People's aspirations had been aroused and they were clamouring for the fulfilment of all the plans and programmes chalked out by the government. People of all castes, religions, professional groups, classes, strata, and region were on an agitational mode. Mishra, himself a college teacher of Economics, spent funds of the state lavishly. Moreover, his being respondent in some serious cases[9] of corruption cost him his popularity and ultimately, the office he held.

C.S. Singh assured the people of Bihar to provide a fair government and ensured that their life and property would be protected. Though these words carried weight, he could not provide good governance to the state as he remained busy in exchanging hot words with his predecessor or in making visits for talking to Delhi leaders. Although Singh tried to look into the problems of the people and attempted to solve them, his tenure was a truncated one and his image was more of a university don or a polished bureaucrat than a politician with roots among the people of the state.

Bindeshwari Dubey, a labour leader tried his best to establish good rapport with the people. He went to the remote areas and looked into the basic problems of the people.[10] Dubey was popular among the people for his clean image, for readiness to listen to public grievances and for trying to find some way out for the development of Bihar. He successfully tried to control riots and violence by Operation Task Force, Operation Two, Black Panther, etc. in the different disturbed areas of the state.

Laloo Prasad and Nitish Kumar, in contrast, have been leaders of the people. They made mass contact through *rallies* and *yatras*. Nitish Kumar meets people in weekly organized *Janata Darbars*, listens to their grievances and receives their petitions. He tries to redress their grievances then or there or as soon as possible. His *Seva Yatras* have been tremendously successful in building bridges between the government and the people. The CM is at the door of the people, listening to their grievances, redressing their grievances, overseeing the implementation of governmental schemes and projects and passing appropriate orders on the spot. This is a fine example of good governance.

CMs AND BUSINESS HOUSES

CMs have had connections with the industrial and

business houses. The Tatas with their big steel industries at Jamshedpur (now in Jharkhand) had vital links with the government and their permanent resident representative in the state capital nursed and maintained the link with the government. The role of Tata's money in the elections as also in making and unmaking of the CMs had been a marked one. Other industrial houses like the Dalmias also operated in Bihar and ran sugar mills, etc, for decades; and maintained links with the CMs but most of the sugar mills of Bihar are closed now and so are the links. The industrial houses also feel secure with a stable government and with smooth maintenance of law and order. They generally had better relations with the Congress party CMs (52-67), though they gave funds to other parties also for election purposes. When the United Front government was in power, the Revenue minister of the CPI breathed fire against the Tata house and took the unprecedented step of the abolition of Tata's *zamindari* to see the step judicially attacked and finally, Tatas retained the *Zamindari* when the Congress government came back to power. But the industrial prospect of the Tatas had worsened to such an extent during the UF government that they had abandoned the plan to expand their factory at Tata and had opened their new branch at Pune. The situation was retrieved when the Congress government came back to power and normalcy was brought back. Laloo Prasad made foreign tours and made appeals to investors to invest in Bihar but got no response. Nitish Kumar has been trying the same. His Finance Minister negotiated with sugar barons to re-open sugar mills. Some positive responses by investors appear to be in offing but no tangible results are visible as yet.

CMs have nexus with big and small businessmen, contractors from class A to C as well as the licensees and permit holders. The Aiyer Commission was seized with the shady deals between a minister of S.K. Sinha's cabinet, M.P. Sinha and the famous business house of Bangalore—the cases lingered on for long between the government and Ramaiyah involving huge misappropriations of public funds. K.B. Sahay was said to have link with Chanchania, a business magnet operating from Dhanbad. The deals are more camouflaged now since the Aiyar and Mudholkar Commissions have taught the politicians to be cautious, if not scrupulous. The deals have had also been made at the middle and lower levels with the tacit connivance of the top leadership. A new class of contractors, *quota* holders and transport operators has emerged which is replacing the feudal landed class in terms of economic, social and political power. The new class thrives with the backing of political class of brokers and bureaucrats which distributes state's funds and opportunities to them. While this happens in gaze of the public, the public remains a mute spectator lacking in both articulation and individual or collective motivation to check it. The CM presides over the system against whose imperatives these things cannot go on happening. For Nitish Kumar also, it is Gordian knot to break the nexus; so the nexus has been operating in the era of good governance.

CMs AND TRADE UNIONS

The relationship of the CM with the labour unions is delicate but important. In the labour fields of Jamshedpur and Dhanbad (both are in Jharkhand now), Congress and Communist parties run labour unions, compete with each other and a class of Union leaders, reinforced by musclemen emerged. In almost each ministry, there is a representative from the party ranks of the union. Bindeshwari Dubey, a Union leader made to the top of state politics from there. However, Union leadership is only a reflection of party leadership and does not stand comparison with the autonomously and independently acting pressure groups of modern Europe. Laloo prasad had broken the backbone of trade unions by dividing their leaders and workmen on caste-lines. So the spirit of the idiom 'My Union is my Union' got replaced by 'with my castemenas CM, my first loyalty is to him and then to any union or organization'. So trade unions weakened and they continued to remain weak in Nitish Kumar's regime also who, too, is a match to Laloo in being adept in social engineering while putting on the cloak which fits those who aspire or clamour for good goverance.

Political parties have their wings among students, teachers, doctors, lawyers and non-gazetted employees. The CM is ever conscious about these wings and Unions; and he tries to refurbish his own image and that of the party through distribution of funds and patronages. Nitish Kumar announced that elections to students' unions would be held shortly. Classes are the offsprings of the newly mobilized society, though they are still rooted in rigid traditional structures. Whereas the political mobilization of the organised sector is behind the scene, the mobilization of the society through traditional structure like religion, caste and regions is on the surface. The CMs, for long, had to contend with the *Adivasi* and *Mithila* regional leaders; the former demanding autonomy and the later a recognition of their language; both of them got what they wanted. The demand for *Mithilanchal* is gaining ground now; whereas other dialects like *Bhojpuri* and *Magahi* are vying for their inclusion in the syllabi of universities or Bihar Public Service Commission. In 1967, the Urdu group secured place in the seventh schedule after hectic electoral mobilization. *Bhojpuri* has also been included in the seventh schedule. *Urdu-Parsi* University has been established in Patna. The mobilized sections make a deal with the CM and the government; and get their demands met. For the last few years, domestic helpers have also been organised and mobilized like tenants of the urban houses and apartments and *bataidars*.

THE CM AND THE PARTY

In a parliamentary democracy; as a matter of fact, in any democracy where people's representatives have to be elected and entrusted with the task of administration of the country and its units, the party system plays a very crucial role. In the absence of a vibrant and healthy party system, the necessary infrastructure for a functional democracy will be missing. For the functioning of a democracy, it is necessary that the parties which function should be permeated by intra-democratic ethos and structural pattern. They must allow the principles of democracy to operate within the party otherwise parties which permit authoritarian trends within lead to the creation of situation of failure in the functioning of democracy beyond. When we look upon the functioning of political parties existing today in India, we rarely find that they are functioning in a democratic manner.[11] In every election, political parties with different programmes compete with one another but that is not enough. The maintenance of inner party democracy party's accountability to its constituents and workers, maintenance of its accounts and its public display on the website as well as annual auditing of funds collected from specified sources are the *sine qua non* of sound electoral politics. It is a pity that the union government has adopted luke ward attitude towards suggestions for electoral reforms put forward by different committees, commissions and even the Election Commission of India.

The relationship between the CM and the party is not a defined one, it is regulated by conventions evolved over the years. As in India, the controversy in respect of the relationship between the PM and the party is the product of the past history of the Congress party and the result of the efforts of its leaders to give continuation to the history. However, in Bihar, the relationship between the CM and the party, for the most part of the period, is the product of the past Congress history. It is evident that right from the beginning, in the history of government in Bihar, the Party's influence over the process of government has been supreme. In 1937, when under provincial autonomy, the Congress party assumed responsibility for governance in some of the provinces (Bihar was one of them), the supremacy of the party and its leadership over the nascent governmental wing was axiomatic. Governments came into existence in the provinces after getting green signal from the All India Congress Committee in 1937. The fact that the leaders of the national stature of the party kept themselves away from these governments reinforced on their part a tendency to treat these ministries as agents or sub-ordinates of the Congress Party. Nehru, the then Congress President, laid down that the governments in the provinces should consult the PCCs, though the later were not to intrude into day-to-day decisions.[12] He also held that ministers and the Congress Parties in the legislatures were responsible to the Congress and only through it to the electorate[13] and that they 'being the creation of Congress can be ended at any time by Congress'.[14] Consequently, all the interim governments tendered its resignation in 1939 at the instance of the party's direction.

The strength of a CM lies in the support he enjoys from his party at the Central and at the state levels. Even when he happens to be a nominee of the Central leaders, he must be able to bring state party organisation within his confidence in order to function effectively and efficiently. The CM is central to party structure, central to its programme formulation, central to ticket allotment, electoral campaign and achievement of electoral victory and finally, to the alround development of the state. He is the chief spokesman of the party in the state and chief representative of the party to fulfil the promises made in its election manifesto. The CM is mainly responsible for putting the party programme and policies into action; the image of both the party and the government depends on his efficiency, sincerity and achievements.[15] The political stability and instability depend *interalia* upon the CM's strong or weak leadership.

For a careful study of the relationship between the CM and party, we can divide the periods into four phases:

(i)	1937-39, 1946-1961 and 1967	The phase of Consolidation.
(ii)	1968-1971	The phase of chaos.
(iii)	1972-89	The phase of Central Domination.
(iv)	1990-2012	The phase of Regional and Backward Domination.

The pre-independence phase appears to be one in which there were feuds but the position of the Premier *vs.* the party president were not compromised.[16] The Premier S.K. Sinha (later called CM) did not face any hardship in enjoying the co-operation from the party. Having a domineering personality and unrivalled position in the party and government in the state, he impressed not only the government and the party in the state but the Centre as well. The relations between S.K. Sinha and the Congress Presidents in Bihar had been good except for a short period. There were teething problems followed by more troubles later on. In the very beginning, there were differences between S.K. Sinha and Mahamaya Prasad Sinha, the Congress Chief. Balchand rightly comments, "the big question that divided S.K. Sinha the leader of government and Mahamaya Prasad Sinha as president of Bihar Congress was one of primacy between government and party. In the long drawn battle, it was inevitable that the leader of the government should do better".[17] It is a fact that in Nehru's time, most of the CMs could consolidate their own position and some of them even ignored Central direction on policies that did not suit them.

S.K. Sinha was also the President of the B.P.C.C. in 1936, a member of its working committee and in fact, the life and soul of the Provincial Working Committee and of the Congress organisation in the state for over thirty years. This long period of service at the help of the state is a proof not only of the great popularity and confidence which he enjoyed in the party but it symbolises also his great qualities as a co-ordinator between party and government. At one time, he developed differences with Lakshmi Narayan 'Sudhanshu', the President of the B.P.C.C. on the issue of inclusion of some followers of Siyaram Singh of Bhagalpur in the Congress whom 'Sudhanshu' did not include on the ground that they were bad elements. S.K. Sinha took it seriously.[18] B.P.C.C. Presidents, Nand Kumar Singh and Prajapati Mishra had very good and cordial relationship with S.K. Sinha. In the early fifties, two identifiable factions developed inside the Congress Party in Bihar. Though Mahesh Prasad Sinha was proposed for a berth in the cabinet by A.N. Sinha at the first instance, Mahesh Prasad Sinha because of personal affinity and primordial affiliation came to be identified as the "weakness incarnet" of S.K. Sinha. K.B. Sahay who, on the other hand, had begun as a minister as a confidant of S.K. Sinha felt that he was being gradually replaced by Mahesh Prasad Sinha and therefore, Sahay became identified in the latter period with A.N. Sinha. These identifications came to the public gaze and also led to open incriminations between the supporters of the two factions. M.P. Sinha and K.B. Sahay started hotly engaging themselves in accusations and counter-accusations against each other under the shadow of S.K. Sinha and A.N. Sinha respectively.[19] The Congress Party in Bihar continued with the politics of factionalism from its beginning. The politics of Congress in Bihar started revolving round individuals, and the process of combination of castes and changes of alliances started operating accordingly.

After the death of S.K. Sinha in 1961, factionalism, groupism and caste combination intensified; their base was broadened and the way was paved for the instability and short tenure of governments in Bihar. Caste leadership became more rigid and entrenched and it no longer remained an upper caste phenomenon as it had been in the fifties. Intermediate caste (particularly *ahir*) leadership was mobilised because they had substantial numerical strength in the capital town, its adjoining rural areas and physical strength in the state as a whole. Reinforced by their physical and material resources, this caste unified under its leader, Ramlakhan Singh Yadav, at that point of time, who, commanded great support structure and huge resources of political mobilization in the traditional society of Bihar.

The mobilization of powerful support structure against the group which had been entrenched in power for about seventeen years was one reason why election for the successor of S.K. Sinha could not be avoided. The non-Bhumihar Congress leadership was groaning under the long spell of a rule which had created feeling of *Bhumiharism*. They now set up B.N. Jha as leader of the CLP as against Mahesh Prasad Sinha who was identified as a caste leader and had following mostly among legislators of his own caste. B.P.C.C. President, A.Q. Ansari called a conference of three top leaders of Bihar Pradesh Congress party viz., D.N. Singh, B.N. Jha and Mahesh Prasad Sinha at *Sadaquat Ashram* to avoid leadership election but the effort failed. Congress politics by now was bereft of the aura of being a party of freedom fighters and of sacrifice-orientedness; the infighting within the Congress had started bitterly. The new leaders of the Congress Party, disgruntled ministers and the followers of the dissident leader were busy in arranging combination of groups and castes with the motive to find place in the government. One could doubt if the Congress as a political party was at all observing the relationship between the homogeneous CM and the party factions. Congress High Command suggested, "In the interest of closer coordination between the governmental wing and the organisational wing, there should be a committee of 7 members, representing the ministry, the Pradesh Congress Committee and the Congress Parliamentary Board. All this is designed to create conditions for the functioning of the ministry on desirable lines".[20]

However, the fact stands out that the Congress party both at the Centre and the state failed to bring out any mechanism or rule to restrain the infighting among the Congressmen. Inside the cabinet, the ministerialist and the dissident groups freely functioned and the party was marked by dissensions or disunity. By 1962, the problem of factionalism in the Bihar Congress had grown worse. A three man committee of Bihar provincial Election committee consisting of the then CM, B.N. Jha, the then dissident leader K.B. Sahay and the then B.P.C.C. President, A.Q. Ansari had attempted to draw up an agreed list of candidates but they too were divided and ultimately, a special sub-Committee comprising Swaran Singh, L.B. Shastri and Indira Gandhi was appointed to work with the then CM, B.N. Jha in finalising the list. After the election again, factionalism in the Congress party continued unabated, Any how, B.N. Jha retained his office only to lose it soon to K.B. Sahay under "Kamaraj Plan" for ostensibly enabling B.N. Jha to serve the organisational wing of the party. No specific organisational work was, however, allotted to Jha as to others except the architect of the plan, Kamraj.

When K.B. Sahay was the CM, the Congress Party in Bihar was divided into four main groups which were functioning freely before the General Election in 1967, respectively led by (i) the then CM, K.B. Sahay himself (ii) a former CM, B.N. Jha (iii) a former B.P.C.C. President, Mahamaya Prasad Sinha and (iv) the Raja of Ramgarh, Kamakhya Narayan Singh. The then CM, K. B. Sahay had acute differences with the top party leaders of the state. He had also vetoed over the inclusion of the Raja of Ramgarh in the Congress party but his views were ignored and thus, the Central Congress party leaders had contributed to the worsening of the situation in the state Congress party in Bihar. The party President, Rajendra Mishra was unsuccessful in managing and maintaining party discipline. The deep rooted factionalism, infighting within the party and lack of coherence in the selection of party candidates contributed to the party's debacle in the state. As a matter of fact, Bihar had been the hot bed of factional politics and in all the elections, large scale bargaining and horse-trading had been resorted to by Congress leaders to get their favourites selected as candidates necessitating the intervention of some Central leaders to arbitrate among the various groups. But the features were more marked in the sixties than they had been in the fifties. In 1961, the groups led by late S.K. Sinha and late A.N. Sinha had jostled together to obtain the largest number of seats in the P.E.C. But the magnitude with which in 1967, the combined group of K.B. Sahay and S.N. Sinha entered into straight contest with M.P. Sinha—B.N. Jha group was spectacular. It is no wonder, therefore, that the Congress defeat in 1967 is largely attributable to the division among the Congress ranks particularly manifested in the defection of Mahamaya Prasad Sinha[21] and the Raja of Ramgarh groups from the Congress; and continued strains in the relations between the K.B. Sahay and B.N. Jha's groups in the party.

The Congress party which had occupied centre stage for twenty-one years was humbled both in the fourth General Elections in 1967 and in the mid-term poll of February, 1969 as a ruling party. Opposition parties from the extreme left to the extreme right and the middle of the centre combined against the Congress, propelled by the common motto of 'non-Congressism'. This resulted in the formation of coalition of disparate parties to come to power and form ministries. The very heterogeneity and lack of unity on the part of the strange bedfellows was such that between March 1967 and March 1972, as many as nine coalitions were formed and functioned for small periods.

THE PHASE OF CHAOS

The precipitating cause of the defeat of Mahamaya Prasad Sinha-led UF Government was that seven members of the ministry belonging to different parties, who were reported to be sore over the distribution of portfolios, had voted against the ministry. With this, a chaotic period appeared in the body politic of the government of Bihar—a period in which several UF Governments came into being, all of them short-lived and concerned only with seeking the support of various constituent parties to remain in power. Since 1967 General Elections, four coalition governments collapsed in Bihar up to June, 1968.

None of these governments had succeeded in giving a clear and a stable government to the state due to the frequent defections, betrayal and polarisation among the parties for satisfying their thirst for power.

In the scenario of chaos and being unseated from power, the Congress had got an opportunity to set its house in order. It is a fact that in the mid-term poll of 1969, the election of the P.E.C. for the mid-term polls was without contest, though not without wrangling. As on previous occasions, this time also, Congress leaders were labelled members of "majority" and 'minority' groups. While K.B. Sahay, M.P. Sinha, S.N. Sinha, A.S. Singh and R. L. Singh Yadav, etc. belonged to the former group; Rajendra Mishra, D.P. Rai, K.N. Tiwari (M.P.), D.N. Tiwari (M.P.), A. Q. Ansari etc, belonged to the latter. The Congress President, A.P. Sharma had been the agreed choice of the majority group leaders and their being in majority in the B.P.C.C. was unquestioned. The minority group leaders had no chances to win even one seat out of ten if they forced a contest. So they agreed to be satisfied if their two terms of having three of their members in the P.E.C. and a fourth general Secretary of the B.P.C.C. of their choice, were met. On September 8, 1968, the B.P.C.C. unanimously authorised its President, A.P. Sharma, to nominate the P.E.C. members and three more names for the executive committee. On September 9, A.P. Sharma nominated the following members of the P.E.C.: K.B. Sahay, M.P. Sinha, S.N. Sinha, R.L. Singh Yadav, A.S. Singh, D.L. Baitha, Nawal Kishore Sinha (all belonging to the majority group) A.Q. Ansari and Rajendra Mishra (minority group).[22] The next day, B.R. Munda (majority group) was nominated as the tenth member. Thus only two out of ten seats went to the minority group. Leaders of the minority group decided to withdraw from the B.P.C.C. executive and the P.E.C. Consequently, Rajendra Mishra and A.Q. Ansari resigned from the B.P.C.C. executive and P.E.C. and D.P. Rai and Prabhu Nath Tiwari resigned from the P.E.C. executive. However, they withdrew their resignations at the request of the then All IndiaCongress Committee (AICC) President, Nijalingappa and in order to appease them, Prabhu Nath Tiwari was nominated fourth general Secretary of the B.P.C.C. This episode proves that the Congress party members, even after losing power in the state, did not see the utility of giving a united show and their bickerings were no less prominent though statements were made from time to time that there was unity in the Congress.[23] But some times, there came damaging statements, too, like one coming from progressive front suggesting that five or seven top leaders should refrain from considering the party as their personal property.[24] After mid-term poll in 1969, formation of a Congress-led government led by Sardar Harihar Singh in Bihar marked a change in Congress politics in the matter of participation in multiparty coalition government.[25] But the C.W.C. was reported to be divided over the issue of the Congress forming a coalition in Bihar without prior agreement on principles and programmes. The inclusion of K.N. Singh, and the refusal of the dissident leader, D.P. Rai particularly caused intense feelings of differences. C. Subramaniam supported by Kamaraj and J. Ram attacked while S.K. Patil and Y.B. Chavan defended the Board's decision to permit the party to enter into a coalition in Bihar. Nijalingappa took full responsibility for permitting Sardar Harihar Singh to include the controversial Raja (K.N. Singh) into the cabinet and even he offered to resign from the Congress presidentship on this issue.[26] His resignation, however, was not accepted. On March 8, 1969, C. Subramaniam resigned from the C.W.C. as a protest against Raja's inclusion. In Bihar, Kedar Pandey and Abdul Ghafoor too opposed this on principle and started a signature campaign to remove Harihar Singh from the leadership of the C.L.P. In the meantime, split[27] in the Congress took place both at the Central level and also in Bihar and accordingly, a new president was elected. K.B. Sahay was the President of the new party known as Congress (Organisation) parallel to A.P. Sharma, who remained with the pro-Indira Congress (Ruling) typically known as congress (R).

THE PHASE OF CENTRAL DOMINATION

Some hopes had been raised by the split but the new B.P.C.C. (R) showed, as its predecessor organisation had in the past, that it was conflict-torn. Even after division of the party, Congress (R) was full of dissension. The same labels of 'majority' and 'minority' groups came into the open. This time,

Kedar Pandey, L.N. Jha, Devsharan Singh, Jamuna Prasad Singh and J.N. Choubey were some of the leaders of dissidents or of minority group. Kedar Pandey openly told the press that if the new Congress failed to give up its old 'dictatorial habits', the future of the party in Bihar was bleak.[28] However, the interference of the Congress high command had sober effect on Kedar Pandey and his cohorts. The Congress high command advised the group not to create a crisis among the Congress rank and file to which they headed. The grip of the Central Wing tightened. It is generally understood that it was not the grip of the wing, but that of its leader, Mrs. Gandhi that had overgrown, that she had a final say in any decision of the party and that she finally checked the list of B.P.E.Cs. and reached a decision as to allotment of Congress tickets to candidates in her own wisdom.[29] She was doubtlessly supreme all over the country in her own party. But in 1971, she was not the one and only one. In the case of Bihar, the list prepared by the P.E.C., was considerably changed and modified to suit the needs and aspirations of the three Central leaders, Mrs. Gandhi as well as Jagjivan Ram's son and *samadhin*. Another notable point was that in the selection of candidates, pragmatism rather than idealism became the guiding factor. In spite of all talks about secularism and the like, congress (R) took care to set up only those candidates whose caste or religion compared favourably with the majority caste of the constituency. In *Brahmin* dominated areas, *Brahmin* candidates were set up; in *Bhumihar* dominated areas, *Bhumihar* candidates were selected and so on. The choices of Muslim for Purnea, of a *Bhumihar* for Muzaffarpur, and of a Brahmin for Motihari examplify the consideration that prevailed in the setting up of candidates. The split did not make much difference; Congress (R) inherited the symptom of identity politics from the undivided congress. Dissidence continued to be organised around personal, familial, feudal and caste loyalties. But the record must be put straight. Not only the Congress but other parties in Bihar, too, have been faction-ridden and the difference between them to the extent is certainly not significant. They are plagued by casteism particularly in the setting up of candidates for elections. This leads to fragmentation of parties. Every fragmentation creates more leaders and every faction with a following of a few legislators makes a bid to a position from which it could bargain with or bully any CM-that be. The CM has to pay the price demanded for the support lest the M.L.A. or men of his group should go over to the other side and strike a bargain with the opposite side. Many M.L.As. in Bihar in this period ceased to represent anything but their own "particular will" (to use Rousseau's phrase); and parties were fragmented to the point of making any show of unity irrelevant. All these features marked the phase which we have, for this reason, termed as 'the phase of chaos'.

After restoration of power in 1972 to the hands of Congress (R) at both the levels of Centre and state, a new ministry was formed under the leadership of Kedar Pandey. A new trend was started to remove the deep rooted tendency of infighting in the party in the states. In order to affect cohesion and unity, resort to "democratic centralism" was taken as the natural course. The appointment of both the CM and the party president in the state passed on not only to be the exclusive domain of the Central leaders but to a single person combining in herself the offices of the PM and party high command- Smt. Indira Gandhi who had stood vindicated by humiliating the old leaders of the Congress party in the election of the Indian President and after the Congress split, by a spectacular military and diplomatic victory in the liberation of Bangla Desh on December 19, 1971 and by electoral triumph in the elections to many state assemblies in 1972. The power of B.P.C.C. President shifted to or were seized by the AICC and Congress Parliamentary Board (CPB) without any notice or murmur by the "loyal royalists". All important decisions of the B.P.C.C. bore the imprint of the party high command and accordingly, the CM emanated from and became responsible to New Delhi rather than to the state's wing of the legislative party or to any wider electoral base of his own. In Bihar, Kedar Pandey down to all the successive CMs of the Congress Party have been the choices of New Delhi and not those of the CLP of Bihar. For twenty years (1970-90), all the party Presidents of the state Congress party from A.P. Sharma down to D.L. Baitha have been nominated by the party high command rather than elected by the B.P.C.C. members. Many of them have been "dark horses", bereft of individual capacity of leadership and talent of administration. Some of them like Abdul Ghafoor and Jagannath Mishra who acquired stature after holding office for some yars were the Centre's nominees to begin with, i.e. when they assumed headship of the government in the state. So in this period, the relationship between the CM and the party relates to the CM of the state and the party at the Centre. And thereafter, no Congress CM influenced the party in any way.[30] They expressed their full devotion to obeying the party's policies, programmes (the Twenty or Twenty-five point) and aims under the instructions given by the Centre from time to time. They even acquiesced to the emerging extra-constitutional authority of the PM's sons who one after the other (not agewise) became decision-makers, youth leaders and real centres of political power emanating from the apex. If a CM failed to do so, he was pushed out of office. In this "dominant-Centre" phase, infighting and dissidence were checked from party politics in the state to some extent but that undermined and adversely affected the CM's power, personality and state's development programmes. Even the administration of the state was affected or checked by the Centre directly or through its political and non-political bureaucrats like Satpal Kapoor and P.M. Haksar—the super-entities of the PM's secretariat.

JANATA PARTY AND ITS CMs

During *Janata* party government in Bihar also, there were Central directives and the extra-constitutional authority of Jaya Prakash Narain had its way during the initial months but the authority was more democratically exercised than in the case of the Congress party. Formal election for the office of the Janata CM was held; and Karpoori Thakur emerged victorious as the leader of the JLP after defeating his rival for leadership, Satyendra Narayan Sinha who became the President of the *Janata* Party in the state. However, bitter relations started between the two and ultimately, the CM, Karpoori Thakur faced political crisis in which a large number of ministers of his own team deserted him and he had to vacate the chair.[31] Central leaders of the *Janata* Party did not make efforts to resolve the issue because they too were facing similar circumstances at the Centre. The successor of Karpoori Thakur,

Ramsundar Das, was the unanimous choice[32] of Thakur's rival group but a crucial role by Thakur and supporters at state level as well as at the Central level was being played. Neither infighting nor tendency of pulling down one's own government could be controlled by the leaders of the party. The CM of Bihar was not in a position to initiate any action which could minimise the poisonous exchanges among the party leaders. Ultimately, *Janata* party government at both the levels-central and state lost its grip over political power showing their inefficiency and calibre in handling the situation and problems despite the great popular enthusiasm with which they had been elected to power in 1977.

RESTORATION OF CONGRESS PARTY TO POWER AND THE CMs

After the revival of the Congress party in 1980 to power in Bihar, the former CM, Jagannath Mishra maintained good relations with the party. But dissidence was present. His rival for leadership (not open), Kedar Pandey was accommodated in the Central Ministry by the PM and high command to put an end to the dissidence that might emerge vigorously in the party. However, Kedar Pandey even from Delhi tried to pull strings and was represented by L.P. Shahi and others in the state Congress who were included in the state ministry and acted as his representatives. But by the passage of time and manifestly till 1983, Jagannath Mishra, who at the time of his elevation to power played second fiddle to Sanjay Gandhi and was most loyal to the dominant Centre, acquired grip over political management of the party in the state and started being arrogant and not as subservient to the Centre as the model demanded from him. There were also charges of corruption against him and his ministers. Consequently, he was replaced by a nominee of the Centre, though Mishra reportedly demonstrated in the full gaze of the Centre's reviewers that he was enjoying full confidence of majority of the Congress legislators. His two successors, Chandrashekhar Singh and Bindeshwari Dubey had been the nominees of the Centre. But C.S. Singh did not enjoy good relations with his predecessor, Mishra who continued to trouble him even against the will of the high command of the party. Dubey started in office as Mishra's man and started his innings as the CM with Mishra's blessings. Dubey's elevation to office was greeted by Mishra at a grand reception party organised by him in which about four thousand persons participated and among the enthusiastic hosts were some of Mishra's old colleagues in the cabinet who had been dropped by him on account of corruption charges and who, having been denied Congress tickets, returned to the Legislative Assembly as independents defeating their congress rivals. The Centre felt uneasy about Mishra's "*Janjagaran Abhiyans*" and his continued popularity. But the Centre was not inflicting direct punishment to him because he had established such a footing in the politics of the state that the Centre was afraid that any action against him might hamper the interests of the party. Chandrashekhar Singh had repeatedly complained to the Central leadership about Mishra's anti-party activities but they were not taken care of. Bindeshwari Dubey, after some weeks of friendship with Mishra, arduously started reshaping his image as an independent CM who was not aligned with any one-not even Mishra. He criticised the former CM, Jagannath Mishra for blaming the Centre to give inadequate aid to the state which had kept the state poor and under-developed. With the change of Central leadership from Indira Gandhi to Rajiv Gandhi, efforts were made to chalk out a compromise formula in the state of Bihar. Many Central party observers had been visiting the state off and on to ascertain the political situation in the state. Dissidence continued to mar the state Congress party. A conference of the supporters of Jagannath Mishra was held on the 14th of February, 1986, at the residence of an ex-minister, Billat Paswan 'Bihangam'. Ostensibly, it was called a compromise meeting but Jagannath Mishra did not attend this meeting because he wanted to test his own strength before launching any plan of action.[33]

Thus, we see that the Congress in the fifties had a strong CM and the Congress president also mattered. In the sixties, it was marred by factionalism but in the seventies, the Congress party developed dictatorial tendencies when decision-making at all levels had become centralised through development of a personality-cult which left all decisions to be taken only by the leader at the Centre. Even the democratic practice of allowing the state legislatures to choose their own CMs had been circumvented by installing the PM's nominee in every state. The result is that when the same party was in power both at the Centre and in the state, federalism practically ceased to exist and became virtually transformed into a unitary system.[34] This is evident with the illustrations of the CM-party relationship from 1972 onwards. This period stands in contrast with the period before 1967 in which some of the CMs of the state were strong leaders like Kamaraj in Madras (now called Chennai), Chavan in Maharashtra, B.C. Roy in West Bengal, C.B. Gupta in Uttar Pradesh and S.K. Sinha in Bihar. None of them was prepared to merely act as a tool of the Congress high command. CMs commanded personality and stature, were able to have their own way in decision-making and administration and above all, were the leaders of the people and legislators; and performers in their own right. The opposition at that point of time was equally non-performer, its commitment to democracy was unsatisfactory and hence, the Nehruvian phase of government-party relationship is remembered as one-party dominant system in which the dominant party itself played the role of opposition as well.

Laloo Prasad not only maintained close grip over his partymen but also kept the Congress and the left parties under lease. That accounted for his political stability. In contrast, Nitish Kumar does not maintain amicable relations either with his party men or his coalition partners except Sushil Kumar Modi. *Kushwahas* and *Bhumihars*, at one time or the other raised banners of revolt against him from behind the party but he was politically astute enough to soothe their feelings of hostility by inducting a few of them in the cabinet-reshuffle and by showing carrots to Arun Kumar, Jagdish Sharma, Sharma's M.L.A. wife and a few others. Arun Kumar is now out of JD(U); and the ex-President of Bihar unit of JD (U), continued to raise the banner of revolt and worked for the Congress party in 2010 Legislative Assembly elections while not deserting JD (U) formally. Even in the early years of his joining as CM, Nitish Kumar's relations with JD (U) Chairman, George Fernandes were far from pleasant and he got him replaced by Sharad Yadav. He denied the M. P. ticket from Muzaffarpur to George Fernandes which George was keen to get. George

Fernandes, an old man, fought the election as an independent and lost. Thereafter, Nitish Kumar made him a member of the *Rajya Sabha* to irritate Prabhunath Singh who, too, wanted the membership. Eventually, Prabhunath Singh left the JD (U) and joined RJD. Nitish Kumar irritated BJP by cancelling an invitation for dinner to BJP leaders and by putting the condition that Narendra Modi and Barun Gandhi would not come to campaign in the Assembly elections, 2010. He is now openly demanding that BJP assure him that it would not make Narendra Modi a Prime Ministerial candidate in 2014. Advani's write up in blog appears to favour Nitish Kumar's case as a PM's candidate which Nitish now aspires to be Nitish talks only to Jaitley and Sushil Kumar Modi of BJP and hardly talks in a friendly manner to any JD (U) leader. His behaviour towards colleagues shows arrogance,though he respects some senior colleagues. But Nitish Kumar has developed a personality cult before which both JD (U) and BJP are forced to acquiesce. On the birth day of Jayaprakash Narain, Nitish Kumar flagged off L.K. Advani's *Rath Yatra* which began from Sitab Diara and moved all over India; This endeared Nitish Kumar to the top brass of the BJP, helped him identify himself with the cause of eradication of corruption which was the avoid aim of the *Yatra*. Above all, Nitish Kumar could sidetrack Narendra Modi in his own party because Modi had to cancel the *Yatra* he was panning because Advani-Nitish stole the show. Meanwhile, Narendra Modi attacked Nitish Kumar for keeping Bihar backward because of addiction to caste-politics. Nitish Kumar retaliated by issusing a statement to the *Economic Times* that only a secular minded person would be acceptable as a Prime Minister in 2014. This started a war of words between the leaders of JD (U) and BJP with RSS chief openly siding Narendra Modi by issuing a statement that a *Hinduvadi* could not be prevented from being the Prime Minister of India.

THE CM AND THE PRESS

In establishing the relationship between the CM and the people, the press plays an important role in addition to personal and mass contacts that the leaders themselves make. Freedom of speech and freedom of press are the *sine qua non* of liberal democracy but the freedom of the press does not mean freedom of editors or of proprietors of press to publish whatever they like. If the latter are left free, they may become hot moulders but misguiders of public opinion. It is essentially the freedom of the public to receive information or in other words, the right of the public to know the correct position as against tainted or biased information in the context of which the press has to play its true role. The press assumes an important role in this case as a major vehicle of communication between government and the people. It is the duty of the press to inform the people as to what is going on not only in the state or the country but even abroad. In a multi-party system like India, where the policies and programmes of various political parties compete and even conflict for democratic legitimatization, the press can do a great deal in influencing public opinion so as to be able to make its ultimate choice of governmental responsibility. It has to reflect public grievances and hardships as also to report acts of omissions and commissions of administration affecting the welfare of the people. In a parliamentary democracy, press has to play a dual role. On the one hand, it has to inform the public as to what is happening in the government and on the other, it has to publicize response and reaction of the public over the government's performance. The task is one that casts heavy responsibility upon the press. Once, Rajgopalachari had said that the Indian press should consider itself to be an active partner with the government in the task of solving the problems confronting the country. A free and independent press is as essential to a democracy as democracy is essential to the existence of free and independent press.

S.K. Sinha, the premier of Bihar was in favour of a free press but at the same time, he asked journalists to create sense of duty among the people. In an impassioned appeal to the press, he called for patience and judgment over controversial issues while expressing his desire that the press should work unfettered. He appealed to the press to create not only sense of rights but also sense of duties.[35] But at times, he had differences with the press for criticising the government's decisions and actions which had no basis or truth as a mater of fact. He had differences with the local newspapers like *The*

Searchlight and *Aryavarta* in 1949 with whose "tainted" publications of news he had felt irritated. His irritation reached such a level that he passed an order to remove the name of *Aryavarta* from the list of approved papers. But later on, he withdrew his own order.[36] The fact was that the *Aryavarta*, one of the leading Hindi dailies of Bihar, occasionally criticised his administration. However, if this was a crime worth punishment in the eyes of the then government, there could be no room for free public opinion in a democracy, and it implied suspension of fundamental rights of citizens. The reason for such an action was also not made specific in the Assembly by the government. The Revenue Minister, K.B. Sahay, denied in the Assembly even the necessity of consulting press Advisory Committee before taking such an action against the said newspaper. However, behind the quick reconsideration of withdrawal of his order by the premier of Bihar, S.K. Sinha lay an appreciation of the approach of not stifling the freedom of the press. Since then, S.K. Sinha, maintained good relationship with the press barring a few instances to the contrary and inspite of the fact that he did not refrain from making suggestions off and on to the press to be impartial and conscious of its own duty.

A peculiar event worth mention took place in the 1950s during S.K. Sinha's regime. M.P.N. Singh (a *Bhumihar*) played a mischievous role. He reportedly incited M.S.M. Sharma of The *Searchlight* to write venomously against S.K. Sinha and later, got Sharma beaten up by the hirelings to impress upon Sharma that this was the handiwork of the hirelings engaged by S.K. Sinha. However, M.P.N. Singh's nefarious act was discovered by Sharma and the CM-press relations could not be disturbed which Singh had designed to do.

B.N. Jha, had good relations with the press. He never blamed the press or any editor for going out of way. Addressing the first conference of editors guild in Patna on the 30th and 31st March, 1963, he stressed the importance of press but advised them to work for accelerating the pace and content of social change.

K.B. Sahay wanted a favourable press for the government. Even when he was the revenue minister in S.K. Sinha ministry, he was against unbridled freedom of the Press. He argued that Press should work with the government; and government was free to put a check on it. During his Chief Ministership, good relationship with the press became a causality. Once his relationship with The *Searchlight* became so much bitter that the editor of The *Searchlight*, T.S. George was arrested on the government instruction.[37] K.B. Sahay strongly believed that press criticized the government to suit the interests of and at the instance of its proprietors, the vested interests. Himself a leading protagonist of anti-*zamindari* system, Sahay believed that a monopoly or *zamindari* press can have no praise for the government's progressive measures. Freedom of the Press, therefore, turns into freedom of the capitalists and the owners of production and perpetuators of reaction to say what they like and not to say what is reasonable, proper and is commensurate with the "common" social good. This is a fact that as the trend towards leftist progress gained momentum, management of the press came under severe criticism from various quarters including the government. Views came to be expressed in favour of a 'committed' and responsible Press.

During the period of coalition governments in Bihar (1967 to 1971), the press took lead in publishing spicy news. Since there was no C.M. having full command over the government, CMs could not influence or check the press in breathing fire. It had become the normal course for the newspaper readers to go through the news of political bickering, polarization and defections of the leaders which the daily newspapers genuinely and tastily reported. The press highlighted the news of the J.P. movement in the years 1974-76 and the photos of Ghafoor were printed reflecting his weakness for toddy. The CMs during the period of coalition were only a silent spectator to the role and performance played by the press. They did not want to invite confrontation with the "Fourth Estate" because they had not found that their feet were politically and administratively strong enough to enable them to take any step for controlling the press. The situation did not alter much in favour of CMs even when the Congress came back to power in 1972.

The worst days for the press and the democracy, however, were witnessed during the emergency. The press during the emergency was muzzled in Bihar as it was elsewhere in North India; and news was published after pre-censorship. However, there are no reports of the kind of overdoing and intimidation to the extent Shuklas and Bansilals were accused of.

The *Janata* Party Chief Ministers started expecting too much from the press. They, at least once, accused the press for non-co-operation. Karpoori Thakur charged the press for adopting a hostile or non-co-operative attitude towards the government. The C.M. wanted that the press should highlight the news favourable to the government and take the line that whatever his government had done in one year was more than what had been done by the previous governments in thirty years. But it was difficult for the press to circulate such news because despite initial euphoria and populism, the *Janata* government was tottering on the front of law and order and good governance.

The greatest jerk to the relationship between the C.M. and the press came during the regime of Jagannath Mishra who made unsuccessful efforts to make the press favourable to the government by curbing the powers of the press. This led to serious differences between the C.M. and the press surpassing the dimensions to which it had reached under the governments of S.K. Sinha had K.B. Sahay who had differences with the press at times as discussed earlier. Inaugurating the Press Guild on January 18, 1981, Jagannath Mishra made an emotional appeal to the press to realize its social responsibility and play a constructive role in the socio-economic development of the country. The CM was very critical of the role of the press in the country in his speech that day. The press, he said, had to be freed from the clutches of the "vested interests" and it must be committed to the Constitution and the society as a whole.[38] The lofty words notwithstanding, Jagannath Mishra actually wanted newspapers of the state to print that Bihar was making a rapid progress in all the spheres under his able and dynamic leadership. The press was not ready to project this picture because that was not true; and newspaper readers wanted criticisms and not only applauds; and the Press had to be sensitive to the realities of the situation and also to what the readers saw and knew by themselves. It may be accepted that the Press, to some extent is dominated by the personal whims of its proprietors. The fight that ensued between the press and the C.M. was, in fact, the culmination of personal differences between the patron of *The Indian Nation, Kunwar* Jeeveshwar Singh (the nephew of Late *Maharaja* of Darbhanga) and Jagannath Mishra, a rich landlord of Saharsa, the two *Maithil Brahmins* who represented two poles of power spectrum-feudal ownership-*cum*-business; and politics while culturally and sociologically, drawing power from the same arena.

The CM, Jagannath Mishra charged that the press was determined in trying to blur the image of the government by flashing "false news". The contradiction issued by government found 'negligible space'. He also charged that freedom of the press was being misused and advised the journalists to keep in tune with the changing society. The things came to such a pass that the role of *The Indian Nation* was brought to the floor of the Assembly for discussion and criticism of that particular press had become a part of on-going state politics. The C.M. was even believed to have encouraged a strike of workers in *The Indian Nation*. The C.M. denied in the Legislative Assembly that his government wanted to curb the freedom of the press, and expressed his full faith in the freedom of the press but the fact was otherwise. Replying to the allegations that government had issued a circular to all the District Magistrates directing them to curb the freedom of the press, the C.M. admitted that his government had issued a circular to all the D.M.s. with a direction to request the newspapermen to get confirmation before publishing any news concerning the government.

Some Mishra-supporters argue that Mishra was conscious of the role of the press from the very beginning; and his actions were calculated to regulate the press so that it could appreciate better the government's thinking and doing. Criticizing the role of some national and state level papers, Mishra himself had regretted the tendency of some newspapers to twist the facts and to try to impose their thoughts and ideas without caring for the consequences. He also expressed himself in favour of a national policy on media. However, it is to be appreciated that Mishra was asking for more than an appreciation of government's views or actions; he wanted the press to behave.

Having repeatedly denied the news of curbing the powers of the press, the C.M., Jagannath Mishra, dramatically announced that the government would be introducing a Bill in the Bihar Legislative Assembly on the pattern of Tamil Nadu to restrain the newspapers from publishing baseless and unfounded reports and to this end, the government proposed to move Indian Panel Code (Bihar Amendment) and Criminal Procedure Code (Bihar Amendment) Bill, 1982. The Bill sought to insert an additional section to section 292 of the Indian Panel Code to discipline the "irresponsible" press and pressmen. It was declared that it would cover 'vulgar' or obscene writings and stories aimed at 'blackmailing' but the Bill was of such a nature that it would have put of the press freedom to great strains. With the thumping majority of the Congressmen behind, the Bill was passed by the *Vidhan Sabha* on July 30-31, 1982 amidst unprecedented chaos.[39] Newspapers and newsmen started breathing fire against the government and particularly, the CM. The Bill was, later on, opposed by several corners of the society.

The widespread feeling was that the government was proceeding towards dictatorial ideology; to stifle the freedom of the press was to abridge an important fundamental right of the people. 43 legislators of the ruling party (Cong. R) comprising Shivchandra Jha, Speaker of the Vidhan Sabha, and Ashwini Kumar Sharma, the then dissident leader, signed a memorandum which was submitted to the CM in which they urged the government not to hasten through the Bill without seeking the permission of Indira Gandhi, the PM. Two *Dalit* MLAs, Ram Ratan Ram and Mahavir Paswan also denounced the proposed bill to curb freedom of the press. The governor and President were urged not to give their assent to such a bill. There was also uproar followed by walkouts in the *Lok Sabha* by the opposition on this issue. On the other side, the CM, Jagannath Mishra went on collecting and establishing facts and arguments in favour of the proposed Bill. The proposed measure, popularly called the 'Anti-Press Bill'[40] hanged in doldrum under president's consideration and ultimately after one year of its passage from the *Vidhan Sabha*, under Centre's instructions, the infamous Bill was withdrawn on the 21st July, 1983 by the same CM who had introduced it and who was replaced from the Chief Ministership after a few days by Chandra Shekhar Singh. CM's action of withdrawal of the Press Bill was hailed by all corners of the society with the proverb "...tter late than never". So traumatic had been the impact of this long drawn out fight between the CM and the press and it assumed such national and popular dimensions that there had been a considerable lull and thereafter, no successive CM played any mentionable role in respect of curbing freedom of the Press. But the Press itself is interested in getting advertisements from the government of the day and therefore, some newspapers deliberately and consciously avoid publishing news and views which are highly critical of the performance of the government of the day, howsoever correct they may be. The Government also hangs the carrot before them and thus keeps the press under siege.

Both Laloo Prasad and Nitish Kumar controlled the press to a great extent. The press, however, published reports of misdoings under Laloo's regime but it wrote eagerly in praise of Nitish's government for one reason or another. Press Council of India Chairman, Justice Markandey Katju alleged in a speech delivered in Patna College in February 2012 that the media in Bihar was targeted if it worte against the government. He also announced that a three member panel had been constituted to probe complaints of Journalists.[41] The Bihar Government, too, would be free to present its views before the probe panel which would comprise mdembers of the Pres Council of India sub-committee consisting of Rajiv Ranjan Nag, Arun Kumar and Kalyan Brua, Justice Katju told PTI. The former Judge said that the panel would inquire into complaints of harassment in newspapers or magazines and would submit their report to him. He hoped that they would be able to ensure "fair, independent and impartial inquiry to find out the truth of the complaints". In a veiled attack on Nitish Kumar, Sushil Kumar Modi and Shivanand Tiwary, Justice Katju said: "I wonder that those who were sent to jail while oposing Emergency have clamped undeclared Emergency on press in Bihar".[42]

JD(U) and BJP objected to Justice Katju's remarks while the Congress and RJD backed the former Supreme Court Judge. Supporting the Judge, Union Minister Subodh Kant Sahay said that there was truth in his observations that release of government advertisements was being used to force newspapers to write positive news about the state government.[43] Justice Katju refused to offer comments against the offensove remarks made against him by Deputy Chief

Minister Sushil Kumar Modi and spokesman of the party, Shivanand Tiwary.[44]

The aforesaid discussion of the relationship between the CM and the Press, based on the assumption that the press is the medium through which people's grievances and government's ignorance or inaction can be highlighted and through which the plans and progress made by the government can be communicated should be read along with the rejoinder that the press too, should play its role in a constructive way and should not turn itself into a vested interest. Sometimes, it works as an agent of somebody to take political vendetta or to deify or tarnish the image of the government in a bid to symbolize its own emergence as a power group in its own right. The other side of the coin is that a strong CM (like S.K. Sinha or Jagannath Mishra) who possessed will power and command over government, cannot tolerate the freedom of the press to that extent. We have looked into destructive and power-seeking role to affect the news and views of the Press by the two CMs. Naturally, this created friction and tension between the two varieties of power bidders and power holders. Besides S.K. Sinha and Jagannath Mishra, K.B. Sahay and Karpoori Thakur too were sensitive towards the role of the press. The arrest of the editor during K.B. Sahay's regime was too much. The final lesson of the friction between the CM and the Press in 1983 is that it is not easy even for a strong CM to annoy the 'Fourth Estate'. After being unseated from power, Jagannath Mishra realized that a top politician should have his own Press. He became patron of a new Hindi daily newspaper *'Patliputra Times'* which had sophisticated printing and colouring machine. Through this newspaper, Jagannath Mishra tried to circulate his and his supporters' thoughts and views even against his Congress successors in the office of the CM and the powers that controled and tried to fiddle him from the Centre. However, the press did not run for long. But a question arises: if a CM bears the same yardsticks for his press, had Jagannath Mishra been ready to accept them? It appears that whoever is in power talks about others' role and duties but when he is out of power, leaves that legacy there and tries to do the same against which he had commented adversely during his tenure of office and power. Such unprincipled stands hamper the process of political institutionalisation which is in need if the government-people nexus is to have wide, legitimate and stable base.

Notes and References

1. *The Indian Nation,* January 17, 1967.
2. *Ibid.,* June 28, 1967.
3. *Ibid.,* March 23, 1975.
4. *Ibid.,* January 30, 1975.
5. *Ibid.*
6. *Ibid.,* April 6, 1975.
7. *Ibid.,* December 14, 1980.
8. *Ibid.,* December 17, 1980.
9. He was charged with signing as CM on a sheet from a back date in Tularam case. But the Supreme Court absolved him of the charge and did not punish him.
10. *The Indian Nation,* January 19, 1986.
11. But so is the experience of the socialist partner. Hence, political sociologists, following Michels' "iron law of oligarchy" have come to accept this to a certain extent.
12. B.P. Singh Roy, *Parliamentary Government in India,* Thacker, Spink and Co. Calcutta, 1943, p. 221; see also Michael Brecher, *Succession in India: A Study in Decision-Making,* Oxford University Press, London, 1966, p. 130.
13. Jawaharlal Nehru, *The Discovery of India,* Drummond. London, 1942, p. 82.
14. W.H. Morris-Jones, *The Government and Politics of India,* Hutchinson University Library, London, 1971, p. 37.
15. H.M. Jain, *The Union Executive,* Chaitanya Publishing House, Allahabad, 1969, p. 212.
16. A.N. Sinha, *Mere Sansmaran, op. cit.*
17. R. Balchand, "Sri Krishna Sinha-Blend of Emotion and Real Politik", *The Indian Nation,* Patna, April 2, 1978.
18. A.N. Sinha, *Mere Sansmaran, op. cit.,* pp. 427-28.
19. Discussed in Chapter 2.
20. *The Indian Nation,* Octobers, 1963.
21. Mahamaya Prasad Sinha was an important dissident leader in the Bihar Congress. He took an active interest in exposing some notorious scandals involving corruption and earned displeasure of the then dominant group in the Bihar Congress.

22. *The Searchlight*, September 10, 1968.
23. *Ibid.*, November, 1968, the Statement was made by Satyendra Narain Sinha.
24. *The Indian Nation*, September 10, 1968.
25. After the 1967 General Election, the Congress party had decided not to seek or be a partner in any coalition although later, it did support from outside minority governments in Punjab and Bihar in 1967-68 and formed a coalition with the Progressive Democratic Front in West Bengal in 1968.
26. Only two days after, on March 9, Nijalingappa said that a majority of C.W.C. including himself had been against Raja's inclusion, but he had to give his consent because Sardar Harihar Singh already stood committed to include him.
27. Discussed in the earlier Chapter.
28. *The Times of India*, January 4, 1971, also *The Searchlight*, January 4, 1971.
29. L.N. Sharma, "Selection of Candidates by Political Parties in Bihar for mid-term parliamentary Polls, 1971". *Journal of the Administrative Sciences*, Vol. XVIII, Nos. 1, 2 and 3, Jan.-Dec. 1973.
30. Discussed in early chapters.
31. *The Times of India*, April 19, 1979.
32. *The Indian Nation*, April 20. 1979.
33. *Jana Satta*, New Delhi, February 14, 1986.
34. Horst Hartmann, *Political Parties in India*, Meenakshi Prakashan, Meerut, 1977.
35. *The Indian Nation*, January 21, 1949.
36. *Ibid.*, April 9, 1946.
37. Vide an interview with a press reporter of *The Searchlight* and some important leaders.
38. *The Indian Nation*, January 19, 1981.
39. *Ibid.*, July 31, 1982.
40. The Bill was then used to be called "The Anti Press Bill".
41. *The Hindu* (Kolkata), 26.2.2012.
42. *Ibid.*
43. *Ibid.*
44. *Ibid.*

9

The CM and the Federal Process

In her long history, except for a brief period subsequent to the Act of 1935, India had never been a federal state. But the vast area, the large population, linguistic, religious and cultural diversities and the clamour of the people for local autonomy—all led the fathers of the Constitution to decide in favour of a federal structure. They wanted to balance the forces of unity with those of diversity; and the powers of the Union with those of the states. So the Indian Constitution well documented its centripetal bias. Article I of the Constitution stipulated in terms of 'a Union of States' but Article 3 granted Union Parliament the right to form a new state, increase or diminish the area of any state, alter the boundaries of any state and alter the name of any state. The backdrop of partition and the recalcitrant conduct of the rulers of princely states of Hyderabad and Junagarh in merging into the Union generated a marked feeling in favour of a strong Union to curb the rise of unruly forces (like Telangana, etc.). The use of the word 'federal' anywhere in the Constitution was intentionally avoided and the word 'Union' was used instead. After decades, the Supreme Court in

Keshavanand Bharati V. Union of India (1973), Minerva Mills *v.* Union of India (1980) and S.R. Bommai and others *v.* Union of India and others (1994) established the doctrine of the unamendability of 'the basic structure' of the Constitution of which federalism was illustratively declared to be a part. Ambedkar had explained that the word 'Union' used in the Constitution conveyed that the Union was lasting and indestructible; and that no state possessed the right to secede from the present Union.

While the Union wanted to maintain its supremacy, states were at the same time anxious to preserve their identity and independence which are not strong in modern times to face industrial expansion, massive economic growth at the cosmic level and the threat of terrorism and nuclear warfare. Indian federations, by their very nature, remained organic and functional.

Scholars have felt inclined to describe India as a "quasi-federation"[1] on the basis of institutional matrix and functioning while some have ridiculed it as a "pseudo-federalism".[2] W.H. Morris-Jones, taking a sympathetic view, calls it a "co-operative federalism".[3] The co-operation between the Union and the states in India particularly between 1946 and 1950 was the result of the state-building and nation-building endeavours of the two "leaders of the leaders" of the nation (called "duumirs" by Michael Brecher[4]) and the trust and co-operation verging to reverence extended to them by the strongest CMs of the Congress Party in the states (like S.K. Sinha, B.C. Roy, G.B. Pant, S.C. Shukla, etc.) followed by the small ones among the CMs. Most of the CMs had stayed with the "duumvirate" in British jails for pretty long time during the freedom movement. They had worked in unison under the leadership of Mahatma Gandhi and taken part as volunteers in Non-Co-operation Movement (1921), Salt Satyagraha (1920) and Quit India Movement (1942) besides day-to-day *Swadeshi Andolan* (Boycott foreign goods movement), use the wheels (*charkha*) movement, remove untouchability movement, etc. and indulged together in activities like service to the lepers, imbibing simple living and using of hands and feet to do all personal work by one's own effort. In one word, they had been partners in constructive programmes for decades before joining governmental work under the leadership of Nehru whom Mahatma Gandhi nominated as his successor in 1946 and by that means, the future PM of the country. To begin with, the relationship between the PM and CMs had thus the heritage of "partnership" in the national movement; since 1946, it extended to the realm of administration and governance. So it was a situation of *bhai-bhai* relationship between the elders; for a young CM, PM Nehru might be the uncle type but a situation of conflict of jockeying of position of power was not present at least till 1962. Even when some power conflict arose on the handling of defence portfolio by V.K. Krishna Menon after the Chinese aggression, it was not in the form of a public debate. Intra-group clashes occurred between Nehru and Patel; Nehru and Rajendra Prasad and Nehru and the Congress President, Tandon which ended in the ouster of Tandon from the office of the Congress President. But after Patel died in 1950 (differences between Nehru and Patel were both temperamental and political), both the Congress and the country were for all practical purposes in the hands of Nehru. In the conflict-torn days, the CM of Bihar, S.K. Sinha favoured Nehru against Patel, Prasad and Tandon. He was a Nehruiite like B.C. Roy, G.B. Pant and S.C. Shukla. Rajendra Prasad was known to be closer to A.N. Sinha, K.B. Sahay and J.P. than S.K. Sinha.

In the historical context of India, the emergence of "co-operative federalism" was a natural development, though Paul H. Appleby argues that the Union was much too dependent on the states for the actual implementation of major national programmes and the Union had little real authority in vital areas of policy and administration.[5] The notable fact, however, is perceptible inter-level co-operation in different fields including legislation. Any instance of co-operation of the states with the Union in the field of legislation is provided by the Estates Duty Act, 1953. Many of the state legislatures passed resolutions empowering the Parliament to legislate in regard to levy of succession duty on agricultural lands which under the constitution is a state subject. In administrative sphere, co-operation is all the more marked. The Union and state organisations worked in the spirit of harmony in carrying out Community Development Programmes and the state planning departments. Another fruitful line of co-operation is the utilisation of water resources. For example, the Damodar Valley Scheme in Bihar was a joint endeavour involving both the Union and the state of Bihar. The Union sends huge funds to run welfare projects to the states without which the states cannot perform meaningful development works. To institutionalise co-operation, the Indian federation acts through conference technique among the units and organizes conferences of the state governors, meetings of the CMs, and Ministers' of states and meetings of the Union and state officials from time to time. The Administrative Reforms Commission Report I on Centre-state Relations favoured the use of such conferences instead of establishing the constitutional forum of Inter-State Council (ISC). Even when different parties came to rule at the Centre and in the states, hopes were pinned on convening CMs' conferences to discuss and settle inter-state issues, specific state's problems or national problems. In a meeting in April 1967, however, the CMs were critical of Union's decision to curtail the overdrafts of the Reserve Bank of India to the states and of the reluctance of the Union to provide more assistance to the states for development plans and payment of Dearness Allowance to their employees. C.N. Annadurai, the then CM of Madras (now called Chennai) wanted the residuary powers residing, according to the Constitution of India, in the Union to be given to the states. Devaraj Urs, the then CM of Karnataka argued that there should be no concurrent list since it had created more confusion, and eroded and taken away the initiative of the states in the development works. Since 1990, the bogey of federalism is being used to flex political muscle and blackmail a 'weak' Union government. In the past, a C.M. like Chandrababu Naidu used to demand asymmetric treatment to his state on a variety of matters. But that did not reach the present stage of stalling every item in the Union government's reform agenda.

The Union and the states are partners in the developmental process; and quite a few co-ordinating bodies are available to facilitate consultation between the two units. The Planning Commission, considered 'super-cabinet' during Nehru's time was then the co-ordinator of planning all over the country. The National Development Council (NDC), formed in

1952, has been another co-ordinating body consisting of the PM and all the CMs. On November 4 and 5, 1962, it met in Delhi to consider the gravity of the situation created by the Chinese aggression and the resignation of the then Defence Minister, V.K. Krishna Menon. The CMs of almost all the states attended the meeting. Nehru called a meeting of a few CMs to discuss the border conflict with China. The CMs decided that they would side the PM in whatever decision he took on this sensitive issue.

The NDC appointed a standing committee in 1954 consisting of members of the Planning Commission and the CMs of nine states. It had also been decided that the CMs of one or more of the remaining states could be invited to attend the meetings of this standing committee. The CMs have been reportedly effective in making claims on the Union Government for larger grant-in-aid for their states, the establishment of public sector units in the Mahalanobis-days and in procuring licences for expansion of the private sector. However, the NDC meets infrequently and so lacks the regularity in making the efforts. Its meetings are more formal.

After Nehru passed away (in 1964), the trust of states in the capacity of the Union to look to the needs of states waned. Mahamaya Prasad Sinha, the then CM of Bihar felt so disgusted with the Union in 1967 that he appealed to the USSR to come to his state's aid to meet the famine situation (in Bihar). There was rise of the food and the language crises under the tenure of Lal Bahadur Shastri as PM. The states started making open defiance of the Centre. PM Shastri made attempts to moderate, reconciliate and negotiate with the states and institutionalise diplomacy by conference to appease the states through what Michael Brecher calls "the grand council" (meaning the conclave of CMs + party leaders, etc.)[6] However, Nehru's phrase of "unity within diversity" came to be turned upside down soon after his death; now it was a case of "diversity without unity".[7] Centrifugal tendencies which were kept under hold during the Nehruvian era came to the fore soon after Nehru was out of sight. During Nehruvian era, both power and political patronage flowed from New Delhi to the states, now the reverse process was on. V.K. Krishna Menon said at a meeting of students at Ahmedabad in January, 1965, "every state is behaving as if it is a separate country".[8]

Smt. Indira Gandhi did not have faith in either parliamentary or federal rule during the seventies. She adopted neo-patrimonial style of governance and dealt with not only the Congress but also the non-Congress CMs in this style. This led to tremendous increase in the power of the Union and the consequent decrease in that of the states. In course of time, this led to the rise of regional parties, regionalism and regional leaders or satraps and consequently, this resulted in their take over in the form of coalition government at the Union level since 1989 either led by V.P. Singh, the UPA or NDA governments.

Shastri did whatever he could to settle the contentious issues and his sending of warplanes to Lahore in the Indo-Pak armed conflict (1965) made him a national hero before his life was cut short suddenly at Tashkent.

India moved from co-operative federalism to bargaining federalism as different parties took charges at the Union and state levels in post-1967 political scenario. The bargaining process was the order of the day after the Fourth, Sixth, Ninth and from Tenth *to* Fourteenth *Lok Sabha* elections in India. Competitive bargaining (to use Morris-Jones' phrase)—formal as well as tacit, was resorted to by CMs in various institutional agencies such as the Planning Commission, N.D.C., Finance Commission, Inter-state Council (I.S.C.), Zonal Councils and a host of statutory bodies. The office of the Comptroller and Auditor-General of India, concerned with the accounts and auditing of not only the Union government but also those of the states, became functional. It has created ripples by submitting reports of siphoning off of huge funds of Central Government due to wrong policies pushed by some Union Ministers or Chief Minister in 2010-2011. Similarly, the Election Commission which conducts elections to the Union and the state legislative bodies, has gained in power and functions with the passage of time. Now it is being demanded that a plural body should appoint persons to the constitutional offices of Election Commissioner and chief vigilance commissioner. The Union has been using its power of control over a large number of state laws by various means which are available to it under the Constitution and used strong will on its part to use them. The constitution of National Investigative Agency to control terrorist acts was an innovative act on the part of the Union. It proposed to constitute National Counter-Terrorism Centre but could not do so due to the oppsition of certain states.

The emergencies declared in 1962, 1965, 1971 and 1977 contributed to making states subservient to the Centre during the period and especially when it was excessively exercised as it was done by Sanjay men particularly in Delhi and North Indian states during nineteen months of emergency in 1975-77.

In 1962, for justifiable reasons, Nehru had wanted B. N. Jha, the then CM of Bihar to get national highways constructed near Purnea in record time so that the Indian Army could pass through it and go on to Darjeeling onwards quickly. Nehru expressed ire when the road was not made ready in time and the army had to be stationed mid-way in Purnea itself. During the internal emergency period (1975-77), the then CM of Bihar, Jagannath Mishra acted at the behest of Sanjay Gandhi, throwing the federal process to wind. According to *India Today* survey, Jagannath Mishra in another spurt in office spent 29 days in the capital city (Delhi) out of 100 total days in office, obviously taking orders from and trying to please the Central bosses.

Since the 1990s, the Indian political system has moved significantly towards greater federalization. Dougles Verney points out that transformation of the Indian party system has led to a regionalized multi-partisan configuration which, in turn, has encouraged the transition of the Indian political system from 'quasi-federation' to 'quasi-confederation'.[9]

Article 263 providing for an Inter-State Council I.S.C. was left unused until 1990 because the Union Government thought that other forums would be more flexible than a constitutional forum like ISC. But the V.P. Singh Government formed ISC in 1990 at the beginning of the era of coalition politics at the Union to respond to an election promise of the Janata-Dal-led manifesto. However, the composition of the ISC overlapped with the N.D.C., so no innovation was achieved. Furthermore, the ISC could not be activated because of two reasons. First, coalition governments that came to be formed in this era tended to be unusually large assortment of parties, some of them heading state governments as well. Since many state governments found direct regional representation in the "federal" cabinet also, most of the intergovernmental matters could be negotiated at the level of the Union Cabinet itself. ISC was needed by those state governments only which were not represented in the Union government. Secondly, the NDC continued to be the forum for approval of economic plans. The recommendation of the National Commission to Review the Working of the Constitution (NCRWC) Report (2002) and the Common Minimum Programme (CMP) of the Congress-led UPA government had underlined the importance of the ISC as the key inter-government forum and had stressed the need to activate it in order to provide true federal spirit. But these recommendations were not paid due regard due to the exigencies of the political situation obtaining at the time which neither needed nor demanded the activation of the ISC.[10]

Formal discussions between the leaders of the constituent units of the Union government and supporting units of the coalition constituted the focal point of governance since 1989. The CMs could exercise influence through their party's representatives, though the bigwigs of the party were present in Delhi cauldron. The bulk of the nitty-gitty of inter-governmental negotiations and decisions since 1989 are carried out by occasional informal conferences of officials, ministers and finally, PMs/CMs. Zonal Councils, too, have by and large become defunct except for the North-Eastern Zonal Council (NEZC).

Finance Commission and Planning Commission provide important inputs but inter-governmental disputes are settled largely by political means. On the submission of the Eleventh Finance Commission Report in 2000, the then Andhra Pradesh CM, Chandrababu Naidu of (Telgu Desam Party) met the PM to register his anguish and dissatisfaction with the Commission's recommendations so far as it related to allotments of finances to his state, Andhra Pradesh. Of late, Bihar, West Bengal, Gujarat and several other states complain of unfair attitued of the Centre in allocating grants to their states or in approving schemes sent by them which required speedy action but the Union government sat on the files for long contributing to mal-development of the states concerned.

Bihar and U.P. got best financial deals from the UPA Government at the centre when these state government leaders supported the UPA's official candidate for the Indian President's office in 2012.

Prior to the emergence of politics of full scale regionalism at the union level during the nineties, Rajiv Gandhi had started pursuing an accommodative approach to regional ethnic demands and movements. During the 80s, anti-Hindi speaking states stood in rebellion against the Union. Except Tamil Nadu and Kerala in the South, peripheral states in the North-East and North-West, *Akali Morchas* and insurgencies in Punjab created insurmountable problems which needed to be solved. Inhabitants of J. and K., Manipur and North-East usually say that they are going to India when they leave their respective places to visit places in North India. Rajiv tried to put balm to the wounds of the angry states. In quick succession, the Union government under Rajiv signed accords with ethnic movements and parties in Punjab and Assam in 1985, Mizoram in 1986, and Tripura in 1988.[11] After nearly a decade of insurgency and repeated spells of Central rule, elections were held in Jammu and Kashmir (J&K) in 1996 and 2002 which can be acclaimed as a remarkable achievement for the revival of democratic process in a state torn by foreign-born terrorism and internal disturbances. It may, however, be noted that Rajiv Gandhi, too, did not pay importance to Congress CMs., he was soft to the non-Congress CMs only. In 2012, the three-members team of interlocutors headed by Dileep Padgaonkar constituted by the government of India has submitted a report which, if implemented, may go a long way in the normalisation of the political situation in J&K.

The installation of coalition and minority governments at the Union has increased the autonomy and prominence of state governments. Federal phase has really started after 1989. An indicator of this fact is that a prominent English Journal, *India Today*, yearly surveys who is the best CM of all and which is the best administered state. Narendra Modi (Gujarat) and Nitish Kumar (Bihar) have found pride of place as the best CMs while Laloo Prasad felt irritated in one of the conclaves of *India Today* because the state of Bihar under his stewardship was ranked very low.

The very style of analysis shifts the importance from how India is governed to how states are governed or institution-wise, from union cabinet/PM to state cabinet/CM. Akhilesh Yadav in UP, Jayalalithaa in Tamil Nadu, Naveen Patnaik in Orissa, Narendra Modi in Gujarat, etc. have emerged as regional sataraps. They demand dignity as CMs and despite their defiance towards the Union government and possessing dubious character, get popular recognition. Deve Gowda's (Karnataka) and Shiv-Sena-BJP government (Maharashtra) represented the federal pattern. The victory of BJP and formation of the party's governments in Madhya Pradesh, Himachal Pradesh, Rajasthan and Gujarat strengthened federal pattern. Similarly, the emergence of a regional party like INLD in Haryana subscribed to the federal pattern and led to the start of the federal process. On a wider scale, on the chessboard, the PM-CM relationship has to be based on a new pattern of federal relationship. In this connection, Supreme Court Judgment in Rameshwar Prasad V. Union of India (2005) against Buta Singh on Centre-State relations is a milestone. In 2007, in Sarvanand Sonwalkar V. Union of India case, the Supreme Court chided the Union government for the fact that though illegal migration in Assam was a "demographic aggression", the Union was not acting to check or protect the inhabitants of the state against aggressors. Thus judiciary has arrogated to itself the task of protecting the rights of states and not only those of the Union in the name of the national interest as used to be the case in the earlier years of independence. Now the argument is that if states are not protected, the nation and its people cannot remain secured. So the states have to be saved from foreign invasion, espionage, terrorist intrusion, internal subversions, and saboteurs, etc.

Nitish Kumar from Day 1 as CM has been vociferously demanding that Bihar be granted special category status like eleven states such as Arunachal Pradesh, Assam, Uttaranchal, Meghalaya, etc. on the basis of lack of electricity, irrigational potential, agro-industrial backwardness, per capita income, etc. He also demanded special package for meeting the ravages created by breaches in Kosi embankment in 2008. PM Manmohan Singh called the breach a "national calamity". But whereas the state had demanded Rs. 14,800 for rehabilitation of the Kosi deluge victims, Bihar got just Rs. 200 crore for the purpose; a suitable grant was not made available.[12] On both the counts, Nitish Kumar and his colleagues have made loud clamour. The CM had personally met the President, PM, Chairman of the Planning Commission, etc. more than once, wrote several letters to the PM which, according to the CM, had not been acknowledged and thus tried to keep the Union in the dock. There has also been a long drawn-out battle on the issue of the counting of BPL families in Bihar between Nitish Kumar and the Union. Whereas according to the count of Government of Bihar, the number of BPL families is round 1.5 lacs, the Centre's count keeps the number at around 65 thousand. The count of 65 thousand made by the Union deprives 85 thousand BPL families of the benefits of getting wheat or Kerosene oil through ration shops, if the count of the state and of some reports are to be put reliance on. Nitish Kumar cites Tendulkar Committee Report and Arjun Sen Gupta Committee Report to buttress his point of view as against that of the Union. However, Bihar procures the requisite fund under *Pradhan Mantri Sadak Yojana* (which has been utilised well by Nitish Kumar since he came to power and for which he has won praise at all quarters). In MGNREGA, mismanagement and corruption are rampant in Bihar as is the case in other Indian states. *Akshar, Anganwari,* etc. are doing comparatively well and the distribution of cycles to 1.70 lac girls for going to schools in 2007 has won popularity for Nitish Kumar. By 2010, the number of girls who got the cycles reached 4.516 lacs. He has also distributed Rs. 700 to secondary school girls under *Poshak* Yojana.

However, Nitish Kumar asserts his autonomy even where it is not required. In the wake of Mumbai terrorist attack, the Union enacted National Investigative Agency Act (2009). The Union Home Ministry convened a meeting of the CMs to discuss the pros and cons of the Act, the ways of its implementation and the proposals of improvement, if any. As the press reported, Nitish Kumar and Narendra Modi took the stand that public order was a state subject. So the Union should not have enacted this Act without the prior consent (read approval) of the states. The role of the states in the investigation of the terrorist acts was also resented. This instance proves that India has come far away from co-operative federalism even on a sensitive national issue like counter-terrorism where they should raise their first foot forward. Narendra Modi had also publically objected that some of his counter-terrorist proposals were not approved for months together despite reminders, requests and even a formal protest by the leader of the opposition, L.K. Advani. When the proposal was finally approved, it was so whittled down that it had become insubstantial for its ostensible purpose of fighting terrorism round the long coasts in Gujarat against the onslaught by Pakistan, Modi alleged. The opposition by the CMs to the Centre's proposal to constitute the NCTC was also not in good taste.

The CMs have thus become vociferous but it cannot be argued that they always have their way because the Constitution has vested more powers in the Union. In 2000, Laloo Prasad, the then CM of Bihar said that Jharkhand would be carved out of Bihar only on his corpse. But Jharkhand was formed as a new state by the Union Parliament and separated from Bihar, depriving Bihar of all the mineral resources and coal (which it badly required for generating electricity and due to the lack of which most of its units had to be closed down after the separation of the state). Despite the request of the Government of Bihar, the Union did not facilitate the transport of coal from Jharia (which falls in Jharkhand now and which abounds in coalmines) to the erstwhile electric generating units in Bihar leading to the plunge of Bihar's large parts in darkness in pick hours.

CM Nitish Kumar rattled out the "injustice" heaped on Bihar on several counts. While Bihar demanded Rs. 3.8 lakh crore from the 13th Finance Commission, it just got about Rs. 1.7 lakh crore only, Nitish complains. It just got Rs. 5,000 crore for primary education which was grossly inadequate. The state government wants to revive sugar mills. The proposal of the Government of Bihar to produce ethanol from sugar has been stalled by the Union which had banned production of ethanol. The state government has a grudge against the Centre's stand.

The spokesperson of JD(U) said that an independent organization in Delhi has proved that opposition-ruled states are getting about 6 per cent less funds than states ruled by the Congress and its allies. Bihar, in particular, is treated as an "internal colony" by the Union. Laloo-Rabri had also raised voices against freight equalisation.[13] In terms of royalty on iron and ore alone, Bihar before creation of Jharkhand was made to lose Rs. 1.10 lakh crore. Economists are cited to prove that Bihar has been ignored and the Central investment in Bihar is just 3 per cent, very low compared to West Bengal and Maharahstra where it is above 15 per cent.[14] Thus mounting resentment and grievances characterize the relations between the state of Bihar and the Union Government also because they are run by different coalition groups.

Centrally sponsored schemes do not render much benefit to states because states have to give matching grants to get the benefit of these schemes. Another factor that hinders growth is instability. Bihar's development became stagnant between 1961 and 1990 due to short tenure (about two years) of CMs. It also did not develop well due to maladministration between 1985 to 1995, the growth rate being about 3.2%. It was much behind the national average growth rate of 6.3% during the period of 1995 to 2005. But it has been registering an average growth rate of 11.4% since the year 2005 (Nitish's period). Growth rate of Bihar in 2008-09 has been declared by the Central Statistical Organisation to be 12%—the highest in India.[15] In 2011-12, it has been declared to be 14.15% and the recent declaration takes it to 13.1% which is the highest in the country. This is a rare achievement for which Nitish's government needs to be lauded. Bihar has shown remarkable improvement in the fields of manufacturing, construction, hotel-motel business and sales tax collection under the regime of Nitish Kumar. Yet, the Government of Bihar is not willing to take the responsibility to implement the Right to Education (RTE). The total budget of the state is Rs. 53 thousand crores in a year. In one year, an amount of Rs. 27 thousand crores will be required for meeting the expenses over the RTE.[16] The state of Bihar wants the Centre to bear the total expenses over the RTE and to hand over the total funds to the state for disbursal.[17] This appears an unfair demand.

This expression of inability despite increase in growth poses a major challenge as Bihar along with U. P. lacks adequate number of teachers and schools to ensure education to every child. The scenario is worst in Bihar where the literacy rate yet is 47.53 per cent.[18] The primary schools have witnessed a negative growth over a period of five years from 2002-03 including the period of Nitish Kumar.[19] The secondary and senior secondary schools have also witnessed negative growth rate.[20] Nitish Kumar's performance in the field of education has been far from satisfactory. The Minister of Higher Education did not find a minute's time to meet a delegation of teachers of universities till four and half years. Many of the promises made to teachers remained unfulfilled for long despite declarations made by the CM himself on the floors of the House. Untrained Primary Teachers were appointed on a poor salary of Rs. 4000-6000. Thus education is the Achilles' Hills of Nitish's period of governance. There are other angles to look at the role of the CMs in the context of the federal process.

A. CM's ROLE IN THE ELECTION OF THE PRESIDENT OF INDIA

As leader of the legislature of their respective states, the CMs tend to play a role in influencing the election of the Indian President. After the expiry of the first term of Rajendra Prasad as the President of India in 1957, Nehru was in favour of getting Radhakrishnan elected in his place. He held private meetings with the CMs of the four Southern states and told them informally that he would prefer a South Indian as President because a north Indian had held the post for a whole term and both the posts of PM and President should not be held simultaneously by north Indians. It would be more appropriate that if the PM was from North India, the President hailed from the South. All the four CMs of the South told Nehru that they were not concerned with regional considerations and were of the view that Rajendra Prasad should be re-elected if he was available.[21]

Much time was devoted to consultation with the CMs in the contentious election of the President in 1969. CMs were divided in their opinion about the choice of the Presidential candidate whom they wanted to have in office. Congress CMs who supported Sanjiva Reddy were Veendra Patil (Mysore), V.P. Nayak (Maharashtra), Hitendra Desai (Gujarat), M.L. Sukhadia (Rajasthan), S.C. Shukla (Madhya Pradesh), C.B. Gupta (U.P.) and B.P. Chhalia (Assam).[22] Brahmanand Reddy (Andhra Pradesh) was the only Congress CM who remained neutral. Bansi Lai (Haryana) and G.M. Sidique (J&K) openly supported V.V. Giri. Even after the two Congress Working Committees came to be formed and met separately, some Congress CMs made the last bid to find a basis for agreement and tried their level best to stop the Congress party from an imminent split but the CMs' formula was late to come. The CM's efforts were wrecked by a propaganda war between the PM and the Congress President over issues they were raising for political reasons such as the bogey of public sector *v.* private sector. The role of Charan Singh of B.K.D. was decisive in the victory of V.V. Giri,[23] though the CM of U.P., C.B. Gupta and the CM of Gujarat, Hitendra Desai had presented a new compromise formula before Nijalingappa's CWC meeting on November 12, 1969.[24]

After the 1977 elections also when the *Janata* Party ruled at the Centre and the Congress Party ran most of the states, the Union found it difficult to elect a favourable President. The election was delayed until the which were Assemblies dominated by the Congress Party were dissolved and until the fresh elections were held in the ten states in June, 1977. After the elections in these states and coming into power of the *Janata* Party in seven states, election for the Presidentship was held and the *Janata* CMs played decisive roles in electing N. Sanjiva Reddy as the President of India.

B. CM's ROLE IN THE SELECTION OF THE PMs OF INDIA

The Congress Working Committee (with all the Congress CMs as its members) has the right to nominate the candidate for the PM's office; and the Congress Parliamentary Party is entitled to ratify it. Nehru had stated on several occasions that the question of choice of PM should be decided by the CWC in consultation with the CMs.[25] The CMs controlled their state contingents in the Central Parliamentary Party. Nehru was the nominee of Mahatma Gandhi and charisma had been transferred to him after Gandhi's death from Gandhi to him. So the role of party bodies in electing him as the PM was a mere formality. Even when Nehru threatened to resign, party leaders were not ready to consider this possibility. But some Congress leaders constituted 'syndicate'—a powerful coalition of Congress leaders from the South, East and West who carried the majority in the Congress Working Committee during the last days of Nehru with a view to dominating and ultimately to settling Nehru's succession (their aim was primarily to keep Morarji Desai out from holding the Prime Ministerial office after Nehru's death.).

Among the canvassers of Shastri as the PM in 1964 were the CMs of Assam, M.P. Mysore and Rajasthan.[26] Kamaraj, the Congress President, was in favour of forging consensus i.e. unanimity in choosing the name of Nehru's successor. He convened the meeting of CWC and CMs, the two most important groups in the party. The Congress Parliamentary Party (CPP) was to follow the lead with the Congress President seeking the consensus. Kamaraj made hectic search for support among the state CMs and Presidents of the PCCs till May 29, 1964.[27]

Bihar Congress, notes Brecher, was split into two almost equal factions. Morarji was supported by the group against K.B. Sahay who was backed by Shastri and Atulya Ghosh. If Shastri became P.M., with Atulya's aid, they feared that they might lose their Assembly tickets. So they did not like to disown newspaper reports of their support for Morarji. While K.B. Sahay had no intention of supporting Morarji, he could not openly alienate the Bihar group of his followers, caught as he was in the web of Bihar factional politics.

Among 57 MPs of Bihar, 30 were in favour of Desai and 27 in favour of Shastri.[28] So far as state contingents of Bihar and Gujarat were concerned, Morarji was in ascendancy. But when Shastri became P.M., K.B. Sahay, the C.M. of Bihar was a member of the grand council during his Prime Ministerial tenure. Conference of CMs was held most frequently during

Shastri's tenure.[29] Brecher calls it "The Chief Minister's Club." He notes, "the most notable accretion of influence .... has been to the State bosses. Through their collective presence in the grand council of the Republic, they have exerted massive power, as the ultimate consensus on food and language amply reveal. The Parliamentary Party, by contrast, has remained inconsequential both in the succession struggle and in the developing pattern of decision on national policy." [30]

CMs played a more pivotal and busier rote in the selection of Mrs. Indira Gandhi as PM in 1966. The CM of Maharashtra, Naik convassed in favour of Chavan before the CM of Mysore, Nijalingappa.[31] The CMs of Andhra Pradesh, Orissa, J&K and Madras confabulated with the Congress President, Kamaraj.[32] The CMs of eastern India met at the house of Atulya Ghosh to stop Desai from becoming Prime Minister.[33] Thirteen CMs attended a meeting of the grand council.[34] Eight CMs issued a statement calling for the election of Mrs. Gandhi as the leader of the CPP on January 15, 1966.[35] Brecher notes, "..... this act assured Nehru's daughter of the Prime Ministership."[36] Seven CMs (of Andhra Pradesh, Assam, West Bengal, Bihar, Mysore, Orissa and Rajasthan) and Punjab's Darbara Singh went to see Atulya Ghosh.[37] Of the nine CMs (those from Andhra Pradesh, Bihar, J&K, M.P., Madras, Maharashtra, Mysore, Orissa and Rajasthan), all but K.B. Sahay from Bihar agreed that they should meet Kamaraj and convey their support for Mrs. Gandhi.[38] K.B. Sahay asked for time to consult his faction-ridden party colleagues. Later, Sahay added his approval.[39] Twelve of the fourteen CMs were now openly identified, only Gujarat and U.P. remained aloof.[40] Thus the CM's club had emerged as a much more effective player in 1966 than it had been in 1964. Indeed, the CMs played a truly aggressive role in 1966. The initative for sponsoring candidates was taken up by the CMs. According to R.G. Ventakeswaran," Most of them not only supported the candidature of Mrs. Gandhi openly but actively campaigned for her by persuading the Members of Parliament from their respective states to vote for her."[41]

CMs exercised power over the contingent of MPs from their respective states. CMs derived power from their control over the *Pradesh* Congress Committees and their pivotal authority in distributing party tickets for elections to the *Lok*

Sabha. As H.M. Jain writes, "The Chief Ministers also enjoyed considerable power of patronage in the states and the Members of Parliament always looking for favours from the Chief Ministers for their constituents, friends and relatives could ill-afford to displease them or disregard their wishes,"[42]

The propriety of CMs coming into the open in the battle for the Prime Ministerial seat was criticized by Morarji Desai, the Prime Miinisterial candidate and H.M. Jain, the political scientist. H.M. Jain argued that "the Chief Ministers had no right to influence the M.P.s." [43] But Atulya Ghosh a prominent political leader of West Bengal rebutted the criticism. He counter-argued," Every citizen of India has the right to express his opinion on this issue. Besides, Chief Ministers are voters so far as the election of the Members of the *Rajya Sabha* is concerned and the Members of the *Rajya Sabha* are voters in the ensuing contest."[44] On the other hand M.R. Masani, a prominent member of the opposition struck a different chord when he stated, "The action of the Congress President and the Chief Ministers in calling M.P.s from different states in small meetings and trying to commit them in advance showed a cynical contempt for the sanctity of the ballot, which is frightening."[45] K. Santhanam also said, "The only safe convention which will stand the test of time is that the CPP should be allowed to elect its leader without external pressure either from the Chief Ministers or the Congress High Command. Until such a convention is established, the relation between the Union and the States and of the Prime Minister and the Congress President will be subject to avoidable risks."[46]

In any case, the CMs were not allowed to be present in the Central Hall of Parliament at the time of polling. Originally, the seats had been arranged in the said Hall to enable the CMs to watch the polling but Morarji Desai objected to this arrangement and so, this arrangement had to be abandoned.[47] L.N. Sharma comments, "Morarji knew that the Chief Ministers were against him and naturally he resented and took exception to the role of the Congress President, the Chief Ministers and other leaders who were not voters taking sides on behalf of one candidate" (read, his rival).[48]

The action of the CMs can be justified on the ground that they do not only have the right but the responsibility to take part in the election of the P.M.; secondly, as CMs, they have an added responsibility to ensure that the person chosen as the PM was acceptable to the states. In an interview to a foreign correspondent, the Congress President defending the role of the CMs in the selection of the PM argued, "Everyone has a free expression of views. Without all the states, where is the Centre"? The Chief Ministers certainly represent the states. Without the states how do you have India and Parliament? [49]

C. CM AND NATIONAL POLITICS

In many ways, CMs hold the position of national leaders and should hold the position legitimately. When they represent sub-nationalism, they become leaders of smaller stature and in a way, represent sectoral or regional interests. By definition, political parties should represent national interest (as Burke argued to differentiate political parties from factions). So CMs in any sense have national recognition and even international eminence which add to their strength. Even foreign experts visit certain states to find out reasons for the success of particular schemes, programmes or projects or to see how and why the rate of success was high or low. Conversely, if a state violates human rights or encourages terrorism, etc., it also attracts the negative attention of international community. So the reputation of CMs is not confined to the boundaries of their states or to the contiguous regions only.

CMs are sometimes invited in the meetings of the Union Cabinet when questions related to their states are under discussion and their presence is considered useful. For example, P.C. Sen, the then C.M. of West Bengal and Biju Patnaik, C.M. of Orissa attended the meting of the Union cabinet on June 6, 1963 when the food problem in the eastern region was causing concern.[50]

Biju Patnaik as the CM was often consulted on defence problems. He was provided a room in the Ministry of External Affairs while he continued to be the CM of Orissa until his resignation in August, 1963 under the Kamaraj Plan.[51] After 1962, defence problems were discussed by CMs.[52] In March 1963, Nehru sent Biju Patnaik, the then CM of Orissa to the US with the approval of the Emergency Committee of the Cabinet to have exploratory talks with the US government on certain aspects of defence.[53] In his talks with the US newsmen, Patnaik disclosed several details of India's military preparations and her requirements of radar, communication facilities and other essential equipments. His disclosures caused resentment among the members of the *Lok Sabha*.

Nehru regarded Kamaraj not only as the CM of Madras but a leader of national eminence. The Kamaraj Plan is an example of the trust Nehru had in Kamaraj. Ashok Chanda aptly commented that the resignations of the CMs and the manner in which they were accepted have no constitutional parallel.[54] Almost all the CMs had been enjoying unqualified confidence of the CLP. But they had to tender resignations under the Kamaraj Plan. Nehru accepted the resignations of six CMs, namely Kamaraj (Madras), Biju Patnaik (Orissa), Binodanand Jha (Bihar), Bhagwat Rai Mandlor (M.P.), C.B. Gupta (U.P.) and Bakshi Ghulam Mohammad (J&K).

The CMs have been closer to the sheet of power i.e. the offices of Presidents and PMs in the coalition era i.e. since 1989. V. P. Singh became PM because of the machinations of Devi Lai for which he had to agree to make his son, Chautala the CM of Haryana. Narasimha Rao was a minority PM and had been preferred silently by Sonia Gandhi over his Congress rivals, Arjun Singh and Pranab Mukherje. But Rao later showed in the AICC that he had hold over the party which endorsed him. Thus the CMs had not to come into the open as they did in 1966 in the selection of the PM, they played a role from behind the curtain. It is a fact, however, that the federal process and the CMs' role have come to be pivotal since 1989 in Indian politics. Though the personality of Atal Bihari Vajpayee in his selection thrice as PM or the choice of Sonia Gandhi in having Manmohan Singh as PM in 2004 and 2009 was the most pivotal factor, the fact is that both Atal Bihari Vajpayee and Sonia Gandhi had been the Supreme and unquestioned leaders of their parties; and CMs had full trust in them.

Notes and References

1. K. M. Munshi, *The President under the Indian Constitution*, Bombay, 1967, p. 1.

2. K. Santhanam, *Union-State Relations in India*, Bombay, 1963, p. 8.
3. K. R. Bombwall, *The Foundations of Indian Federation*, Bombay, 1966, p. 96.
4. Michael Brecher, *Succession in India: A study in Decision-Making*, Oxford University Press, 1967, p. 99.
5. Paul H. Appleby, *Report of a Survey*, New Delhi : The President's Press, 1953, Sections V and VII.
6. D.C. Gupta, *Indian Government and Politics*. Delhi : Vikas, 1972, p. 328.
7. Brecher, *op. cit.*
8. G.S. Bhargava, *After Nehru : India's New Image*, Delhi : Allied Publishers, 1966, pp. 177-202.
9. *Press Trust of India Report*, January 23, 1965.
10. Doglas Verney, "From Quasi-Federation to Quasi-Confederacy? The Transformation of India's Party System", *Publius*, Vol. 33, No. 4, Fall 2003, p. 171 and Lawrence Saez, *Federations Without a Centre : The Impact of Political and Economic Reform on India's Federal System*, Sage, New Delhi, 2002.
11. For a good discussion on these points, see M.P. Singh and Rekha Saxena, *Indian Politics : Contemporary Issues and Concerns*, Delhi : Prentice-Hall, 2008, pp. 147-52.
12. *Ibid.*, pp. 152-53.
13. "Change of Centre's apathy towards state gains ground", *The Times of India* (Patna), 9.4.2010.
14. *Ibid.*
15. *Ibid.*
16. *Hindustan* (Patna), 9.4.2010 (in Hindi).
17. *The Hindustan Times* (Patna) 10 4.2010.
18. *Ibid.*
19. *Ibid.*
20. *Ibid.*
21. H.M. Pandit, *The Prime Minister's President*, Delhi: S. Chand, 1971, p. 8.
22. T.V. Kunhi Krishnan, *Chavan and the Troubled Decade*, Somaya Publishing Pvt. Ltd., 1971, p. 324.
23. Subhash C. Kshyap, *The Politics of Power: Defections and State Politics in India*, Delhi: National, 1974, p. 303.
24. T.V. Kunhi Krishnan, *op. cit.*, p. 339.
25. H.M. Jain, *The Union Executive*, Allahabad : Chaitanya Publishing House, 1969, p. 165.
26. Brecher, *op. cit*, p. 43.
27. *Ibid.*

28. *Ibid.*
29. *Ibid.*, p. 168.
30. *Ibid.*, p. 169.
31. *Ibid.*, p.197.
32. *Ibid.*
33. *Ibid.*, p. 199.
34. *Ibid.*, p. 205.
35. *Ibid.*, p. 209.
36. *Ibid.*
37. *Ibid.*, p. 210.
38. *Ibid.*, p. 211.
39. *Ibid.*, p. 212.
40. *Ibid.*
41. R.G. Venkateswaran, *Cabinet Government in India*, London: George Allen and Unwin, 1967, p. 167.
42. H.M. Jain, *op. cit.*, p. 175.
43. *Ibid.*
44. Cited in *ibid.*, p. 178.
45. Cited in R.G. Venkateswaran, *op. cit.*, p. 169.
46. Cited in L.N. Sharma, *The Indian Prime Minister*, New Delhi : Macmillan Co. of India, 1976, p. 25.
47. R.G. Venkateswaran, *op. cit.*, p. 168.
48. L.N. Sharma, *op. cit*, p. 25.
49. R.G. Venkateswaran, *op. cit.*, p. 168.
50. *Ibid.*, p. 44.
51. *Ibid.*, p. 61.
52. *Ibid.*, p. 63.
53. *Ibid.*
54. *Ibid.*

10

The CM and Aspiration for Good Governance: Retrospect

The responsibility for providing good governance rests on the shoulders of the CM primarily and as a matter of course, he is accountable if there is maldevelopment or inadequate development of his or her state. In *Arthashastra,* Kautilya enunciated the doctrine that the ruler's happiness lies in the happiness of his subjects; and his welfare lies in their welfare; the king considers as good whatever pleases his subjects. He held the ruler directly responsible for promotion of agriculture, animal husbandry, trade and commerce and maintenance of law and order, that is protection of life and liberty. The ruler has to carry out preventive and punitive measures against corrupt officials and provide good governance even amidst instability. These may be treated as a catalogue of routine functions for those CMs who aspire to provide good governance.

In spite of the fact that like Maharashtra, Bihar from 1946 to 1960 was a well-governed and well-administered state, it cadme to be plagued by instability of governments and bad administration (economically, was called a *BIMARU* state) between 1961 and 1989. By 1967, the Congress party lost its aura of being the party of freedom fighters and people of all castes and classes held it responsible for rising prices, unemployment and corruption. All classes of people united under ideological exhortation by Ram Manohar Lohia and mobilisation at the grassroots level by Karpoori Thakur against the Congress in 1967 Vidhan Sabha and Lok Sabha elections. The Congress party became a butt of the "revolution of rising frustration" and was displaced from power leading to the era of coalitions (1967-1989). But backward castes had not learnt to coalesce the right way and thus coalitions interchanged between those led by the Congress and non-Congress ones for twenty-two years (1967-1989).

Between 1990 and 2012, backward castes came to be empowered. In two phases, the CMs came from intermediate castes-*ahir* and *Kurmi*. The difference between 1990-2005 and 2005-12 phases was that in the former phase, weaker sections got self-respect, dignity, self-esteem and the benefits of using space meant for *Charwaha Vidyalayas* and *rikshaw* sheds. Muslims got security as there were practically no communal riots and as a result, a social and political combination of Muslims and *ahirs* merged during that period. During the latter period, reservation was made on 50% seats for women and on 20% seats for extremely backward castes in *Panchayati Raj* institutions and UCBs. In addition, a *Mahadalit* Commission was constituted and the government resolved to provide 20 decimals of land or Rs. 20,000 to each *Dalit* family for constructing home. Provisions were made for rendering benefits to *Pasmanda* Muslims. In addition to provisions for social justice, school going girls were provided uniforms and bicycles for going to schools; and general public happiness was sought to be raised through constructing roads, ensuring law and order, appointment of primary school teachers (though on poor salary) and those of *anganwaries*, nurses, etc. Inclusive growth and good governance were thus to some extent, the hallmarks of the latter phase.

As a whole, Bihar passed through the following four phases between 1946-2012:

1. One-party-dominant-system;
2. Coalition system;
3. Imperial Prime Ministerial System Phase I and Phase II; and
4. Upper/Backward Caste Dominant System/Regional Party Dominant System.

S.K. Sinha was the best specimen of one-party-dominant-system. He was a charismatic personality inasmuch as he transcended his class interests. He was socially and economically, a progressive and endeared himself to BCs and minorities, ensured their vote and support along with those of upper castes/classes for the Congress party to which he belonged. He had started his innings in 1946 with criticisms from his party colleagues and press but he established himself as one of the powerful CMs in the country of his times. His position, however, started waning after the second General Elections in which his close confidants like Mahesh Prasad Sinha and Dasu Singh lost their Assembly seats. His differences with a senior Congress minister Ram Charitra Singh, proved embarrassing for him. The fact that S.K. Sinha retained the CM's office in a contest within the party against A.N. Sinha in 1957 kept his morale high but the on-going debate in the houses between 1957-60 indicate that anti-incumbency factor had started working against Sinha.

Like S.K. Sinha, Jagannath Mishra too enjoyed security with Sanjay Gandhi (Mrs. Indira Gandhi's son) behind him who was the General Secretary of the Congress party and who goaded his mother, Mrs. Gandhi, the then PM to support him. But with Sanjay Gandhi gone, Jagannath Mishra lost support from New Delhi and in spite of the fact that he enjoyed support of the majority of the members of the Legislative Assembly, he had to resign as CM. He had to reckon with several charges of corruption which were heaped against him.

Laloo Prasad did not have majority in the Assembly in 1990-1995 but he cobbled enough support to remain in the saddle. His ability to survive caused his strength to grow; and he emerged most powerful as CM in 1995. He remained party president and as party supremo, managed to hand over the charge of the Chief Ministership to his wife, Rabri Devi. Laloo's position underwent a diminution after the fodder and Disproportionate Assets Cases were lodged against him and the latter also against Rabri Devi. Similarly, Nitish Kumar had an unsullied image and identification with good governance for the first three and half years of his rule. But as 2010 Vidhan Sabha elections came nearer, he identified himself, with caste combinations and manipulations and crafted the image of a social engineer for himself. He had vowed that he would not tolerate familism but in 2010 elections, he gave tickets to sons or relatives of ministers. He made bridges with criminals and renewed their position in the party. His dithering on land reforms proved that he was no ideologue. The continuation in office of Nitish Kumar uninterruptedly for the last seven years and his continued popularity thus (though suffering diminution in 2012) are due to both pragmatism and good governance.

Despite variations in position and powers; in theory, the CM remains a miniature PM. There is no doubt that his position and powers have remained circumscribed by the overarching constitutional role of the Union Government, by the patriarchical role of the PM in one party dominant system (1946-64), by the imperial Prime Ministerial system of Mrs. Indira Gandhi (1972-77 and 1980-84), by the second phase of imperial Prime Ministerial system of Rajiv Gandhi (1984-89) and also by CMs' own personalistic traits interacting with the situation obtaining at the time of their incumbency. The nature of the Congress system under Nehru was such that it allowed freedom of action to CMs particularly to stalwarts and loyalists like S.K. Sinha (1946-61) who enjoyed comparative freedom in choosing his colleagues. Sinha was chose K.B. Sahay as a minister even against Mahatma Gandhi's wishes. He had no difficulty whatsoever in any electoral contest for a seat in the Legislative Assmebly; he hardly visited the constituency at the time of polls to beg for votes and yet, came out victorious. He had to face contest for the post of the CM within the party only once (in 1957). His personal reputation as a good orator, a voracious reader and a sound administrator (who though having been beaten brutally by the police during the freedom struggle and jailed for about eight years, praised the police in public if they performed well and got public order machinery greased with their support) also accounted for putting him in the high office of the CM for the longest period of time so far uninterruptedly for fifteen years as CM and for about two years as the premier of the state (1937-39).

After S.K. Sinha's death in 1961, the two Congress CMs to step into his big shoes- Binodanand Jha and K.B. Sahay came to occupy the office after a hot contest in the CLP. They did not command the loyalty and confidence of his partymen or the masses to the extent their eminent predecessor did. Binodanand Jha was ridiculed for making frequent trips to Delhi to consult the high command. He was made to resign after a little more than two years in office (in 1963) under the Kamaraj Plan. K.B. Sahay tried to encourage intermediate castes re-organize into a conglomeration. Instead of pursuing S.K. Sinha's method of co-opting backward caste members, he included a majority of members of backward castes in his cabinet and gave an upper hand to them under his leadership but this stragegy failed to mollify the backward castes who were on the verge of tasting power on their own. Personally, K.B. Sahay's administration had become unpopular because of poor law and order; and firing on students at Patna and Nawadah had inflamed the passion of students against him. The Congress by 1967 had become the butt of criticism for running permit, licence and *Quota raj* and for making rich richer and poor poorer. The *Zamindari* abolition had not substantially altered land relations in the countryside because big land holders still held sway. The Congress had not implemented the Land Ceiling Act and other progressive measures of land reforms strictly even though they had been passed and amended by the Legislature from time to time. So inequities continued on the rural scene and Sahay's strategy of using the social division on the lines of intermediate and other castes did not pay dividends and they remained disgruntled.

By 1967, the growth rate and administrative efficiency in Bihar had started dipping. Anti-incumbency factor worked against the Congress and the Congress cap had become the symbol of hatred. Hence, the general mood of the electorate was that the Congress must go out of power and K.B. Sahay-led government became a scapegoat of the negative mood of the public.

Mahamaya Prasad Sinha and Ghulam Sarvar used the emotional rhetorics to swing the youth and students to defeat the Congress. Bihar remained under multi-party rule between 1967-89. Most of the times, it was under coalition model of the multifarious parties but at times, the Congress-led coalition ruled. For two years (1977-79), the *Janata* Party rule was established but the *Janata* Party was also faction-ridden and a conglomeration of ideologically divergent parties. So the whole period, broadly speaking, comes under the coalition model.

By definition, CMs of coalition governments were weak, marked as they were by inherent instability, ideological divergence, administrative inefficiency and maldevelopment. The life span of each government between 1967 and 1989, led either by the United Front, the Congress or the *Janata* Party, was on an average of two years and this small period was marred by constituents of the government quabbling over seats in the cabinet, better portfolios, undue favour (as Kamakhya Narain Singh, a minister in Kedar Pandey's cabinet pressed for), etc. Nine coalition governments existed between 1967 and 1972 with parties as disparate as the CPI and the *Jana Sangh* and the outside support of the CPI (M) and the *Swatantra* Party as well as regional outfits owing allegiance to diverse local groupings and having heterogeneous character.

Political instability of governments went hand in hand with unsavoury manipulations in order to survive and CMs were left with little time for governance. Good governance went abegging. This happened irrespective of the nature of parties or alliances ruling the state. Political instability also went hand in hand with gradual collapse of administration in the state. The people of the state had outvoted the Congress mainly on the ground of it being corrupt. But some CMs of the coalition government outdid their Congress counterparts in the matter of providing corrupt and inapt governance.

The end of co-operative federalism even when the same party ruled at the Cenre and in the state was a special feature of rule by coalition governments. The Congress CMs particularly were dependent on the Congress high command to get permission to form governments in the state as a partner in coalition governments or to sit in opposition, if not permitted to form their government.

A motley of parties, under the nomenclature of *Samyukt Vidhayak Dal* (SVD) formed government under Mahamaya Prasad Sinha as the CM and Karpoori Thakur as Deputy CM in 1967. Mahamaya Prasad Sinha's emotional jingoism symolized by beginning his speeches by addressing the youth as his "*Jigar Ke Tukre*" (pieces of heart) and declaring his policy of not permitting the police to enter into the university campus except under emergent situations were the hallmark of the UF government. Jagannath Mishra had started the process of downgrading the standards of education by converting a large number of colleges into constituent ones, by introducing the schemes of non-aided colleges and time-bound promotion of University and college teachers ludicrously called "Jagannatha Professors." But it was left for the SVD to accelerate the process of degradation of standards of education. Students became so incensed that some students left examination hall in A.N. Sinha College at Patna because they were not permitted to copy from *chits*, etc. raising slogan like *'Chori se Sarkar Bani Hai, Chori se Hum Pass Karainge'*. The quality of education was downgraded by enunciation of the policy by the then Education Minister, Karpoori Thakur that a student would be declared to have passed Entrance Examination even if he failed in English with the proviso that a note would be appended in his Certificate and marks sheet that the candidate had passed without English. These gimmicks failed, as expected, to fulfil the desire of the masses who had outvoted the Congress in 1967 for getting better administration, good governance and a more democratic ethos. As the dissatisfaction with governance came to the surface, the UF government lost its elan to govern and the heterogeneous stuff of which it was made started taking its toll. Defections which were to become so common in the coming years that even old non-Congress leaders were seen reverting back to the Congress Party had its first manifestation when B. P. Mandal, a member of the S.S.P. and a minister of the then cabinet refused to resign from the cabinet against the explicit advice doled out to him more then once by no less a person than the eminent leader of the S.S.P., Lohia himself. B.P. Mandal chose to defect from the party with his men which led to the fall of the first coalition ministry led by Mahamaya Prasad Sinha (5.3.1967-25.1.1968) after it lasted for only thirteen months. The second ministry led by Satish Prasad Singh lasted for four days and performed its sole purpose (for which it was constituted) of paving the path for B.P. Mandal to take charge as CM by recommending his name to the governor for nomination as MLC prior to making it possible for the governor to invite him to take oath as CM. But the ministry of B.P. Mandal, too, suffered from inherent contradictions and gave way after 47 days' rule. On March 22, 1968, another UF Ministry came into being under the Chief Ministership of Bhola Paswan Shastri but it lost majority in three months i.e. on June 25, 1956 and recommended imposition of emergency under Art. 356 which the governor accepted. The imposition of emergency was followed by a 'mini-general' election in 1969 but it failed to improve matters since no party secured absolute majority once again. However, in the changed post-election scenario, the Congress Party got chance to form government and amidst intense political activity, it requisitioned the support of *Janata* Party, BKD, *Jharkhand* Party, *Soshit Dal*, *Swatantra* Party and six independents. Sardar Harihar Singh-led ministry was installed on 26.2.1969. He took a month in settling the wrangle over the distribution of portfolios among his ministers. The meetings of the CLP were reportedly turned into "regular battle fields". The administration came to standstill. In the midst of heightening internal bickerings, Sardar Harihar Singh resigned as CM on 19.6.1969, leading to the re-installation of Bhola Paswan Shastri as the CM of UF government. But the cracks between the major partners like *Jana Sangh*, SSP, CPI and PSP re-surfaced. Shastri complained that the Jana Sangh faction opposed the inclusion of non-Hindus into the government. Under the circumstances, the second Shastri ministry too fell in July, 1969 itself necessitating the re-imposition of President's rule in Bihar which was revoked on February 16. 1970. After the revocation of the President's rule, a Congress (R) ministry under the chief ministership of Daroga Prasad Rai came into being with the support of the BKD, *Shoshit Dal*, PSP, CPI and *Jharkhand* Party. With the process of internal dissension going unchecked, Rai's government ended on 18.12.1970 when it was defeated in a trial of strength in the house. Thereupon, a new SVD ministry under the chief ministership of Karpoori Thakur of the SSP was installed which received a rude shock by the results of Lok Sabha elections, 1971 which provided the Congress (R) two-thirds majority in the Lok Sabha as the "Indira Wave" swept all over the country. This new development enthused the Congress (R) leaders of Bihar to form a new alliance called *Progressive Vidhayak Dal* under the leadership of Bhola Paswan Shastri. The trend of counter-defection to the Congress (R) was so quick that it portended imminent danger to Karpoori Thakur ministry which was counting its days. The Karpoori Thakur ministry was the last of the nine coalition governments to fall down between 1967-72 leading to the next Assembly elections in 1972 which provided Bihar Congress hegemonic rule once again but due to agitation and imposition of internal emergency to quell it during which excesses were committed in parts of north India which ended the rule of the Congress party in 1977.

Since the Congress party had resumed ascendancy in 1971 under Mrs. Gandhi after defeating her political rivals in the party and after attracting the masses with her *'garibi hatao'* slogan, she launched the era of imperial Prime Ministerialism. The practice of PM (Mrs. Gandhi) nominating the CMs and removing them as soon as they appeared to gain strength on their own became the usual practice in this era. Later on, after the assassination of Mrs. Gandhi in 1984, when the reigns of power came to the hands of her son, Rajiv Gandhi, he too continued the practice of his mother (Mrs. Gandhi) and thus in the second imperial Prime Ministerial era (1984-89) also, the Congress CMs were the nominees of the PM and dependent upon him for survival and were dutybound to consult him on all governmental or party matters and swore loyalty to the "crown" lest they should lose their Chief Ministership. There was no trace of co-operative federalism or 'government by discussion'. In the long run, this practice proved disastrous for the Congress Party. The Congress CMs did not find it necessarilly to build contact with people at the grassroots, to hear and listen to them, to explain the policies or problems of the party and to take the masses along with them. The duty of bringing a political balance into play had passed from the hands of CMs to those of the PM in this phase of extreme centralization within the party and beyond. Under the circumstances, the cabinets that the CMs formed in consultation with the high command were not cohesive, open-minded and the governance was exclusive. It is no surprise if the institution of CM lost its aura, stature, self-esteem, dignity and position. In this changed scenario, the CM did not remain the hub of state government and administration and his responsibility for providing good governance was partial because he was no longer accountable to the legislature or the people of the state but to the imperial Prime Minister of his or her party.

In 1972, Kedar Pandey was nominated CM after the CLP of Bihar authorised Mrs. Gandhi to nominate the leader of the CLP and hence, the CM. But his rivals in the party made it difficult for Pandey to govern, though he initiated some laudable steps to make education qualitative. Internal bickerings did not allow Pandey to stay in office for more than one year and odd months. After his exit, Abdul Ghafoor was nominated CM by Mrs. Gandhi. After Ghafoor's exit, the CLP knew beforehand that Jagannath Mishra (the younger brother of L.N. Mishra, Union Minister of State for Foreign Trade who had been assassinated) had acquired the sympathy and blessings of Mrs. Gandhi (he was known as a man of

Mrs. Gandhi's second son, Sanjay Gandhi who had acquired prominence in the party) and therefore, the CLP unanimously elected Mishra as its leader and thereby, as the CM. His reign coincided with the imposition of internal emergency in the country and he became identified with much of the execesses of emergency besides his own personal misdoings.

Mishra's rule ended in 1977 when the electorate of Bihar hardly returned any candidate of the Congress (R) to the *Lok Sabha* in the elections held that year. Following the Congress debacle in 1977, the Bihar Legislative Assembly was dissolved (along with Legislative Assemblies of other eight states where the Congress (R) had met similar fate) and fresh elections were ordered. The *Janata* Party secured absolute majority in the Bihar Legislative Assembly and formed government with Karpoori Thakur as the CM in 1977. Two factors are worth mentioning about the nature of the Janata interregnum. Firstly, the Janata Party had a coalitional character in view of the fact that it was a conglomerate alliance of several heterogeneous elemetnts. The 214-member Janata Legislative Party (JLP) was distinctly divided into three factions- 84 MLAs were loyal to the Congress (O) leader, S.N. Sinha; and equal number of MLAs including the Socialist Party loyalists were behind Karpoori Thakur, and the rest belonged to the *Jana Sangh*. Under the factional feud, no consensus to elect the CM was possible and a contentious electoral battle between Karpoori Thakur and S.N. Sinha ending in the victory of the former was not a good beginning for the Janata Government. In fact, it coincided with a vicious campaign by S. N. Sinha and his loyalists alleging that the *Jana Sangh* faction had tilted the balance in favour of Karpoori Thakur and had devised the plan to divide all the eight CMs' posts in North India between the two erstwhile factions of the BKD and the Jana Sangh. The circumstances which withstood high voltage turmoil weakend the party organization. Secondly, the Janata Party had come riding on people's general enthusiasm which transcended the barriers of caste, class, region and community, etc. But in 1978, Karpoori Thakur initiated the step to implement the policy of reservation in jobs for OBCs as recommended by Mungeri Lal Commission. Though it was mentioned in the manifesto of the Janata Party, upper caste youth who had enthusiastically supported the Janata Party in 1977 elections had not bargained for it. So when Karpoori Thakur was at it, they started agitating against its implementation. The backward castes stated counter-agitation to press for its implementation. Karpoori Thakur faced storm on that account and had to give way to a suave and modest socialist Janata leader, Ram Sundar Das (a *Dalit*) who continued as CM between 21.4.1979 to 6.6.1980 and who did not press for reservations. The Congress rule was revived again due to the bickerings and unimpressive show of the Janata regime in 1980 elections.

With Mrs. Gandhi in the PM's chair again between 1980 and 1984, the practice of nomination of CMs was revived as before. Due to her blessings and more due to that of her son, Sanjay; Jagannath Mishra was re-elected CM by the CLP on June 7, 1980. But as soon as Rajiv Gandhi took over as the General Secretary of the Congress Party (after Sanjay's death in an air crash), Mishra lost favour of the party high command. Finding himself defenceless against a host of charges levelled against him, he had to vacate the CM's office on 14.8.1983. Mrs. Gandhi and the high command, thereafter, chose C.S. Singh as the CM since the party was looking for a man with a non-controversial and clean image. But Singh failed to produce impressive output either in the fields of administrative or agrarian reforms and pulled the yoke of state's governance till the next general election of *Vidhan Sabha* in 1985.

Mrs. Gandhi was assassinated in 1984 and Rajiv Gandhi's term (1984-1989) which we have designated as 'the second imperial Prime Ministerial era' started. Continuing his mother's practice, he too, started nominating CMs. In 1985, his choice fell upon a tried trade union leader, Bindeshwari Dubey. Rajiv changed CMs at frequent intervals; so Dubey was replaced by Bhagwat Jha Azad (a Central Government minister hailing from Bihar) on 14.2.1988; Azad by S. N. Sinha on 11.3.1989 and Sinha by Jagannath Mishra for a three months' stint (6.12.1989-9.3.1990). Mishra has been the last CM of the Congress party so far. The Congress party's electoral fortunes have been on decline since 1989.

One of the reasons for the electoral decline of the Congress Party has been that it made its CMs puppets of the PM whenever it got the chance to rule between 1967 and 1989, making them rootless. The Congress party structure at the state and local levels became hollow and withdrawn from its supporters, members or voters. The Party could not build itself as a potential opposition party after 1990 and became an ally of the ruling party—the J.D. or *Rashtriya Janata Dal* (RJD) whose credentials as a governing party were suspect. Rajiv Gandhi, during his hey day was soft to non-Congress CMs but he was not soft to Congress CMs who remained dependent upon PMs of the day for survival and sustenance. The Congress party is even now heavily dependent upon one person —Sonia Gandhi and she has become the first President in the long history of the party to be chosen its President in 2010 for the fourth time; and *Pradesh Congress Committees* were found queueing to request her to nominate Presidents of their state's PCCs. Rahul Gandhi is made the star campaigner in elections particularly and heir designate for the PM's post. The fall of this national party is apparent and its prospects in 2014 elections to the *Lok Sabha* are not rated high.

As the national party vacated space, the Union came under the minority or coalition mode since 1989 and there has been a spurt of regionalism and regional parties. Regional satraps ruled the roost as CMs, members of the Union cabinet, MPs, members of NGOs or as leaders of agitaional movements launched against the Centre on policy or implementation issues. The advantage was taken among other regional parties by R.J.D. a regional party which replaced the Congress in Bihar in 1990. The support of Chandra Shekhar and Raghunath Jha (the two upper caste leaders) influenced the outcome of the contest for the Chief Ministership in 1990 and Laloo Prasad became the CM. He was a minority CM in 1990-1995 but he was astute enough to muster the support of the Congress and the left parties. He emerged as the symbol of the empowerment of the OBCs, having in the past (as a member of the Lok Sabha) supported V. P. Singh in implementing Mandal Commission recommendations. Laloo's rustic mannerisms and jokes made him popular particularly among the rural folk. In 1995, the R.J.D. won the Bihar Legislative Assembly election with a thumping majority. He had outwitted his rivals including Nitish Kumar who had not counted on the support Laloo Prasad had gained from among the EBCs in addition to his command over MY (Muslim+Yadav) combination. Having won the election, Laloo wanted to give a policy thrust to his administration and was thinking of ways to do so. But as things would have it, he was chargesheeted in fodder scam by the CBI and taken on remand under the orders of the Patna High Court. With his clout in the party and control over the levers of power, he was able to hand over the charge of the Chief Ministership to his wife, Rabri Devi in 1997. RJD's position deteriorated in the 2000 *Vidhan Sabha* election which gave a hung Assembly. Laloo who had association with the Congress since 1990 continued to see that Rabri remained the CM. He continued to back the UPA ministry at the Centre even after 2000 and himself joined the Union Ministry. The UPA, in turn, supported Rabri's ministry in Bihar. Laloo-Rabri duo, however, suffered defeat at the hands of JD (U)-BJP combine in 2005. JD(U)-BJP Combine got a pro-incumbency vote and was re-elected in 2010.

PERFORMANCE AS AN INDICATOR OF GOOD GOVERNANCE

The growth rate of Bihar was not impressive either during the coalition period or during the Laloo-Rabri regime. Bihar grew at the rate of 3.2 per cent during 1985 to 1995 as against the average national growth rate of 5.5 per cent during the same period. The growth rate during the period of 1995 to 2005 was 4.75 per cent which again was much behind the national average growth rate of 6.3 per cent during the same period. So the Laloo-Rabri period can be assessed positively only for its contribution towards providing self-esteem to OBCs as a means of their empowerment. It is spoken of negatively as a *'Jungle Raj'* (to quote an observation of the Patna High Court) because kidnappers, ransom seekers and criminals had a field day; and governance and public order had taken a back seat. Laloo Prasad put much hope on his craft of maintaining MY+other caste combinations. He was proved wrong in 2005 when the people of Bihar refused to vote on caste lines alone and instead gave chance to JD (U)-BJP combination with the hope that it would provide good administration. It was good governance combined with pragmatic electoral tactics that led to the re-election of this combine in 2010.

Nitish Kumar started his innings as CM in 2005 with the promise of good governance and repeatedly told the people that if he did not produce specific results by 2010, he would not ask for votes in the 2010 Assembly elections. In keeping with his promise, he built a good number of roads, lanes, by-lanes and flyovers covering large parts of the state. He got 3000 km highways and 9000 km rural roads constructed in five years. He ensured speedy trial of criminals; and about 55,000 criminals were convicted through such trials and they included MLAs and MPs even of his own party. He also ensured that ministers or MLAs did not interfere in administrative work. This ensured better law and order. Cycle and *Poshak* distribution to lacs of girls in schools and the implementation of *Akshar Anchal* enthused girls to study in schools. *Hunar Yojana* enthused students to learn skills. One lac school rooms were constructed; new primary schools were opened. Many new educational institutions like NIT, IIM, Chanakya National Law University, Nalanda International University, etc. were opened. Rural women have been benefited through their appointment as nurses, teachers, *Anganwaries, Asha Karyakarta* and (two lac) Panchayat representatives; schools and hospital buildings were repaired; teachers were appointed in schools. The step to open centre for generation of electricity at Nabinagar in collaboration with NTPC has added ferther to his cap. But in the absence of coal linkages, thermal power projects at Chaura, Pirpainty and Kajra are stalled. The overall picture is that generation and higher education, irrigation, industries, agriculture, etc. have not improved. Corruption is rampant in the implementation of MGNAREGA, PMGSY and *Sarvasiksha Abhiyan*. The government of Nitish Kumar failed to give land to even a single tribal in the state as progress report on the Scheduled Tribes and other Traditional Forest Dwellers (Recognition of Forest Rights) Act, 2006 pointed out. Indeed, he has not succeeded in doing much to banish poverty or diminish disparities of income among people of the state.

Controversy shrouds over the fact of real economic development that took place in Bihar under Nitish government. On the one hand, according to the figures of the Central Statistics Organisation, the growth rate under Nitish is said to be on an average of 12.3 per cent; on the other, the state demands since 2005 that Bihar be granted special category status because of poverty. Development is not integrated. Agricultural development index reached up to the negative in the last five years. UNDP reported that in the matter of hunger, Bihar exceeds Somalia. In human development index, Bihar stands on the 22nd position and in educational index, on the 35th position, next only to Pondichery. Higher education has got the worst deal. In public perception, the level of corruption increased in government offices during Nitish raj than it was during Laloo-Rabri raj. Law and order situation has deteriorated after March-April, 2012. Nitish claims that the Centre does not grant the requisite funds to Bihar due to which Bihar lags in equitable development. But C.P. Joshi, Union Minister of Rural Development cites figures which contradict his contention. Joshi points out that under MGNREGA, Bihar received Rs. 2,358 crore during the fiscal year 2009-10, while the fund utilised was just Rs. 1,816 crore. Similarly, under *Pradhan Mantri Gramin Sadak Yojana,* the state received Rs. 493 crore for the same period but the fund utilised was just Rs. 173 crore. In *Indira Awas Yojana,* the state had received Rs. 4,484 crore, and the state just spent Rs. 2,996 crore. Whereas the national manday average is 54 days under MGNAREGA; in Bihar, it is barely 28 days which is far from below. However, Joshi cannot refute the fact that when Bihar demanded massive aid from the Centre for the rehabilitation of *Kosi bandh* breach victims, the Centre allotted a meagre fund. The work started with gusto with the financial help from the World Bank. Similarly, financial help from Asian Development Bank (ADB) helped the Government of Bihar a lot in the building of roads.

Nitish Kumar can be credited for providing teeth to the empowerment of OBCs, EBCs, women and *Dalits*. Bihar is known widely for the empowerment of weaker sections. There have been four messiahs of backward politics in Bihar: Jagdeo Prasad (who pioneered in raising the slogan and rose to occupy the office of a minister, Karpoori Thakur (as CM, who tried to implement the Mungeri Lal Commission Report in 1978), Laloo Prasad (having become CM in the post-Mandal phase, he exhorted the OBCs to have self-respect and initiated certain programmes for their welfare) and Nitish Kumar (who reserved 50% seats for women and 20% for Extremely Backward Castes in *Panchayati Raj* Institutions even against single posts, promised to give 20 decimals of land or Rs. 20,000 for every *Dalit* family to construct home and thought of ways to improve the condition of *Pasmanda* Muslims). Thus in 65 years, politics of Bihar tended to move away from elites to masses. But the movement is away from the poor and tilts in favour of the neo-rich. Almost all the politicians have recorded a manifold increase in their assets in their affidavits to the Election Commission submitted in 2010. Whereas the son and daughter-in-law of Jagannath Mishra and himself a former minister, Nitish Mishra has registered a growth of Rs. 92 lakh in his property in five years, Bijendra Yadav, a minister who was in debt previously had 14 lakhs in 2010, and the Congress MLA from Simri Bakhtiarpur is in possession of property worth Rs. 3 crore besides Rs. 8 lakh in cash. Agriculture Minister Renu Kumari Kushwaha submitted in her return along with the nomination papers for 2010 polls that she is the owner of 32.45 lacs as against Rs. 1.71 lakhs shown during the October 2005 polls. Thus poll aspirants of the 2010 *Vidhan Sabha* elections have asset boom and elections led to elite turn over even in the era of Mandalisation under Nitish's dispensation.

There has been increase in GDP between 2004-05 to 2008-12 and between 2005 and 2012. Law and order situation had become better bringing better feelings of safety and security to citizens between 2005-2011. Dons like Mohammed Shahabuddin, Pappu Yadav and Anand Mohan had been placed behind the bars through their speedy trials by competent courts, though Anant Singh is out. However, the statistics about the increase in GDP does not tally with the increase in the level of happiness or well-being indicated by levels of literacy, nutrition, healthcare, educational care, agriculture, industry, irrigation and other areas which make people's lives worth living. Development means integrated development—social, economic and political which is not being seen. Nitish Kumar would have been given full credit for good governance only when he was able to bring perceptible improvement in the conditions of living of the poor and marginalised sctions of the society.

Some problems were invited by Nitish Kumar and some came his way. He invited problems with the appointment of Bandopandhyay Commission whose report on land reforms favoured transfer of land titles to sharecroppers. Either he should not have appointed the Commission (knowing the Yeoman's views beforehand) or he should have had the courage to implement the report or at least some urgent measures of land reforms like updating land records, etc. concerning which he got law passed in late 2011. By doing nothing in land reforms, he had got himself placed in the category of a reluctant socialist (only a Mandalite) if his performance in the first term on this front is assessed.

The picture on the law and order front is also a mixed one. According to the report of the National Human Rights Commission for 2007-08, the Commission received a total of 4,595 cases related to human rights violations from Bihar. Of them, 560 cases are related to custodial deaths, while six are encounter deaths. This figure is second to Delhi which sent the highest 6,210 complaints. In 2005, less than a dozen districts of Bihar were affected by Naxalism. By 2010, 33 out of 38 districts are Naxal-affected; and Nitish Kumar takes a soft approach towards the Naxals which the Centre resents and which results in the loss of many lives of police officials and destruction of public and citizen's property. Nitish Kumar's image took beating when the Patna High Court ordered a CBI probe into unaccounted withdrawal of funds to the tune of Rs. 11,000 crores since 2006 from the treasury. Similarly, in matters relating to purchase of stamps also, his government received a thrashing. The mercurial political temperament particularly shown from time-to-time to Narendra Modi and his ilk and the reaction of the upper castes and the neo-rich intermediate castes towards his propensity to land reforms do not add to his popularity index. Nitish has been clever enough to blend his slogan of good governance with all the tried tactics of identity politics. Both he and Laloo Prasad promised a certain percentage of reservation to poor upper caste in 2010 Election

Manifesto. Both he and Laloo Prasad claim that they did not allow any communal riot to occur during their regime, reminding the Muslims of the carnage that the Congress party had failed to control against them at Bhagalpur in 1989. Nitish Kumar takes the credit for getting the accused of Bhagalpur riots of 1989 including Kameshwar Yadav punished whom Laloo had allowed to remain unpunished. Laloo Prasad takes cudos for arresting Advani at Samastipur, stopping *Rath Yatra* and not allowing any communal riots following the demolition of Babri Masjid in 1992. Nitish Kumar is accused of not doing enough to prevent the carnage of Muslims at Kishanganj but by and large, Nitish nurses the Muslim constituency astutely and does not go amiss on occasions where hs presence is required. He is putting strong pressure on the BJP for not setting Narendra Modi as a Prime Ministerial candidate in on the ground that this will alienate Muslims from the NDA.

INTER-RELATIONSHIPS

In previous chapters, we have examined the relationship of the CM with the governor, the cabinet, the people, the party, the media as well as we have seen how the CM interacts with the federal process.

The CM has the constitutional duty to keep the governor informed on matters relating to the administration of state or proposals for legislation as the governor may call for under Art. 167. It is, however, observed that CMs do not want the governor to have any direct dealing with any state official even in most ordinary matters except through them. In One-party-dominant system, the CM-governor relationship had been on an even keel. But when coalition governments came to be formed, the governors started playing an effective role in the formation of governments, dismissal of ministries, dissolution of Legislative Assemblies either on their own or as agents of the Centre. It was expected that with the passage of time, sound conventions governing CM-governor interrelationship would develop but it has been noted that personal egos have marred the interrelationships. For example, the relations between governor G.N. Singh and C.M. Bhagwat Jha Azad; and those between governor S.S. Bhandari and Rabri Devi were so strained that they caught public eye. Rabri Devi even used unparliamentary language with reference to governor Bhandari in public. The Centre has not institutionalised the constitutional process with the CMs in the appointment of governors. The cause of friction between G.N Singh and B.J. Azad related to the appointment by Singh of several Vice-chancellors without consulting the state governors which the Universities Act demanded of him in his role as Chancellor. Nitish Kumar does not impose consultation on the chancellor in this matter but Education Minister, Deputy Chief Minister and party spokesperson have publically complained against this. Meanwhile, the Patna High court has cancelled the appointment of two V.C.s on the ground that the state government was not consulted in their appointment. The episode vitiates the atmosphere in higher education.

The formation of the cabinet is said to be a prerogative of the CM. But some leaders appoint themselves and even dictate the choice of their portfolios. This is particularly true of leaders like A.N. Sinha in Dr. S.K. Sinha's cabinets, of the representatives of constitutent parties in coalition governments or of the leaders imposed by the PMs in Prime Ministerial governments. Every CM took care of the socio-economic and regional factors as well as cared about factional representation in his cabinet. A marked fact is that till 1963, cabinets were dominated by upper caste members. For the first time, K.B. Sahay's 11-member cabinet in October, 1963 had the dominance of those who were not upper castes. Since 1967, backward castes continued to have reasonable representation but they have overwhelming presence in cabinets since 1990. In addition to S.K. Sinha, Jagannath Mishra became the CM of Bihar thrice and Bhola Paswan Shastri, Laloo Prasad and Nitish Kumar twice. Even while Mishra was out of power, he either controlled the CM (as he did Bindeshwari Dubey in the beginning) or he made the life of the CM, Kedar Pandey miserable. Kedar Pandey was shifted to the Union Council of ministers so that peace could reign in the state Congress but Pandey created trouble through his representatives in the state cabinets. So the Congress party or for that matter, all the parties, suffer from internal feuds; and ideological coherence and discipline have been lacking.

CMs like S.K. Sinha, K.B. Sahay, C.S. Singh, Jagannath Mishra, Bhagwat Jha Azad, Laloo Prasad and Nitish Kumar handled the houses well. They have had debating skills and spoke eloquently backed by facts and figures. However, those CMs who always feared that they might lose majority in the lower house felt shaky; and governance under them was also not smooth.

A CM's greatest asset is his rapport with the people. S.K. Sinha's mass meetings brought hordes of people to hear him. He was known as '*Bihar Kesari*' for his lionlike roars when he rose to address the masses. K.B. Sahay, though a progressive and a good draftsman, could not make rapport with the people. Mahamaya Prasad Sinha dramatized when he spoke and entertained the audience with the recitation of couplets in Urdu. The political system turned populist as time passed. Karpoori Thakur was a serious speaker. But the most jovial entertainer for the rural folk has been Laloo Prasad. One reason for his and his wife being in power for fifteen years is their rustic style which endeared them to the illiterate masses. Nitish Kumar is a serious speaker and a bureaucrat type personality who also uses puns for recreation of the audience.

Before Aiyar Commission and Mudholkar Commission submitted its reports and indicted certain ministers for their nexus with the business or the bureaucracy, ministers did not act with that much of caution. Now though it is a fact that politicians' known bank balance jumps high every five years (as declared by them if they stand for election in which submission of return of assets is compulsory), ministers act behind a curtain.

The CM-party relationship has been analysed in this study by dividing them into the following phases:

(i)	1937-39, 1946-61 and 1967	The Phase of Consolidation
(ii)	1968-71	The Phase of Chaos
(iii)	1972-89	The Phase of Central Domination

(iv) 1990-2012 The Phase of Regional and Backward Domination

S.K. Sinha, K.B. Sahay, Karpoori Thakur and Jagannath Mishra wanted a responsible and sympathetic press and so they wanted to put curbs on the press; other CMs allowed the press to remain free and did not interfere.

At the end, we may point out that India moved from co-operative federalism to bargaining federalism as different parties took charges at the Union and state levels in post-1967 political scenario. States were subservient to the Union during the emergencies declared in 1962, 1965, 1971 and 1977, more particularly during the nineteen months (1975-77). Since the 1990s, the Indian political system has moved significantly towards greater federalization. A regionalized multi-party configuration is ruling the Centre and the Indian political system is making a transition from 'quasi-federation' to 'quasi-confederation'. Rajiv Gandhi in the 1980s was pursuing an accommodative approach to regional ethnic demands and movements. He was paying importance to non-Congress CMs. The trend is now wide open. *India Today* (the popular periodical) is not interested in presenting data about who is the best Union Cabinet minister but who is the best CM. Narendra Modi and Nitish Kumar, often, get pride of the place and since Laloo is left out, he grudges. Mayawati, Gogoi, Patnaik, Jayalalithaa, Mamata Banerjee etc. often hog the headlines in the media. The states speak in a voice of parity with the Centre and often, there is a tug of war between the two as to which between the two is guilty for keeping a state under-developed or for passing a law without taking other's consent. In this context, the offices of the CM, not only of Bihar, but of all states, have assumed an unprecedented aura. The CM of Bihar has an added significance because he is the vehicle of development in a state which seven years ago, was considered fit enough to be included in the 'Fourth World'. But to cite one instance, one ex-CM of Bihar passed an order allowing each MLA to seek the transfer of two Block Development Officers; leading, in course of time, to the collapse of the Community Development Programme in the state. So the CM can as easily cause collapse of public order and development as augment them through his leadership qualities and acumen.

While the statistics points out that the extent of redistribution of wealth in India was a negligible six per cent, the position of Bihar can be imagined to be worse because of tardy implementation of land reforms to reduce rural poverty. Some primary and high school buildings have been built and repaired but no teachers come to teach and where there are teachers, they are not qualified. Parents in rural areas complain that teachers generally do not turn up to perform their duties in schools. There may be canals, pumps or computers but insufficient power. There may be midday meals (though of quality and quantity) but no textbooks, toilets or water. Equal rights in all respects or the right to education are mere slogans. Yet favoured politicians or bureaucrats serve themselves at the expense of masses and hence, the level of corruption goes on increasing. Despite all the tensions, the weaker sections have been empowered. We hope to see if the general population is provided better opportunities of life by the present and by succeeding CMs.

11

Post-2010 Developments in Bihar Politics

Nitish Kumar-led JD (U)-BJP alliance won a landslide victory in the Bihar Vidhan Sabha elections held in October-November, 2010. Out of a total of 243 Vidhan Sabha seats, party-wise breakup of seats won was as follows:

JD(U)	-	115
BJP	-	91
RJD	-	22
LJP	-	03
INC	-	04
CPI	-	01
JMM	-	01
Others	-	06
		243

JD (U)-BJP alliance captured 85% of seats; whereas its rival RJD-LJP alliance a mere 10% and the Party Congress which, unlike other previous few elections fought it alone (i.e. not with RJD) contented itself with a mere 2% of seats in the Bihar *Vidhan Sabha* constituted in 2010. Nitish Kumar started his second (consecutive) stint as the Chief Minister and the head of the JD (U)-BJP alliance on 26.11.2010.

Several factors are attributed to the spectacular electoral show of JD (U)-BJP alliance. The image of Nitish Kumar as one who was identified with good governance (*sushashan*)— confirmed subsequently by a report submitted to the US Congress Committee by the India-based Congressional Research Service in the second week of September, 1911 which counted Nitish's governance as next only to Narendra Modi's; Nitish government's taking Bihar from the status of a BIMARU state to a growth rate of 14.15% or 13.1% per annum, his state showing some signs of improvement in law and order and public safety, road construction to the extent of 3000 kms. between 2005-10, initiatives that led to women's engagement and consequently, empowerment (through reservation of 50% of seats for women in *Panchayati Raj* Institutions even against single posts- Bihar was the first state to introduce reservation at this high scale and of this nature after winning legal cases after seven year's wrangle in courts), appointment of women as *Anganwari sevika* and *sevikas* (whose monthly payments have been raised since November 2011), school teachers, workers in MGNREGA or helpers in the preparation of mid-day meal schemes for school children, initiatives aimed to encourage young girls to go to schools (through schemes like free distribution of bicycles and school uniforms to them) and the decision of the cabinet to distribute three decimals of land or Rs. 20,000 to each *Mahadalit* family for house construction, promise and (later allotment) of land of the state to establish Aligarh Muslim University at Kishanganj endeared women, *Mahadalits*, EBCs and *Pasmanda* Muslims in particular to the JD (U)-BJP alliance. The persistent demand for granting special status to Bihar since the Nitish government came to power enticed the votes of the elites, intellectuals and the masses. The exhortation of the Nitish government led the Centre to form a committee to examine the issue of special status of Bihar, though nothing tangible came out of the meeting of the NDC which has the authority approve it.

Awarded by NDTV Indian of the Year-2010; Forbes declared him to be the Indian person of the Year; CNN-IBN also declared him Indian for the Year-2010. He was made NDTV Indian of the Year (Political) -09 and Business Reformer of the Year-2009 by Economic Times in 2009. In 2007, he had also received the best Chief Minister Award and in 2008, CNN-IBN had declared him the Great Indian of the Year (Politics).

Apart from catering to the civil society's aspiration for good governance, the wonderful electoral outcome of 2010 was the result of dexterous combination forged before the election by Nitish Kumar of voters belonging to the four upper castes (*Brahmins, Bhumihars, Kayasthes* and *Rajputs*), and three intermediate castes (*Banias, Kurmis* and *Kushawahas*), EBCs, *Mahadalits* and *Pasmanda* Muslims. The factor of good governance attracted fleeting votes and legitimized voting in general; for example, this became the reason for some Muslims who generally do not vote for BJP voting in favour of BJP candidates. Such Muslims voted for the reason that Nitish Kumar had secular credentials, had got those found guilty in Bhagalpur Communal riots of 1989 punished in no time (whom Laloo Prasad and Rabri Devi had not got declared guilty and hence, had been going unpunished) and no communal strife had taken place during his five year's tenure as CM. But not only had the performance of the NDA-I but the weaknesses of opposition parties and groups also contributed to the stupendous victory of Nitish Kumar. Shortly before Nitish Kumar had to face election, a commission on Land Reforms (popularly called Bandopadhyaya Commissiton) submitted a report to the government which, among other things, recommended implementation of *bataidari* laws and their provisions. The Congress party and a group of JD (U) started campaigning against the impending danger to the land owners if the laws came to be implemented while left parties and groups started organizing rallies to implement the recommendations of Bandopadhyaya Commission. Nitish Kumar who had appointed Bandopadhyaya, a man known for his leftist leanings, sensing that this may turn his upper and intermediate caste votes against him, made a U-turn; and members of his government started saying in chorus that the government had no intention to implement *bataidari* laws. The Congress, by turn of events, at that momentous time became engaged in internal bickering and JD (U) dissenters got factionalised or were won over by supporters of Nitish Kumar. In this way, pragmatism in Nitish Kumar had sway while he wore his apron of good governance. He succeeded in cornering upper and intermediate caste votes because of his volte-face on *bataidari kanoon* and also the TINA factor. The RJD-LJP alliance could not make dent in the electoral fray and the Congress and left parties were also rejected by voters because they were seen as allies of Laloo-Rabri's fifteen years' misrule. Yet, it is notable that on about hundred seats, the margin of victory of the NDA over the opposition or the independent candidates was not substantially high. JD(U)-BJP alliance was higher by just three to four per cent over their opposition rivals.

A most notable and unprecedented factor in the Bihar *Vidhan Sabha* elections in 2010 which was most visible on electoral booths was that women voters were the first to arrive to cast votes in general and they were said to have cast votes in a large number for JD (U)-BJP alliance. Women outnumbered men in casting votes with 54.05 per cent women voting against 50.07 per cent men. There has had been perceptible increase in women's awareness, participation, self-perception of dignity, increase in income through self-employment, self-help like shop keeping, employment, etc. and there can be found a distinct glow of pride in their eyes during Nitish's regime (2005-12) due to Nitish's policies. Laloo-Rabri had paved the way for the emancipation of OBCs but they did not do much for their economic development and not at all for women empowerment. Nitish stole the show in all the three directions.

The success of JD (U)-BJP alliance has also to do with some other factors. Since practically nothing was done in Bihar by Laloo-Rabri as CMs between 1990-2005 and law and order had come to a *nadir*, people felt happy even if routine functions like construction of roads, lanes or flyovers were being done and general maintenance of law and order was being observed.

Zamindari bandhs were constructed in rural areas. It had become common during 1990-2005 under the regime of Laloo-Rabri that ministers or MLAs' hands or hands of party workers were behind criminal incidents, kidnapping or misappropriation of property. Now ministers, as a common practice, did not talk to DMs or SPs in connection with criminal incidents. The one or two instances of ministers making statements in favour of a criminal or to favour a criminal were condemned by Nitish Kumar. Nitish Kumar as the CM himself took particular notice of the fact that ministers or MLAs remained aloof from interfering in criminal activities. People felt sharp relief that political interference in crime became a thing of the past. Laloo Prasad and Rabri Devi were accused in Disproportionate Assets cases and Laloo Prasad along with many of his cohorts were accused in Fodder Scam. Laloo's kins and close associates were engaged in many highhanded activities. Nitish Kumar, by contrast, presented himself as Mr. Clean which improved the delivery system to a reasonable extent in Bihar. Nitish Kumar took a politically risky and amazingly bold step to encourage speedy trial of more than two dozens of politically influential personages who had been MLAs, MPs, ex-MLAs, ex-MPs or even ministers. He allowed law to take its due course and justice was meted out in time. Some of the persons involved were men of his ruling party and some were dreaded criminals. All these acts of Nitish Kumar won laurels for him.

According to the India Human Development Report 2011, Bihar and U.P. have done better in improving the lot of its marginalised *Dalits* and tribes, thanks to social movements launched by deprived classes and governmental encouragement. The per capita social sector expenditure had increased significantly in Bihar between 2005 and 2010. The share of expenditure on welfare of Bihar's SCs and STs had almost doubled during 2005-08 from 0.4% to 0.8%. Despite these improvements, the condition of lower castes is still not comparable with other states. According to Santosh Mehrotra, the report's lead author, though there is greater social inclusion, high incidence of malnutrition among children is still found. The case of violence in Khagaria over *Musahars* perpetrated by intermediate castes over possession of *Bhoodan* land was a blot. A lot, therefore, is yet to be done to eliminate social disparities.

The change in scenario is reflected by the fact that there has been spurt in land deals, property deals, increase in rent of houses and prices of land because of perceived nature of atmosphere of public safety and better law and order situation. Multiplexes and malls have come up in good number in cities; people are buying cars and luxury goods as if money is afloat. This is also a sign of growth in black money due to misappropriation of development funds and growth in inequality along with increase in the growth of few houses.

There is hype propaganda in 2010-11 about social development and infrastructural development in Bihar and almost every week, international conferences or national conferences in praise of developed Bihar-Vision 2015 or 2020 are organized. There is truth in some of the propaganda done. The Right to Services Act is being implemented innovatively. A large number of petitions have been received under it out of which a good number have been dealt within the stipulated timeframe. Right to Information is being punctually observed. Government officers, employees and ministers have declared their assets this year, though the perusal of files is pending. But it has been notified that if people complain against false declaration by any body, the matter will be referred to the vigilance for inquiry. JD (U) has launched *Bihar Harit Abhiyan* to which JD (U)'s and some BJP's M.Ps and MLAs are contributing generously and it is hoped to be a success. Since environmental protection is a general concern, it could have been better to launch it as a governmental programme. But Bihar gains even if the party does it. A final indicator of the continued popularity of JD (U)-BJP alliance is that almost a year after the general elections in 2010, the Bihar by-poll in Daraundha (Siwan) returned the JD (U) candidate with 7% more than her mother-in-law, the ex-JD (U) candidate (who died in June 2010 precipitating a by-election) received in the last election in 2010. But there is more to the story to which we shall refer at the end of the chapter. JD (U) also retained Purnia and Laukaha seat (the latter by a margin of over twenty thousand votes), bypolls to which have been held since 2010. The Nitish government has thus demonstrated that it retains the confidence of the electorate and JD (U) continues to rule the roost.

There is not only positive side of Nitish Kumar's governance as CM. Bihar is still ruled by three upper and three intermediary castes as the composition of its ministry reflects. Out of 31 ministers in Nitish's NDA-II ministry, 12 belong to the upper castes and 9 from the intermediate castes; thus the distribution is not equitable populationwise whatever be the slogan the alliance of electorally. Caste has been increasingly used in political realignments, employment, postings and transfers and dispensation of other benefits. People holding government positions prefer people from their castes in bureaucratic offoces—a practice politicians in 1950s shied away from. It is alleged that bureaucratization is ruling the roost under Nitish's regime; he acts more by the advice of secretaries than by that of his colleagues. There were leaders in Laloo Prasad's *Janata Dal* in 1990-94 who could tell him on his face that he was going wrong and he would listen. Sushil Kumar Modi was consulted by Nitish Kumar in NDA-I but even he is least consulted in NDA-II.

According to Transparency International Corruption Index- 2008, Bihar was the most corrupt state in 2006 and 2007. It is popularly said that corruption has been existing in the period between 2007-12. It is visible in secretariat, collectorate, circle offices and *Panchayati Raj* Institutions, etc. In the distribution of funds for *Indira Awas Yojana*, MGNREGA, *Vridha* Pension, various contracts, etc., corruption has been rampant and supervision has been scant. *Gram Kutchary* has been generally non-functioning, even though till decision has been taken by the state government to ask the police to refer cases to it. Nitish Kumar has been trying to correct the situation with regard to corruption through punitive and preventive measures. The Bihar Special Court Act was passed in 2009 to open schools in seized properties and property declaration of ministers, MLAs and bureaucrats every year to curb corruption is a good precautionary measure. In two to three instance, a primary schools for *Dalit* children were opened in palatial buildings of officers who were found to have amassed wealth beyond their earnings by using corrupt methods. Their buildings were confiscated by the order of the District Magistrate. Nitish Kumar not only has been meeting people in his *Janata Darbars* weekly, hearing complaints and redressing people's grievances to the extent possible, his *Seva Yatras* to distant corners of the state have brought him in contact with the people and officials on the spot. He has been seeing corruption, delay or nepotism from his naked eyes or hearing complaints about them, holding on the spot inquiry leading in some cases to instant suspensions of officials or warnings. Thus corruption may be a thing of the past if he and his ministers move in eradicating corruption in the style they have adopted . Special Vigilance Units, formed in 2006 are in action. The scrapping of MLA Local Area Fund Scheme has been a positive decision to curb corruption.

Notwithstanding the fact that the growth rate in Bihar had risen tremendously due to rise in construction work and trade, per capita income of individuals in Bihar remains much behind those in other states. This is proved by the number of BPL families Bihar presents to the Centre, though the Centre does not accept the figure. The improvement in agriculture, industries, irrigation facilities, energy, agro-industries, literacy and urbanization is not impressive. Industrialisation in Bihar is 6%, whereas it is 20% in Maharashtra and 17% in Gujarat. The establishment of Agriculture Cabinet has been a positive step. Though Nitish Kumar had promised to check migration from Bihar, according to a survey in 2009-10, one person in 57% families had migrated due to lack of heavy investments and employment opportunities in Bihar. Brain drain also continues because brainees find better prospects elsewhere. But a N.G.O., Bihar Institute of Economic Studies has come out with the statistics that in comparison to 2001-03, there has been downfall of 26.53% in 2006-08 in the migration of workers of Bihar to Punjab, Delhi, etc. Labourers are returning to Bihar.

As Dreze and Ritika Khare, speaking in Patna on 1.10.2011 remarked, the functioning of PDS is far from satisfactory in Bihar and needs improvement. *Gram Sabha* members do not meet generally and they do not perform the functions of planning, supervising schemes or controlling the administration. Doctors do not report to the PHCs or dispensaries in the villages or semi-urban areas. The Government of Bihar in Education Department admits that less than 50% students are present in schools; and schools do not open or close in time due to lethargy and lack of sense of duty of teachers as well as lack of supervision over them and in a large number of cases, corrupt deals between teachers and supervisory staff. The Government has constructed more rooms of bigger size in schools and provided a few incentives to students to reach schools but the Government still vies to see that 75% students come to the school.

The state of higher education is no better. Speaking in an international seminar organized in Patna on 20.10.2011, A.K. Rath of Gurgaon opined that the state of education in Bihar had been very bad seven years ago but it has improved considerably now, though it still needs considerable reforms. Rath's statement conveys the impression that it was bad during Rabri's regime and it is better during the regime of Nitish Kumar. It is a fact that Nitish Kumar established or helped establish Chandragupta, Chanakya, IIT, a branch of BIT (MESRA) and Aryabhat Universities along with three central universities but most of them are not in good shape due to various causes.

The state of higher education particularly as typified by the quality and method of appointment of V. Cs and Pro-V. Cs of state universities is in a poor state for which both the Chancellor and the state government are to blame. The point needs elaboration. In Pramod Kumar Vs Chancellor of Bihar in PIL case no. CWGC 822/824, the appointments of Magadh and V.K.S. Universities came for hearing first before the single bench of Patna High Court, then before the joint bench of the Patna High Court and then before the Supreme Court which referred it back to the joint Bench of the Patna High Court. Both the appointments were quashed on the ground that the Chancellor had not consulted the state government which was statutorily binding for him to do before making the appointment. A file containing the note of Nitish Kumar as the Chief Minister was produced before the Court of Justice A. K. Tripathi of the Patna High Court which betrays the mind and attitude of the Chief Minister on the issue of the process of appointment of V. Cs and Pro- V. Cs of state universities. His note read that though no consultation was made, the matter may be dropped since it involved the high office of the *Mahamahim*. It connotes that Nitish Kumar as CM cared for the magnanimity of the office and two hoots for the Acts and the statutes of the Universities framed by the legislature of Bihar. The CM has either been conniving at or taking a defensive attitude since his very appointment as CM when the Chancellors appointed V.Cs and Pro-V.Cs who were not men of learning and scholarship as required by Sec. 9 of the Universities Act of 1976 and without consulting the state government as required by Sec. 10 of the aforesaid Act. After the Departmental Minister, party spokesman of JD(U) and Deputy Chief Minister spoke against the procedure adopted by the Chancellor the CM spoke rather modestly and his words lacked the warmth of protest that characterised the words of Yeddyurappa or Narendra Modi against their UPA- appointed Governors when those Governors indulged in acts that irked the decision making process at the level of their state governments. This led the Chancellor of the universities of Bihar to ignore the advice of the state government to remove one particular acting V.C. when the latter was facing prosecution under sections of IPC and Cr. P.C. and the Chancellor persisted in appointing six V. Cs and four Pro- V. Cs ignoring totally the panel submitted by the state government i.e. he made appointments again "without full and effective consultation". Ram Tawakya Singh through a writ dated 9.9.2011 (SLP Civil Case No. 16205/2011) has challenged these appointments on the aforesaid ground.

The question of how the universities are managed is intimately connected with two repercussions. The appointment through single man is identified with arbitrariness, corruption and lack of academic leadership qualities in the head of the universities (V.Cs) resulting in colossal deterioration in the standard of higher education in the last seven years. It is an anachronism that no mechanism for appointment of a large number of vacant posts of lecturers (after long exercise by the state government to fix the number of posts after the process of rationalisation of posts), after Nitish government cancelled the previous arrangement, exists due to rift between the Governor's office and the state government. The governor did not sign the Bill passed by the legislature constituting a three member panel to select V.Cs. The governor also did not sign the Bill stipulating the papers of appointment of teachers in colleges and universities. The method of appointing *ad hoc* teachers in colleges and universities on nominal salaries is a sure recipe to further reduce the standard of teaching and research in higher education. Payments to non-aided colleges create hurdles every now and then. Rift continued between the Centre and the State government over the site of the CBU for three years resulting into its maldevelopment. The state government spends a large amount of money on court cases involving teachers of colleges and universities (working and retired) and non-teaching employees.

At the level of primary education, the teachers were appointed without due qualification and due checking of certificates and at much lower pay. This went against the canons of ensuring quality education. Thus in the matter of providing basic amenities like education, health, sanitation, etc., all is not well from the point of view of good governance. It is claimed on behalf of the state government that super speciality hospitals have come up but that is hardly a solace because that does not serve the suffering poor masses. In Bihar, only twelve universities are functioning to date though populationwise, Bihar needs thirty-two universities. Commentators rightly comment that higher education has gone off the track and it is sliding down with each passing day. More medical universities are needed with a good number of para-medical staff in government hospitals. Administration of health and sanitation require a lot of improvement. The government's decision to establish 609 dispensaries in MCAH centres is laudable because it can take care of mother's and children's health. But the number needs to be increased to cater to the vast population of mothers and children. The threatening voice of the Minister of Health in respect of doctors was not a sign of good administritive acumen.

The policy of getting private schools registered and ordering private schools to admit poor students on 25% of their seats is, no doubt, a positive step as it encourages the Right to Education. But simultaneously, the government will have to strengthen government school system because the private school management is fighting the case in the Supreme Court and is resisting through *bandhs*, etc.

By flagging off L.K. Advani's *Rath Yatra* from Sitab Diara against corruption on 11-10-2011, Nitish Kumar tried to set aside Narendra Modi as the No. 1 Prime Ministerial candidate (as predicted in the report to the US Congress Committee) and tried to enhance his chances, though many hurdles are in his way. He tried to score a point by trying to enact *Lokayukta* Act in the winter session of the legislature in December, 2011. He deferred to the popular criticism against the draft of the bill which had provided that the Chief Minister will be a member of the Selection Committee of the *Lokayukta*. Later, provision was deleted. Like Uttarakhand, Bihar also brought its Chief Minister within the ambit of the *Lokayukta*. Nitish Kumar might have waited for the Centre to pass the *Lokpal* Act providing for a comprehensive *Lokayukta* Act for starting but after Uttarakhand passed the Act, he did not afford to wait to become a late runner in the game of one-upmanship. The winter session of legislature, 2011 passed the Bihar *Lokayukta* Bill and it has already been notified and regulations have also been made. So Selection Committee can start its function of establishing the office of *Lokayukta* as soon as the search committee is constituted and makes the recommendations.

Nitish Kumar has, however, been mired in few constitutional and financial controversies. The governor has returned more than a dozen bills passed by Bihar legislature without signing and some of the bills have been returned by the governor on the ground that since they are Money bills they required the prior consent of the governor prior to their introduction in the House. The JD (U) mildly protested against these acts of the governor but they created difficulties in governance. After higgling, a number of bills have been signed by the governor but some important bills pertaining to education, etc. are still pending at the table of the governor.

One financial deal relates to non-finalisation of A/c, D/c bills about which the Patna High Court had once remarked that they require an inquiry by the CBI. But the case has since been cleared by the Patna High Court. Another scandal relates to the allotment of industrial plots by BIADA to wards of persons close to the Chief Minister. The then Chief Secretary who was authorised by the CM to submit a report after conducting the affair on telephone admitted that in one case, the application was processed on the day it was submitted. C.K. Anil, IAS raised some pertinent points to be looked into in connection with these allotments. It is to be investigated why BIADA changed the policy of allotment of land from bidding and advertising as provided in the BIADA Act of 1974 (which could benefit common unemployed persons willing to enter into entrepreneurship in a land committed to social justice) to first-come-first-served policy in 2007 (which caused 2G spectrum allotment scandal). Indeed, this policy needs change but the present government is not inclined to change the policy. The amended BIADA norms are suspected to facilitate nepotism. The government's inquiry report lists the allotment details of eight persons including Rahmat Fatima, daughter of Social Welfare Minister Parveen Amanullah and senior civil servant, Afzal Amanullah; Urvashi Shahi, d/o Education Minister P.K. Shahi, Rahul Sharma, son of M.P. Jagdish Sharma; Saurabh Agarwal, son of BJP MLC Ashok Agarwal, and S. Siddharth, Secretary to the CM. Satish Paswan, P.K. Sinha and Sarwar Warsi have filed a PIL case in the Patna High Court urging the court for a CBI inquiry into preferential allotments of prime governmental land at sub-par rates without "tender and advertisement" which they allege has cost the state exchequer thousands of crores of rupees. The Patna High Court on 20-10-2011 ordered the BIADA to reply immediately to the petitions but disposed of the case in favour of BIADA subsequently. The case is now being heard at the level of the Supreme Court.

The government has had to answer allegations against human rights also. In December 2010, NHRC, Bihar Chapter had ordered for payment of compensation to a widow for death of a prisoner in judicial custody. The same body ordered an inquiry into cases of assault by jail staff of Beur on the inmates of Beur jail on 13-09-2011. According to National Crime Record Bureau, 781 prisoners died in jails of Bihar between 2004 and 2009 i.e. one prisoner died every third day.

This is not a good record from the point of view of observance of human rights.

The state government under Nitish Kumar has decided to undertake survey of land and *chakbandi* within stipulated period. Bihar had been lagging in implementing the provisions of uptodating its land records which many other states in India had already done. If the Nitish government is able to undertake this task, it will be a service to the state but, Nitish government might find itself at loggerheads with *benami* land holders and occupiers of *gairmazarua* or *bhoodan* lands who may organize to create hurdles in the way.

To conclude, electoral endorsement legitimizes the functioning of democracy. In that sense, the ruling alliance may pat itself on the increase in the number of votes gained between 2010 Vidhan Sabha and 2011 Vidhan Sabha by-election at Daraunda and Laukaha. But the story of the by-election at Daraundha is not too flattering from the point of view of good governance. Jagmato Devi who was the sitting JD (U) MLA died in June, 2011 precipitating the by-election. Her son, Ajay Singh, a bachelor was a contender for the JD (U) ticket. He was, however, reportedly rebuffed by the party bosses because of his criminal antecedents. To retain the reign of power in the family, he married Kavita during *Pitrpaksha* (a period during which Hindus, by convention, do not marry) when the dates of filing nomination papers were still on. Critics point out that Kavita Singh's victory was not only a popularity vote but a sympathy vote as well as vote for a so-called criminal's wife. Thus we often come across zigjags in Bihar politics under Nitish Kumar (2010-12) dispensation where there are intersections of pragmatism with propaganda of good governance and some genuine amount of intentional, motivatedly and pointedly implemented good governance.

The bad plight of the state of Bihar was seen during 1961-90 in which 25 CMs changed hands in 29 years; and the CMs remained engaged in saving their chair. After this phase of political instability, financial flagrancy was seen during the Eighth Five Year Plan (1992-97) when only Rs. 5404 cr. could be spent out of the planned allocation of Rs. 13,000 cr. But during Nitish Kumar's regime, the state presents demand before the

Centre for much greater allocation under different schemes and spends money efficiently well in time. The state has a master plan for the development of cities, towns and villages and things seem to be in upswing. Where the Centre dithers to advance funds as it usually does, the state has built financial rapport with several other national and international funding agencies because of its quality of work and timely submission of utilisation certificates. Nitish Kumar's educational background of a technocrat and personality of a sophisticated and well-mannered humanist help his aura of good governance while his practical sense of politicking keep him going so far ascending the stairs of popularity (with slow noises of murmuring) as the most successful Chief Minister after S.K. Sinha.

Bibliography

Books

Agrawala, R.C., *Constitutional History of India and National Movement*, New Delhi: S. Chand and Co., 1964.

Ahluvalia, Sagar, *ANNA: The Tempest and the Sea*, New Delhi: Young Asia Publications, 1969.

Ahuja, R., *Political Elite and Modernisation*, Meerut: Meenakshi Publications.

Alderman, R.K. and Cross, G.A., *The Tactics of Resignaion*, London: Routledge and Kagan Paul, 1967.

Ali, Sadique, *A Survey of The General Elections of 1967*, New Delhi: A.I.C.C., 1969.

Almond, Gabriel and Coleman, James S., *The Politics of the Developing Areas*, New Jersy: Princeton University Press, 1964.

Amery, L.S., *Thoughts on the Constitution*, Oxford: Oxford University Press (2nd ed.), 1953.

Anandam, M., *Tryst with Destiny*, New Delhi: Arnold Heinemann, 1975.

Anwar, Ali, *Sar Ke Bal Khari Muslim Siyasat*, Amarte-Ahale Ansar, Alhind: Patna, 1998.

Azad, Maulana Abul Kalam, *India Wins Freedom*, Calcutta: Orient Longmans, 1959.

Banerjee, A.C., *The Cabinet Mission in India*, (1946).

Barker, E., *Essays on Government*, London: Oxford University Press (2nd ed.), 1951.

Basu, Durga Das, *Commentary on the Constitution of India*, Calcutta: S.C. Sarkar & Sons Ltd., (3rd ed.), 1955.

Brass, Paul R., *Caste, Fraction and Party in Indian Politics*, Vol. I and II, Chanakya Publications, Delhi, 1984, And *The Politics of India Since Independence*, Cambridge University Press, 1990.

Birch, A.H., *Representative and Responsible Government*, London: George Allen & Unwin Ltd., 1965.

Brecher, Michael, *Succession in India: A Study in Decion-Making*, London: Oxford University Press, 1966, *India and World Politics: Krishna Menon's View of the World*, London: Oxford University Press, 1968. *Political Leadership in India*, Delhi: Vikas Publications, 1969.

Butter, David, Ashok Lahiri and Pranoy Roy, *India Decides: Elections 1952-95*, New Delhi, Books and Things, 1995.

Chakravarty, Saroj, *With West Bengal Chief Ministers*, New Delhi, Orient Longman, 1978.

Chanda, Ashok, *Federalism in India: A Study of Union-States Relations*, London: George Allen & Unwin Ltd. 1965.

Coondoo, Mrs. Ranjita, *The Division of Powers in the Indian Constitution*, Calcutta: Bookland Pvt. Ltd., 1964.

Das, Arvind, N., *The Republic of Bihar-1992*, New Delhi, Penguin, 1992.

Datta, C.L., *With Two Presidents*, Delhi: Vikas Publications, 1970.

Deutsch, Karl J., *The Nerves of Government*, London: The Free Press of Glencoe, 1963.

Diwakar, R.R., *Bihar through The Ages*, Bombay: Orient Longman, 1958.

Drucker, Peter F., *The Effective Executive*, London: Hainemann, 1967.

Dutta, K.K., *History of the Freedom Movement in Bihar*, Patna: Government of Bihar, 1957.

Finer, M. *The Theory and Practice of Modern Government*, London: Mathuen (4th ed.), 1961.

Francine, R. Frankel, *India's Political Economy 1947-1967: The Gradual Revolution*, Delhi: Oxford University Press, 1978.

Frankel, Francine R. and M.S.A. Rao, *Dominance and State Power in Modern India*, Vol. I; Oxford University Press, 1987.

Gadgil, N.V., *Government From Inside*, Meerut; Meenakshi Prakashan, 1968.

Gajendragadgar, P. S., *The Constitution of India: Its Philosophy and Basic Postulates*, Bombay, Oxford University Press, 1969.

Gamson, W.A., *"Coalition Formation" in International Encyclopaedia of the Social Sciences*, Vol. 2.

Gandhi, M.K., *Letters to Sardar Vallabbhai Patel*, Ahmadabad: Navajivan Publishing House, 1957.

Gledhill, Alan, *The Republic of India*, London: Stevens and Sons, 1951.

Gupta, R.L., *Politics of Commitment: (A Study based on 5th General Elections in India)*, New Delhi: Trimurti Publications, 1972.

Hartman, Horstman, *Political Parties in India*, Meerut: Meenakshi Prakashan, 1977.

Ismail, M.M., *The President and the Governors in the Indian Constitution*, Madras: Orient Longmans, 1972.

Jain, C.M., *State Legislature in India*, New Delhi: S. Chand & Co., 1972.

Jain, H.M. *The Union Executive*, Allahabad: Chaitanya Publishing House, 1969.

Jennings, Sir Ivor, *Cabinet Government*, Cambridge: Cambridge University Press, 1969.

Jennings, W.I., *The British Constitution*, Cambridge, Cambridge University Press (4th ed.), 1961.

Jha, Shashishekhar, *Political Elite in Bihar*, Bombay: Vora & Co., 1972.

Kale, B.B., *Chavan: Man of Crisis*, Bombay: Sindhu Publishing Pvt. Ltd., 1969.

Kapur, Anup Chand *Constitutional History of India (1765-1970)*, New Delhi: Niraj Prakashan, 1970.

Karanjia, R.K., *Indira—J.P. Confrontation—The Great Debate*, New Delhi: Chetana Publications, 1975.

Kashyap, Subhash C., *The Politics of Power: Defections and State Politics in India*, Delhi: National, 1974.

Keith, A.B., *The British Cabinet System*, London: Stevens & Sons Ltd., 1952.

Kohli, Atul, *Democracy and Development in India*, Oxford University Press, 2009.

———, (ed.), *India's Democracy*, Orient Longman, Princeton; 1996.

———, (ed.) *The Success of India's Democracy*, Cambridge University Press, 2001; and

Kohli, Atul, *Democracy and Discontent: India's Governing Crisis of Governability*, Cambridge University Press, 1990.

Kothari Rajni, *Politics in India*, New York: Little Brown & Co., 1970 and

——, *State Against Democracy*, New Delhi, Ajanta

Krishna Anant V., *India Since Independence*, Delhi: Pearson, 2009.

Krishnan, T.V. Kunhi, *Chavan and the Troubled Decade*, Somaniya Publishing Pvt. Ltd., 1971.

Kochanek, Stanley A., *The Congress Party in India*, Princeton University Press, 1968.

Kulkarni, V.B., *Problem of Indian Democracy*, Bombay: Bhartiya Vidya Bhavan, 1972.

Kumar, Shanta, *Rajniti Ka Shatranj*, Delhi: Rajput & Sons, 1982 (in Hindi).

Lal, A.B., *The Indian Parliament*, Allahabad: Chaitanya Publishing House, 1956.

Lal, Munni *Profile of a Chief Minister (A Biography of Bansi Lal)*, New Delhi: Vikas Publishing House Pvt. Ltd., 1975.

Laski, Harold J., *Parliamentary Government in England*, London: George Allen & Unwin Ltd., 1959.

Mackintosh, John P., *The British Cabinet*, London: Stevens & Sons Ltd., 1962.

Mahajan, Vidya Dhar, *Fifty Years of Modern India (1919-1969)*, New Delhi, S. Chand & Co., 1970.

Maheshwari, S.R., *State Governments in India*, Delhi: Macmillan, 1979.

Manor, James, *Political Change in an Indian State*, Columbian Missouri: South Asia Books, 1978.

Mazara, S., *Bihar and Punjab*, New Delhi: Economic and Scientific Research Foundation, 1973.

Mill, L.S., *Representative Government*, Basil: Blackwell, 1946.

Mishra K.P. and Avasthi, R., (ed.) *Politics of Persuasion*, Bombay: Manaktalas, 1967.

Mishra, Jagannath, *Bihar Ke Pira Se Judiye*, Patna, Bharti Bhawan, 1985 (in Hindi).

Moraes, Frank, *India Today*, New York, Macmillan, 1960.

Morris-Jones, W.H., *The Government and Politics of India*, Hutchinson University Library, 1971.

———, *Parliament in India*, Longmans, Green & Co., 1957.

Mitra, Roma, *Caste Polarisation and Politics*, South Asia Books, 1992.

Munshi, K.M., *Indian Constitutional Documents: Pilgrimage to Freedom (1902-1950)*, Bombay: Bhartiya Vidya Bhavan, 1963.

Narain, Govind, *Leadership in Administration*, New Delhi: Department of Personnel & Administrative Reforms, Cabinet Secretariat, 1973.

Narain, Iqbal, (ed.) *State Politics in India*, Meerut, Meenakshi Prakashan, 1967.

Narasimhan, V.K., *Kamaraj: A Study*, Bombay: Manaktalas, 1967.

Nayar, Kuldip, *India- The Critical Years*, Delhi: Vikas Publications, 1975.

Neutstadt, Richard E., *Presidential Power*, Delhi: Allied Publishers, 1960.

Ogg, F.A., "Coalition" in *Encyclopaedia of the Social Sciences*, Vol. 2.

Palmer, Norman D., *The Indian Political System*, Boston: Houghton Mifflin Co. (2nd ed.), 1971.

Pandey, Jawaharlal, *State Politics in India*, Delhi: Uppal Publishing House.

Pandey, L.B., *State Executive Under Indian Polity*, Delhi: Amar Prakashan, 1985.

Pandit, H.N., *The Prime Minister's President*, New Delhi: S. Chand & Co., 1974.

Pavate, D.C., *My Days as Governor*, Delhi: Vikas Publishing House Pvt. Ltd., 1974.

Prakasa, Sri, *State Governors in India*, Meerut: Meenakshi Prakashan, (2nd ed.), 1975.

Prasad, Rajendra, *Autobiography*, Bombay: Asia Publishing House, 1957.

Pasmanda Muslim Agenda 21 vin Sadi Ki Ore, *Main Office of Pasmanda Muslim Mahaj*, Patna, 1999.

Puri, Rajinder, *A Crisis of Conecience*, Delhi: Rajendra Puri, 1971.

Rao, K.V., *Parliamentary Democracy of India*, Calcutta: The World Press, 1965.

Rau, B.N., *India's Constitution in the Making*, Allied Publishers Pvt. Ltd., 1963.

Ray, Bharati, *Evolution of Federalism in India*, Calcutta: Progressive Publishers, 1967.

Rudolph, L.I. and S.H. Rudolph, *In Pursuit of Lakshmi*, The University of Chicago Press, 1985.

Seervai, H.M., *Conatitutional Law of India: A critical Commentary*, Bombay: N.M. Tripathy & Co., 1967.

Sen, Pulinbihari, *Towards A Prosperous India* (Speeches & Writings of Dr. Bidhan Chand Roy), Calcutta: Pulinbihari Sen, 1964.

Sethi, J.D., *India's State Power Structure*, Delhi: Vikas Publications, 1969.

Sengupta, Nirmal and Arvind N. Das, *Agrarian Change, Agrarian Tensions, Peasant Movements and Organisation in Bihar*, Patna: A. N. Sinha Institute of Social Sciences, 1984.

Sharma, L.N., *The Indian Prime Minister*, New Delhi: The Macmillan Co. of India, 1976.

Sharma, M.P., *The Governement of the Indian Republic*, Allahabad: Chaitanya Publishing House, 1957.

Sharma, C.Y., *Ek Aur Mukhya Mantri*, Delhi: National Publishing House, 1969 (in Hindi).

Singh, M.M., *The Constitution of India (Studies in Perspective)*, Calcutta: The World Press Pvt. Ltd., 1975.

Sinha, A.N., *Mere Sansmaran*

Sinha, Mahamaya Prasad "*Jab Main Mukhya Mantri Tha*" (When I was a Chief Minister).

Siwach, J.R., *Office of the Governor*, New Delhi: Sterling Publishers, 1971.

Varma, R.S., *Bureaucracy in India*, Bhopal: Progressive Publishers, 1973.

Venkateswaran, R.J., *Cabinet Government in India*, London: George Allen And Unwin Ltd., 1967.

Wainer, Myron (ed.). *State Politics in India*, New Jarsey: Princeton University Press, 1968.

Unpublished Thesis

Mazhar Hussain, *Office and Powers of Chief Ministers: A Study of Some Aspects of Indian Administration*, submitted to Patna University in 1979.

Arjun Sharma *The Chief Minister of Bihar: Office and Powers*, submitted to Patna University in 1986.

Reports and Documents

Administrative Reforms Commission, *Report of the Study Team on Centre-State Relationships*, Vol. I, 1968.

Report of the Committee of Governors, New Delhi: President Secretariat, 1971.

Report of the Centre-State Relations Inuiry Committee, Government of Tamil Nadu, 1971.

Constituent Assembly Debates, (Government of India, Constituent Assembly, Official Report), 1946-50, Vols. I-XII, Relevant Parts.

Government of India, Ministry of States: *White Paper on Indian States*, 1950.

Lok Sabha Debates (New Delhi: Lok Sabha Secretariat), Relevant Parts.

Aiyar Commission, *Reports of Inquiry against One Chief Minister and Five Ministers*, Patna: Government of Bihar, 1970.

Mudholkar Commission of Inquiry, *Report on the Charges against 14 ex-United Front Ministers of Bihar*, (Patna: The Superintendent, Secretariat Press), 1970.

The Constitution of India, Delhi: Government of India Publications, 1969.

Bihar Through Figures, Patna: Government of Bihar Publication.

Bihar Legislative Assembly Debates, Patna: Government of Bihar.

Selected Articles in Journals

Aiyar, P., "Union-State Relations in India- Post-Election View", *United Asia*, 19 (2) March-April, 1967.

Appadorai, A., "Guidelines for Governors", *Eastern Economics*, Delhi: May 23, 1969.

"The Demand for State Autonomy", *Eastern Economist*, October 2, 1970.

Bacon, James C., "Leadership of the Systems Development Team", *Journal of Systems Management*, May, 1976.

Badal, Prakash Singh, "No More President's Rule", *The Illustrated Weekly of India*, March 26-April 1, 1978.

Balchand, R., "Sri Krishna Sinha- Blend of Emotion and Real Politic", *The Indian Nation* (Patna), April 2, 1978.

Banerjee, D.N., "Discretionary Powers of the Governor", *Swarajya*, November 1, 1969.

Bhatia, Prem, "Dilli Chalo", *The Tribune*, April 7, 1959.

Blair, H., "Structural Change, the Agricultural Sector and Politics in Bihar" in Boulder J. Wood (ed.), *State Politics in Contemporary India: Crisis or Continuity?*, Westview Press, 1984.

Bombwall, K.R., "Federal Relations in India", *Secular Democracy*, Nehru Number, New Delhi, 1976.

Brass, Paul R., "Coalition Politics in North India", *American Political Science Review*, December, 1968.

Chandrashekhar, "There is no Need for Change", *The Illustrated Weekly of India*, March 26-April 1, 1978.

Chaudhary, N.C.B. Ray, "The Politics of India's Coalition", The Political Quarterly (London), July-September, 1969.

Clements, P., "Rawlsian analysis of the plight of Bihar", *Studies in Comparative International Development* (SCID), Springer, New York, December, 2005.

Costa, Benedict, "Elections in Five States", *The Illustrated Weekly of India*, February 18-25, 1978.

Das, Durga, "Political Confrontation of Centre & States", *Economic Times* (Calcutta), April 22, 1969.

Frankel, Francine R., "Caste, Land and Dominance in Bihar", in F.M.S.A. Rao (ed.), *Dominance and State Power in Modern India*, London: Oxford University Press, 1989-90.

Gadgil, V.N., "Coalition Politics in India and Abroad", *Politics India* (Delhi), October, 1996.

Gandhi, Indira, "A Weak Centre Would Not Do", *The Illustrated Weekly of India*, March 26-April 1, 1978.

Jha, Chetkar, "Caste in Bihar Congress Politics", in Iqbal Narain (ed.), *State Politics in India*, Meerut: Meenakshi Prakashan, 1968.

Karunanidhi, M., "You Can't Run India from Delhi", *The Illustrated Weekly of India*, March 26-April 1, 1978.

Krishna, Gopal, "One party Dominance Development and Trends" in *Party System and Election Studies*, Occasional Papers of the Centre for the Study of Developing Societies, New Delhi, 1967.

Kohli, Atul, "Breakdown in a 'Backward' State: Bihar", in *Democracy and Development in India*, Delhi: Oxford University Press, 2009.

Kothari, Rajni, "Forms and Substance in Indian Politics", *The Economic Weekly*, June 3, 1961.

"The Congress 'System' in India", *Asian Survey*, December, 1964.

"Party Politics and Political Development", *Economic and Political Weekly*, February, 1967. "Caste and Political Recruitment in Bihar", in—(ed.), Caste in Indian Politics, New Delhi: Orient Longman, 1970.

Kumar, Avinash, "Illegitimacy of the State in Bihar", *Economic and Political Weekly*, October 31, 2009.

Lalvani, Mala, "Coalition Governments: Fiscal Implications for the Indian Economy", *American Review of Political Economy*, March, 2005.

Markandan, N.K.C., "Governor's Discretionery Powers: A Study in the intention of Constitution-Makers", *Journal of Constitutional & Parliamentary Studies*, (Delhi), October-December, 1968.

Mehta, Ashok, *Politics of Planned Economy*, Hyderabad, 1953.

Mithal, D.N., "Governor as a Component Part of the State Legislature", *Journal of Constitutional and Parliamentary Studies*, (Delhi), Jan.-March, 1970.

Mohanty, Niranjan, "Bihari Blues: A Riches to Rags Story", *The Times of India*, December 12, 1997.

Minocha, O.P., "Coalition Government—Experience and Prospects", Fortieth Annual Conference of Members of IIPA, Delhi: IIPA, October 27, 1996.

Morris-Jones, W. H., "Dominance and Dissent", *Government and Opposition*, August, 1966; and

"The Indian Congress Party", *Modern Asian Studies*, Vol. I, No. I.

Namboodiripad, E.M.S., "State Autonomy Will Not Endanger Unity", *The Illustrated Weekly of India*, March 19-25, 1978.

Narain, Iqbal, "Office of the Governor : The Problem of Role Identification", *Journal of African & Asian Studies*, Spring, 1968.

Nayar, Kuldip, "States Deserve a Larger Share of Authority", *The Statesman*, Calcutta, April 22, 1969.

Ogg, F.A., "Coalition", *Encyclopaedia of the Social Sciences*, Vol. III, New York; The Macmillan Company, 1963.

Prasad, R.C., "Bihar: Social Polarization and Political Instability", In Iqbal Narain (ed.), *State Politics in India*, Meerut: Meenakshi, 1976.

Rai, Haridwar & Pandey, Jawaharlal, "Political Process and Coalitional Politics: The First United Front Government of Bihar", *Journal of Bhagalpur University*, Vol. VI, 1973.

Rao, K.V., "The Governor in the Constituent Assembly", *Journal of the Society for the Study of State Governments*, Varanasi: January-June, 1968.

Ray, Ashwani K., "Governor in Indian Constitution", *Mainstream*, January 26, 1968.

R.G.K., "Who Should be More Powerful: Centre or State", *The Illustrated Weekly of India*, March 19-26, 1978.

Riker, William R., "The Study of Coalitions", *International Encyclopaedia of The Social Sciences*, Vol. II, 1968.

Roy, Ramashray, "Dynamics of One Party Dominance in an Indian State", *Asian Survey*, 1969 and "Caste and Political Recruitment in Bihar" in Rajni Kothari (ed.), Caste in Indian Politics, New Delhi: Orient Longman, 1970.

Santhanam, K., "Dual Role as PM and Party Leader", *The Hindu*, Madras, July 18, 1970.

Sen, Sachin, "Role of the Administration in Indian Democracy", *The Journal of the Administrative Sciences*, Institute of Public Administration, Patna University, January-December, 1966, Vol. XI; and "Political Parties in India", *The Indian Nation*, December 17, 1976.

Shankar, V., "Portends of Current Centre-State Relationship: Drastic Change after 1967", *Jana Deep* (Souvenir): New Delhi, 1971.

Sharma, L.N., "Selection of Candidates by Political Parties in Bihar for Mid-Term Parliamentary Polls, 1971", *Journal of the Administrative Sciences*, Institute of Public Administration, Patna University, January-December, 1973.

Sharma, V.V.P., "Chief Ministers as I Saw Them", *The Hindustan Times*, January 10, 1997.

Shiviah, "The Governor in the Indian Political System", *Journal of Constitutional and Parliamentary Studies*, October-December, 1968.

Singh, Dalip, "The Role of the Governor under the Constitution and Working of the Coalition Governance", *Indian Journal of Political Science*, January-March, 1968.

Singh, L.P., "Learning from Experience", *Seminar*, June, 1984.

Siwach, J.R., "Appointment and Dismissal of The Chief Minister", *Mainstream*, January-March, 1986.

Thakur, C.P., "The Governor and Centre-State Relation", *The Indian Nation*, March, 1986.

Thakur, Raghu, "They create differences in the Janata Party", *The Illustrated Weekly of India*, March 19-25, 1978.

Timberg, Thomas A., "Bihari backwardness: Does Feudalism Frustrate?", *Asian Survey*, May, 1982.

Weiner, Myron, "Congress Restored: Continuities and Discontinuities in Indian Politics", *Asian Survey*, April, 1982.

Zakaria, F.R., "Turmoil in Indian Politics", *The Illustrated Weekly of India*, May 20-26, 1979.

Newspapers

Aryavarta (Patna)—in Hindi.
Asian Recorder
Congress Bulletin
Hindustan (Patna)—in Hindi.
The Hindustan Times (Delhi and later on from Patna also)
The Hindu (Kolkata)
Indian Backgrounder
The Indian Express (Delhi)
Indian Recorder
The Illustrated Weekly of India
The Indian Nation (Patna- now closed)
Link
The Patriot (Delhi)
The Statesman (Delhi)
Sunday Times (London)
The Tribune (Ambala)

Index